# Economic Development and Women in the World Community

Muslim 9
  Gender Constraint
            Purdah

# Economic Development and Women in the World Community

Kartik C. Roy, Clement A. Tisdell
and Hans C. Blomqvist
*Editors*

Westport, Connecticut
London

**Library of Congress Cataloging-in-Publication Data**

Economic development and women in the world community / edited by
   Kartik C. Roy, Clement A. Tisdell, and Hans C. Blomqvist.
      p.   cm.
   Includes bibliographical references and index.
   ISBN 0–275–95134–0 (alk. paper)—ISBN 0–275–96631–3 (pbk.)
   1. Women in development.   2. Women—Economic conditions.
   3. Economic development.   I. Roy, K. C. (Kartik Chandra), 1941–
   II. Tisdell, C. A. (Clement Allan)   III. Blomqvist, H. C. (Hans-
   Christer)
   HQ1240.E28   1996
   338.9′0082—dc20      95–23225

British Library Cataloguing in Publication Data is available.

Library of Congress Catalog Card Number: 95–23225
ISBN: 0–275–96631–3 (pbk.)

First published in 1996

Praeger Publishers, 88 Post Road West, Westport, CT 06881
An imprint of Greenwood Publishing Group, Inc.
www.praeger.com

Printed in the United States of America

The paper used in this book complies with the
Permanent Paper Standard issued by the National
Information Standards Organization (Z39.48–1984).

10 9 8 7 6 5 4 3 2 1

**Copyright Acknowledgment**

Chapter 12 is an extensively revised version of an article written by Helen I. Safa that
originally appeared in *Women's Work and Women's Lives: The Continuing Struggle Worldwide*,
edited by Hilda Kahne and Janet Giele, © 1992. Reprinted with permission from Westview
Press, Boulder, Colorado.

# Contents

# Preface

In eliminating obstacles to sustainable development, women of the world community play a central role. The socioeconomic status of women is a major influence on economic development and, conversely, the socioeconomic status of women is significantly altered by economic development. This book explores these relationships both for developed and less developed countries. While the importance of these relationships have been recognized as a result of the World Conference on the International Women's Year in Mexico in 1975 and the active involvement of the United Nations in women's issues during and after the U.N. Decade for Women (1976–1985) they have been given less attention than they deserve.

Women contribute greatly to poverty reduction and to economic security within the family. They are the major providers of food for millions of families and contribute more than 50 percent to total food production and about 25 percent to the total industrial workforce in the developing world. At the same time, they are very aware of the value of preserving natural resources and would not abuse them were there an alternative for them. They are usually the carers in the family, for example, for family members who become ill.

Poverty reduction also depends on reduction in population growth. Here again women play the crucial role. Education, as well as knowledge of and access to health care will make them aware of the benefits of fewer children, and economic independence achieved by raising the marriage age and providing greater control over their own lives would impact favorably on the rate of fertility.

Thus women are the most important agents of change. As such, the differences in their roles in economic development in the developing and developed world are a matter of degree. Sustainable economic development of the world community, including the developed countries, therefore, requires significant improvement in the socioeconomic status of women. On the other hand, improvement in the socioeconomic status of women cannot be achieved without economic development. Women's central role in development and the need for improvement in their economic conditions have been reemphasized again in the recent U.N. Conference on population and development held in Cairo in August 1994.

The aim of this book is to examine the current socioeconomic status of these agents of change, the impact of economic change on women, and measures to empower women in the economic development process in the world community.

This book, which is unique in the sense that it presents a comparative picture of the status of women in all five continents, is the product of shared interest of the editors in the field of economic development, poverty, and environment and their belief that women play a central role in the preservation of environment and sustainable development of the world community. The editors wish to thank their respective home institutions, the University of Queensland in Brisbane, Australia, and the Swedish School of Economics and Business Administration in Helsinki, Finland, for their support of this project and to Praeger Publishers for publishing this volume. We also wish to thank all others who have been associated with the publication of this book, and first of these, of course, the numerous contributors to chapters on various countries.

It is hoped that this volume could be of use to researchers and students in development economics, sociology, and women's studies in universities, to planners, policymakers, and implementors in governments, to women's grassroots organizations, nongovernment organizations, bilateral and multilateral aid agencies, and all others genuinely interested in uplifting the socioeconomic status of women both in developing and developed countries. Finally, we dedicate this book to the women of the world community, the most important but neglected agents of change.

# 1

# Economic Development and Women: An Overview of Issues

*Kartik C. Roy, Hans C. Blomqvist, and Clement A. Tisdell*

## INTRODUCTION

Since the World Conference on the International Women's Year in Mexico in 1975, which declared the period 1976–1985 as the U.N. Decade for Women and the World Conference in Nairobi in July 1985 to review and appraise the achievements of the U.N. Decade for Women, women's issues have been firmly placed on the agenda for world development. As the concern for the preservation of the world's natural resources and environment has been growing, women's issues are gaining further prominence due to the increasing realization by the world community that a strong and an intimate bond exists between women and nature and that addressing women's issues will also help the preservation of nature.

In the development studies literature, the problem of poverty in individual countries has sometimes been sought to be understood in terms of inequality in the distribution of income between different income groups. From 1950 to the mid-1960s, development economists tended to ignore the problems of poverty and inequality on the assumption that the growth in income will automatically solve the problem. However, since the late 1960s, new income distribution statistics revealed that in many developing countries inequality was rising, the mass of the people were not at all benefiting, and the poor were actually becoming worse off from development. In the 1970s, although interest in the problems of inequality and poverty among income groups began to wane, renewed interest in the problems was created with the growing realization that pervasive poverty of a different kind exists within each income group due to the discrimination practiced against women on the basis of their gender. In this chapter we present an overview of issues influencing women's development in the world community.

## GENDER: PHILOSOPHICAL, HISTORICAL, AND CULTURAL DIMENSIONS

The conceptual distinction between sex and gender as developed by Anne Oakley (1987) recognizes sex as biologically determined and the gender identity of men and women as socially and psychologically as well as historically and culturally determined. Gender is learned through a process of socialization and through the culture of the society concerned. In various cultures, boys and girls are encouraged in the acts considered to display their respective male and female traits through toys given to them, such as guns to boys and dolls to girls (Brett 1991). Children learn from birth about how they should behave in order to be perceived by others and themselves as either masculine or feminine. This learning is further reinforced in subsequent years by their parents, teachers, peers, culture, and society. Once this differentiation is established, the role of gender, however, tends to differ considerably between cultures.

In Indian culture, every living entity owes its origin to the primordial energy, which is the substance of everything and pervades everything. The manifestation of this power is called nature (Prakriti). Nature, both animate and inanimate, is thus an expression of Shakti, the feminine and creative principle of the cosmos, and in conjunction with the masculine principle (Purusha), nature (Prakriti) creates the world. Therefore, women are an intimate and integral part of nature, which embodies the feminine principle on the one hand and is nurtured by the female to produce life and provide sustenance, on the other.

In ancient Indian civilizations since the Vedic era, women enjoyed far greater freedom and respect than they seem to enjoy in today's society. History records that women played crucial roles in household as well as state affairs. Today, gender discrimination and the ideology of seclusion is more widely practiced in upper caste and scheduled caste families than in tribal families. Thus it would seem that the subjugation of the female gender by the male gender in India may have started with the onset of Islamic rule in India and reinforced further by the spread of Western knowledge and culture. Vandana Shiva (1989), the nuclear physicist turned philosopher and feminist, described the program of Bacon (1561–1626), the father of modern science, as benefiting the middle class, European and male entrepreneurs through the conjunction of human knowledge and power in science. Modern science was a consciously gendered, patriarchal activity. As nature came to be seen more like a woman to be subjugated, gender too was re-created. Science as a male venture, based on the subjugation of nature (Prakriti), provided support for the polarization of gender. Patriarchy, as the new scientific and technological power, was a political need of emerging capitalism. In Adam Smith's writings, the wealth created by nature and women's work did not receive explicit recognition. Labor, particularly male labor, became the fund which originally supplied it with all the necessities and conveniences of life. As this assumption spread to all human communities, it introduced dualities within society and between nature and man. The importance of nature as a source of wealth, of women in subsistence production, of peasant and tribal societies became marginal to the framework of the industrial society primarily as resources and inputs. As the productive power was associated only with the male Western labor, economic development became a program of remodeling the world along that line (Shiva 1989).

Theology legitimizes the existing economic structures of patriarchal exploitation as well as the cultural gender role division and socialization for "feminine" behavior which internalize and sustain such exploitation. Thus according to the capitalist patriarchy, women's work in the home is not recognized as work and therefore not paid at all, although reproduction and child bearing are important for survival and for the state. Discriminatory pay scales for women was also advocated in the New Testament (1 Tim. 5:3–16) where the Pastoral Epistles stipulate that the widow/elder should receive only half of the payment or honor which is due to the male presiding elder. Whereas male elders of the community should be remunerated independently of their family status and income, widows/elders should only receive financial support from the community when they are absolutely without family support (Fiorenza 1987). Socialization of women into domesticity is further reinforced through a "theology of women" which insists that women's nature and vocation is to be a loving housewife and self-sacrificing mother. Although recent papal statements insist on the equal dignity and responsible equality of women, they also make it clear that these ought to be realized in their self-giving dedication to their husbands and in their loving service to their children.

In the Third World, in the second half of the present century, the spread of commercial capitalism with the adoption of "green revolution technology" in agriculture may have further marginalized women's role in rural societies as the planning for its adoption and the designing and deployment of apparatus were undertaken by men.

Many institutions grow out of social customs, traditions, and so on. Many of these social customs and traditions are manifestations of the economic structure of a society at a particular time. These institutions provide social and legal validity to these customs and traditions. However, with the passage of time, many of these customs, traditions, and institutions become outmoded. They need to be replaced with those which reflect the current social and economic realities. Replacing these customs and institutions require creating appropriate social and political environment. This is where the developed countries have been more successful than developing countries. As a result, gender discrimination would appear to be less prevalent in developed countries than in developing countries today. Thus one example of gender constraint which may not be justified by current economic and social realities but still persists with institutional backing is the ideology of seclusion practiced by Muslim women under purdah. Purdah is the outward manifestation of the operation of classic patriarchy which implies the control of younger males by the old and the shelter of women in a highly hierarchical domestic realm. It also implies the control by men of some form of viable joint patrimony in land, animals, or commercial capital (Kandiyoti 1985; Burnstein et al. 1992). Purdah, a Persian word for curtain, is an institutionalized system of seclusion and veiling which operates at three levels: the physical segregation of women's living space; social segregation, which permits women's interaction only with the immediate kinship circle; and the covering of the female face and body. The purdah system keeps women secluded and isolated from the wider world and confines them to the surroundings of their home, family, immediate kinship circle, and neighborhood (Dankelman and Davidson 1989). Even in urban centers, the segregation of women at work, on public transport, and in hospital, schools, and colleges continues. This sheltering is a cultural ideal most formalized in Islamic countries and even in northern India where there is a large Muslim population. These separate worlds of men and women dictate the division of labor in the family, and innate differences are presumed between the protector and the protected from which an assumption of fundamental sexual inequality is generated. In families where physical segregation does not exist, purdah manifests itself in clothing, gestures, and silent movement of women (Papanek 1982).

Although purdah is practiced by many households that can afford it, the economic and social realities of the present day may not justify the continuation of the practice. However, interestingly enough, the economic realities of landlessness and poverty forces many rural Muslim families in India and Bangladesh to abandon the practice. The studies by Agarwal (1986, 1990) on India and by Kabeer (1990, 1991) on Bangladesh lend support to Kandiyoti's (1985) observation that the intensified commoditization which produces processes of proletarianization, semiproletarianization, or sheer pauperization erodes the material bases of classic patriarchy.

At the other extreme, in Thailand economic impoverishment provides the rural parents with the justification to condone their daughter's involvement in the sex trade and the lure of foreign exchange inflow provides the justification for the country's political elites to let the practice continue, although it is culturally and morally condemned by the society. Prostitution is also a form of patriarchy under which the parent-daughter relationship is appropriated to serve the economic interest of the family and oppression is inflicted on them through economic injustice, male dominant culture, and tradition (Lewis 1987).

Thus in the case of institutionalization of prostitution in Thailand it may be said that the current economic and social realities have prevented the creation of the appropriate social and political environment for the abandonment of the institution and for the restoration of old traditions and customs. What all these suggest is that although gender discrimination is morally wrong and should be eliminated from the society, in some cases there might have been economic and social justification for its continuation.

## WOMEN'S ROLE IN ECONOMIC DEVELOPMENT IN LESS DEVELOPED COUNTRIES

Women, representing slightly more than half the total population of the developing countries, actually contribute more in economic terms to economic development than is usually recognized. They account for over half the food produced in the developing world, and even more in Africa; they constitute one-fourth of the developing world's industrial labor force; they carry the main responsibility for child-care and household chores; they head one-fourth or more of the families in many developing nations; and they usually collect most of the household's water and fuel wood.

Furthermore, because of their responsibilities to provide food, to gather fuel and water, and to care for the sick and elderly, they often have valuable knowledge and experience about their environments. This knowledge, so crucial to the success of programs of sustainable development, is often overlooked or ignored by develop- ment agencies as well as governments and international agencies because women are very rarely consulted about any of their expertise (Wallace 1991).

Also indirectly, women are in a strong position to influence economic growth by slowing down the growth of population. Education and fertility are two important and interacting factors affecting development. Greater education and more social awareness of the need to plan families help reduce fertility. At the same time, while the employment opportunities for women increase with education, the cost of caring for children also increases. With the increase in the cost of caring, the preference shifts toward fewer healthy children rather than a large number of them. This shift in preference in turn helps lower fertility.

Education, by making women more aware of the need for better prenatal and infant nutrition, helps reduce infant mortality, which in turn tends to reduce fertility over the long run. Education also makes women more conscious of better health practices, specially nutrition and contraception. Thus the social returns to females' education in terms of better health for future generations and slower population growth far exceed the private benefits for the parents who pay for their education. Yet women's contribution to economic growth and development remains substan- tially underestimated, partly because women's work often does not count and partly because much of it is home based. Being underpriced, it is difficult to value, and being often immediately consumed, it quickly ceases to be visible (Hertz 1989).

Since about 75 percent of the world's population are among the poorest and women make up the majority of the poor, procuring food for their offspring and their families is probably the most important task they undertake. Women produce more than 80 percent of the food for Sub-Saharan Africa, 50–60 percent for Asia, 46 percent for the Caribbean, 34 percent for North Africa and the Middle East, and more than 30 percent for Latin America (Foster 1986). However, throughout the developing world, women also contribute substantially to the family budget through such income-generating activities as food processing, trading of agri- cultural products, and the production of handicrafts. This is specially so for the growing number of female-headed households which account for about 22 percent in Sub-Saharan Africa, 20 percent in North Africa and the Far East, and 15 percent in Latin America (Dankelman and Davidson 1989). Women make up the majority of subsistence farmers. In most rural societies women's labor provides a family with its basic diet and with any supplementary food that may be obtained from barter or from selling surplus goods. In some countries, women's participation in cash crop production is greater than that of men.

For example, in Nigeria, women work more than men in the cocoa and coffee plantations as well as in the production of rice, maize, grain, and cassava which are not destined for the export market. In Nicaragua, women make up a sizable proportion of the total workforce in coffee and cotton production.

Women, as the world's most important food producers, are directly dependent on a healthy environment and possess valuable knowledge about their environment, soil conditions, and crops. In fact, women's agricultural practices, which do not cause any long-term damage to the land and environment, were practiced in both India and China for many centuries (Shiva 1985). The knowledge and experience gained through generations allow them to exercise great flexibility in cropping practices, which provides security for themselves and for others.

Water, which is acknowledged as the basis of life, is scarce in supply in rural areas in most developing countries. But women, with their specialist knowledge, do collect water and cope when supply is scarce and in the process have developed unique customs in regard to water collection. With their knowledge of water quality, health, and sanitation and by exchanging information, they often create their own effective primary health care networks. For centuries women have been the primary gatherers of forest products such as fuel, food, and fodder. While this is an important activity for women in tribal households, women in millions of other rural households in Africa, Asia, and Latin America undertake this task. In the process they have learned the many uses of trees.

Although poor rural women and young girls migrating to urban centers in search of employment and a better life end up in slums and are largely excluded from the benefits of the formal economy of the cities, they form the backbone of the urban informal sector. There is no accurate official estimate of how many women eke out a living in informal sectors of such vast agglomerates as Calcutta, Lagos, and Mexico City, but their number would run into millions. The availability of a wide variety of goods and services at a very low cost at this sector helps the not-so-well-off formal sector city dwellers, and these women in their roles as housemaids and cooks provide an invaluable service to middle class and upper class housewives who can more effectively utilize their time to obtain greater benefits from the formal sector of the urban economy. Apart from all these, women still perform all the other household chores and their reproductive roles.

Women, whether they live in villages or towns, whether they are of poor families or rich families, tend to perform three distinct roles in the society. The first is their reproductive role, which includes everything that is necessary for reproduction of the workforce. The second is their productive role, which involves producing goods and services as part of the workforce, and the third is their community management role, which includes tasks necessary for maintenance of social relations. Women, whatever their class, assume responsibility for tasks such as cleaning, cooking, shopping, and looking after the children, husbands, family elders, and so on. They also play a key role in transmitting the culture, socializing children, and caring for the ill. Domestic tasks are varied and demand constant attention. The total time spent in doing domestic work is probably the same as, and sometimes more than, the time spent in income-earning activities (Lopez 1991).

## DEVELOPMENT IMPACTS ON WOMEN AND
## GENDER DISCRIMINATION

In developed countries women in general have been able to derive considerable benefits from growth and development. Economic growth opened up greater opportunities for education, health care, employment, and other amenities of life. Efforts have also been made by governments, voluntary organizations, and women's lobby groups to lessen considerably the force of gender discrimination from all spheres of activities. With growth and development, the concept of the nuclear family has almost been universally accepted in developed countries. This, of course, led to a significant transformation in family culture and environment. Dependent on themselves to bring up a family and to build up a future for themselves and their children, men now recognize and appreciate the value of women's contribution to the family's income and therefore have come to accept the fact that women are also independent living entities with a mind and a voice of their own. Girls brought up in this culture and environment, therefore, are significantly less subjected to discrimination on the basis of their gender than in other cultures. The growth of such a nuclear family culture and environment can, of course, be attributed to industrialization, increasing urbanization of industrial societies, and the concomitant breakdown of the old extended family system. With the breakdown of the old system, old social customs, traditions, and prejudices embodying gender restrictions and enforced by family elders also gradually began to disappear. In the whole process, education and media have played a crucial role by making women aware of the contribution they make to their families and to the wider society and of the discrimination they experience in their family, social, and economic spheres, thereby helping them to organize into powerful groups with considerable electoral clout. In both the United States and Australia, where women account for slightly over 50 percent of the total population, women's votes were crucial in the Democratic Party's success in the U. S. presidential election in 1992 and the Labor Party's success in the Australian federal election in 1993.

Nevertheless, gender bias still persists in industrialized societies. Schröder (1987) observes that even in the United States, single mothers are the real poor. First, motherhood without a financial contribution from the father means that the responsibility for bringing up a family rests entirely on the mother. Second, due to extreme segregation on the labor market, they receive a poverty line wage for a working day of sixteen hours. Mothers not (any longer) in families form a class, the members of which together with their children are sinking into poverty. In the United States, the number of single-mother families run into several millions. In the European Communities (EC), it exceeds four million. In North America, as in many other developed countries, women workers are concentrated in a small range of poorly paying occupations—primarily clerical and service jobs. Changes brought about in the availability and conditions of work in these predominantly female occupations by computers and telecommunications technologies produce significant effects on the precarious economic welfare of millions of women and their children. A Georgia Institute of Technology study forecasts a reduction in clerical employment of 22 percent for the insurance industry and 10 percent for banking by the year 2000 in the United States (Andolsen 1987). It is also noted that in the United States, minority women are disproportionately concentrated in those clerical jobs most vulnerable to elimination through technological change. Minority women are also more likely to have stressful, highly routine, and rigidly monitored jobs. Many of these jobs are being shifted from urban locations with high minority populations to rural and suburban communities where employers can hire comparatively well educated married women willing to work part time. Furthermore, as more routine works are completely automated, those clerical workers who manage to retain their jobs and those newly appointed perform duties in a closed environment isolated from other workers. Such a system produces a social isolation which diminishes the quality of work life for many clerical workers and weakens workers' solidarity. These are just a few examples.

In developing countries also economic development has helped improve many women's socioeconomic status. Expansion of educational opportunities and improvement in health care facilities have opened up better employment opportunities for women and have helped reduce the fertility rate, infant mortality rate, and so on. Much of these benefits have been enjoyed by women in urban areas. But the picture in rural areas, where the overwhelming majority of the total population and women live, is markedly different. It is fascinating to observe that as we move from extremely traditional villages to semirural villages, to rural towns, to midi cities, and, finally, to megacities, the intensity and pervasiveness of gender bias against women within the surroundings of their home and outside tend to lessen gradually and considerably. In large cities, the prospects for educated women gaining economic independence are considerably better than in towns and rural areas. Education and greater exposure to media have made women more aware of the value of the contribution they make to their family's sustenance. With the rapid expansion of the nuclear family in the cities, the value of the wife's contribution to the family is being increasingly recognized by the husband.

Furthermore, the frequency and severity of enforcement of gender discrimination against women in their social and economic spheres seem to have lessened considerably due to the disappearance from the nuclear families of the upholders of old traditions, customs, and prejudices, for example, the extended family elders such as grandparents. Also, although the custom of marriage by negotiation is still practiced widely in urban centers in many Third World countries, the economic and social pressure of finding a suitable match for their offspring has been forcing an increasingly larger number of parents to accept the practice of marriage by choice. By accepting this, the urban society is gradually recognizing that women are independent living entities.

On the other hand, in rural towns and villages, such conditions as outlined above are not present in any measurable extent. Accordingly, gender discrimination against women in the social and economic sphere within their homes and outside reigns supreme. In India the extended family system is widely prevalent and the influence of family elders on the lives of women is still quite strong. During the fieldwork in 1992 in a rural town in India for the present authors' (Roy and Tisdell) ongoing research project on technological change and rural poverty, a number of unemployed unmarried female university graduates reported to K. C. Roy that while the economic independence of women is extremely important for lessening the gender bias against women, the story does not end there. Even if the employment opportunities are there, they are prevented from utilizing these opportunities by their parents because they (parents) cannot go against the wishes of their grandparents, and also neighbors in the street and locality will ridicule their parents for allowing their daughters to go outside their home for employment.

Also, since the presence of young unmarried daughters in the family seems to be unacceptable to the neighbors, the daughters, although educated, are forced to marry any groom the parents can get. Many of those unmarried educated women who have managed to achieve economic independence but live in extended families find gender restrictions imposed on them by the family elders. This situation exists in upper caste families in India. But on the other side of the rural spectrum, while some poor women in many developing countries have benefited from increased employment opportunities due to the adoption in agriculture of technological change and expansion of export crop cultivation, millions of other landless and land-poor rural women have suffered: The technological change in and the increasing mechanization of agriculture have displaced these women from their traditional tasks in agriculture and the degradation of environment, disappearance of forests and village commons due to increased population pressure, commercial exploitation of forests, increasing demand for raw materials from industries, and illegal expropriation of village commons by powerful villagers have robbed these women of the traditional source of supply of free goods for their families' sustenance. The displacement of women from their traditional work in agriculture by contributing to the diminution of their economic independence may have further accentuated the preexisting gender bias against them, although their overall work burden has not lessened. Absence of the right to inheritance and other legal and institutional barriers and the presence of gender bias in the design and implementation of development programs appear to have prevented women from realizing their full potential under economic development and have contributed to the persistence of gender discrimination against them in the social and economic sphere.

## SOME INSTANCES AND IMPLICATIONS OF GENDER DISCRIMINATION IN DEVELOPING COUNTRIES

Even with the initiation of agrarian reforms in many countries, the politics of land ownership often work to ensure that the most productive land remains in the hands of a few, particularly men. Many of the effects of industrialized agriculture are confined to women because of the gender-specific division of labor in rural agricultural societies. In most cultures, rural women are responsible for food processing and fuel and water gathering. But the performance of these tasks becomes more difficult as with diminishing access to fertile lands they are displaced to more distant, fragile, and less fertile lands and are increasingly marginalized to the status of landless laborers.

In Africa, women's subsistence agriculture suffers from neglect where large-scale agriculture absorbs land and economic resources. At the same time, the labor necessary for survival increases. In Cameroon, for example, men were given land, water, seeds, and technical training to enable them to produce rice for sale. Women were then expected to carry out their traditional agricultural tasks in the cash-crop rice fields, as well as cultivating sorghum for their families (Foster 1986). The work that women are expected to do in growing cash crops, planting, and in weeding is often more gruelling than men's work, as men generally run the farm machinery. In Sierra Leone the introduction of tractors and modern ploughs resulted in a decrease of the working day for men in the rice culture, but women had to work 50 percent more to finish weeding and maintaining the larger fields. In Kenya and Uganda widespread use of insecticides and fungicides made many women redundant who previously performed by hand 85 percent of the task of weeding (Dankelman and Davidson 1989). Under large-scale agricultural expansion, those women who have access to land would rarely have access to capital or credit to invest in agricultural inputs. As Taylor (1985) observes: "When you cannot afford to drink the milk from your own buffalo, but must sell it to buy wheat, what possibility is there of purchasing fertilizers and imported seeds?"

When rural women do participate in the wage labor economy, they face discrimination and lower wage rates. In countries that are trying to meet rural needs through the development of agroindustry, discrimination in job classification and wages is specially intense. In food-processing industries for export, women are employed in the vast majority of jobs because they can be paid at significantly lower rates than men. This situation is widely prevalent in Mexico where young rural women, as wage workers in agriculture or agroindustry, face unfavorable conditions due to the lack of legal and union protection, are discriminated against in the labor market, are conditioned to behave in a docile manner, and accordingly are more vulnerable than men to exploitation (Arizpe and Botey 1987). Moreover, they face a fluctuating labor market controlled by unscrupulous middlemen and agents. Peasant women are still required to carry out their responsibilities for feeding, protecting, and socializing their children and families, often without the support of their partners, who have migrated. They are also exposed to sexual violence both within the home and outside. Their gender subordination in social and political life makes it even more difficult for peasant women to improve their situation. In Brazil, a study (Guazzelli 1985) reported that the unplanned effects of development forces rural women to leave the countryside for the large cities, but the limited options for work there intensifies their poverty. Many women are forced to work in the informal sector selling food and other goods on the streets or doing domestic work. Others are forced into prostitution. Other women in subsistence agriculture who have not been part of the mainstream educational activity and have been out of reach of extension workers are specially vulnerable to the injudicious use of dangerous chemicals. In Central America, an increasingly larger number of women are found with poisoned milk from pesticides. The consequences of such development impacts on women and children have been largely overlooked (Dankelman and Davidson 1989).

## MEASURES TO ADDRESS THE ISSUES AND PROBLEMS

With the recognition of the importance of the role of women in development, policies, programs, and projects designed to assist low-income women have proliferated throughout the Third World. The widespread dissatisfaction emanating in the 1970s from female professionals and researchers, development economists, and planners and the U. N. with the welfare approach, which, with its assumption that women are passive recipients of development rather than participants in the development process, was primarily concerned with relief aid for socially vulnerable groups, led to the development of such other approaches to women's issues as equity, antipoverty, efficiency, and empowerment.

The equity approach encountered problems from the outset due to its underlying logic that since women beneficiaries have lost ground to men in the development process, in a process of redistribution men have to share in a manner that entails women from all socioeconomic classes gaining and men from all socioeconomic classes losing, through positive discrimination policies, if necessary.

With its assumption that the origins of women's poverty and inequality with men are attributable to their lack of access to private ownership of land and capital and to sexual discrimination in the labor market, the antipoverty approach aims to increase the employment and income-generating options of low-income women through better access to productive resources. Projects designed under this approach often ignored problems such as access to raw materials, markets, and so on. Moreover, unless employment leads to greater autonomy, it does not meet strategic gender needs.

The efficiency approach has found favor with international agencies and the Oranization for Economic Cooperation and Development (OECD) governments because of its adherence to the objectives of structural adjustment policies.

Finally, the empowerment approach, while acknowledging the origin of women's subordination in the family, emphasizes that women experience oppression differently according to their race, class, colonial history, and current position in the international economic order. Its action is focused in terms of the capacity of women to increase their own self-reliance and internal strength. Increase in women's self-reliance can be achieved by enhancing their ability to gain control over crucial material and nonmaterial resources. However, this approach maintains that women will have to challenge oppressive structures and situations at different levels. Owing to this potentially challenging nature of the empowerment approach, it has remained largely unsupported by national government and bilateral aid agencies (Moser 1991).

The World Bank approach to women's development combines essential elements of the antipoverty approach, efficiency approaches, and the empowerment approach. Much of the research on women's issues and also, for example, our fieldwork in rural India point to women's economic independence being a key factor in women's development. To this end, the World Bank's efforts are directed to make productive inputs, credit, and information more readily available to women farmers and rural and urban entrepreneurs, to expand or improve education at primary and secondary levels, and to strengthen local maternal health and family planning services. This may require bringing services physically closer to women; involving women more in the design, management, and delivery of services; and strengthening and working with women's groups as contact points and to give women greater influence. Since the existing extension services often fail to reach women, an overhauling of the existing services by involving women in the delivery of services and by using women's groups and contact points (Hertz 1989) is necessary. However, realizing these requires enormous legal, financial, technical, and manpower support from national governments, as well as active support and involvement of nongovernment organizations (NGOs), international donor agencies, donor governments, and women's groups both at international and local levels.

Governments in both developed and developing countries have tried to improve the status of women through top-down legislation which has tended to meet potential gender needs. While the financial and other supports from the government have been forthcoming, the resource-strapped less developed country (LDC) governments implementing structural adjustment programs find it easier to cut funding to those areas which are supported by politically weaker lobby groups. Hence efficiency in the use of resources assumes importance.

Empowerment of women would require them to be actively involved in the development process. But existing institutional barriers may prevent that from happening. For example, in a rural household, a woman may try to gain her economic independence by earning an income, but in keeping with the local culture and tradition, the husband may take the whole income. If the woman seeks justice from the council of village elders (dominated by male members), her grievances may receive no sympathetic hearing. Hence measures to empower and utilize women in the economic development process ought to be accompanied by actions to change the society's perception of women and their needs, which is deeply rooted in the culture. Something which is rooted in culture can be changed gradually by education of women, family, and village elders and by actions by NGOs and women's grass-roots organizations. Many such organizations have grown during the last fifteen to twenty years in Asia, Africa, and Latin America and have achieved results. But their number and resource capacity are also limited. There are more than 6,000 women's groups in Africa alone. Enabling rural women to change their lives would thus require a restructuring of the existing social and political setup. Although it will be a long process, progress toward the goal is not impossible.

Therefore, this overview of issues affecting women in the development process sets the scene for the discussions to follow in succeeding chapters. The rest of this chapter briefly summarizes the central theme of each of these chapters covering women in development in five continents.

## SUMMARIES

In his theoretical survey on the relation between economic development and the status of women, Clem Tisdell organizes his discussion around pessimistic and optimistic views about the nature of this relation. In the former case a common view seems to be that primitive societies are more egalitarian and in some cases even matriarchal. According to the author, it is doubtful whether such a generalization is adequate. European colonialism and the social and economic institutions introduced by the colonial powers do seem to have affected the situation of women in the colonies in a predominantly negative way. Even if the era of colonialism is now behind us, some authors still use the center-periphery paradigm as a device for explaining the allegedly deteriorating status of women. There are also examples of other traits of the development process that may impair the status of women. Not least the tendency of women to be concentrated in a rather small number of industries and occupations appears to militate against a positive relation between the status of women and the level of economic development.

According to the optimistic view subsistence economies are generally patriarchal and in the absence of growth women cannot gain independence, while the proliferation of the market system—which is inherently nondiscriminating—opens up new opportunities for activities outside the household and, hence, for improving the women's socioeconomic status. This development is reinforced by the fact that economic growth regularly results in better education opportunities, health care, and so on, also for women. This in turn improves the employment possibilities for women and is likely to lead to smaller families.

In developed countries some problems related to equality remain, despite extensive legislation. There is no final explanation for this, but for one thing, a woman's career is frequently interrupted by childbearing. Hence their level of work-related skills tends to be lower than that of men. In addition to this there may be outright discrimination, although it has proved difficult to show exactly how important this is. The perceived role of women as homemakers is definitely a major reason for their subordinate status on the labor market. However, there is evidence that gender-based discrimination has declined during the last few decades and this decline has been correlated with economic growth.

All in all, Tisdell concludes that there may be a U-shaped relationship between economic growth and the socioeconomic status of women. At low levels of income the relation may well be negative, but as growth continues, it is likely to turn positive.

In their chapter on women in Taiwan, Cal Clark, Janet Clark, and Bih-er Chou also note that economic development is often ambiguous as to its effects on women. On the one hand development may create new opportunities, but on the other hand development patterns have often been such that women have lost their traditional role and still are unable to secure more than a marginal role in the labor market. Taiwan as a case study of this problem is interesting as its culture is largely based on Confucianism, which is quite patriarchal. On the other hand, the country has shown a very rapid economic development, which should have put enormous pressure on the traditional way of life.

According to the authors, the Taiwanese women seem to have done quite well in international comparison. In terms of fertility, infant mortality, and life expectancy for women the figures show without any doubt that Taiwan has done very well as compared to an "average" country at the same level of gross domestic product (GDP) per capita. A closer look at the position of the Taiwanese women in the country's socioeconomic structure reveals a more nuanced picture, though.

The labor force participation rate for women increased from 36 percent in 1961 to 46 percent in 1988. Having examined the figures on the share of women and men in different occupational strata, the authors conclude that women do not seem to be particularly disadvantaged. This picture is somewhat misleading, however, since only 7 percent of women were able to secure managerial or professional positions. Furthermore, women suffer from wage discrimination. In the mid-1980s women earned on average only two-thirds of the earnings of men with a comparable education.

Another indicator of women's disadvantaged status is the fact that 36 percent of employed women now work in industrial production, where they often form a "part-time proletariat." These women are mostly still dependent on the traditional family structure. Women are particularly disadvantaged in commerce and agriculture, however, where most of them are either unpaid family members or self-employed.

The analytical framework used by the authors presumes that economic, social, and political institutions evolve historically, thus shaping the socioeconomic conditions and policy responses to them. In the case of Taiwan, agricultural and industrial development contributed strongly to the advancement of women due to some special characteristics of this development. Land reform created a highly egalitarian small-scale agricultural structure where the relatively low degree of mechanization prevented a gender-based division of labor. Industrialization was also predominantly small scale in Taiwan and thus did not disrupt the traditional support system and family ties as much as in many other countries. In fact, rural families often participated in both agricultural and industrial activities simultaneously.

The third crucial institutional feature was the compulsory education system put in place in the early 1950s enabling women as well as men to take advantage of the new opportunities created by agricultural and industrial development. By the 1980s the gender differences between enrollment ratios at all levels of education had virtually disappeared. On the negative side, however, women with little or no education and usually older and/or rural women suffered a loss of status as a consequence of economic development. As agriculture declined, it became more and more "feminized," while the upgrading of the industrial structure tends to leave the unskilled woman workers behind. The institutional changes that by and large benefited women as well as men were not specifically aimed at improving the status of women. Hence, when negative effects appeared, the authorities did not envisage any specific measures to counter the problems.

In her chapter on the situation of women in China, Gao Kun concentrates on pinpointing remaining problems after the establishment of the People's Republic, which in principle guaranteed equal rights for women and men.

As to participation of women in politics and government affairs, the share of women has been unambiguously on the increase, even if it is still far from equal to that of men. Further advancement is aggravated by pending political reforms and, not least, by the Chinese cultural heritage that presupposes women to maintain a low profile as regards public affairs.

Women now officially comprise 45 percent of the total labor force, up from 7 percent in 1949. Most women employees have now completed secondary-level education, although their average level of education is slightly lower than that of their male counterparts. As to vocational training, women are gradually catching up with men even if they still lag behind the male employees on average.

The Chinese women's expectations concerning work are to a great extent geared toward lifetime employment. According to surveys, the main motive for working is the economic one, but economic independence is an important motive, too. The recent economic reforms in China have opened up possibilities to choose occupation and workplace more freely, but still the opportunities are considered far from satisfactory as, for example, it is not unusual that husband and wife work at locations distant from each other. Moreover, discrimination against women in terms of enrollment, employment, and promotion is still common. The problems are now being seriously addressed, not least by utilizing existing and newly established mass media, but also through surging research on women's issues.

In the rural sector the economic reforms have greatly increased production efficiency. Hence, much labor is being released, paving the way for rural enterprises, which in turn can offer new possibilities for emancipation and new job opportunities for women. According to available studies, women's share of employment in the rural industries is very high, especially in the "light" type of industry. Moreover, women employed in these emerging rural industries are younger and better educated on average than women workers in general. As the share of these rural industries in production was as high as 48.5 percent in 1992, it is obvious that these new developments are very significant for the national economy of China.

Education of women has made great progress during the last decade. In spite of the impressive figures that can be presented in this context, serious problems remain. The average duration of education is still markedly shorter for women as compared to men. Women's educational rights are often violated, and it is not uncommon for girls to drop out of school. Female college students, although only a small proportion of all women, face difficulties finding jobs after having completed their studies. Among students in tertiary institutions women account for 33.7 percent of the total (1992); at the secondary, technical level their share was 46.1 percent, in ordinary secondary schools 43.1 percent, and in primary schools 46.6 percent.

Jamilah Ariffin analyzes the relation between the export-oriented industrialization process of Malaysia, women's entry into paid employment, and how this process can be understood in terms of gender. For Malaysian women there are no serious sociocultural norms to keep them out of the labor force. Hence, the industrialization of the country has to a significant extent relied on female labor. This is especially prevalent in the affiliates of multinational companies, particularly in specially designed export processing zones. In the electronics and electrical industries, for example, 76 percent of the workers were female in 1990. In the garment and textile industries the female workers are a majority as well. According to the author, this cannot be explained only in terms of a "normal" development process but is related to a changing international division of labor where it has been advantageous to locate certain industrial activities in, for example, Malaysia and to rely on female labor to a great extent.

Production in the export processing zones was labor intensive and highly specialized (but did not require a high level of skill). The inputs were imported and the goods produced were mostly exported. Due to their personal qualifications, such as dexterity, patience, and docility, and to the fact that they were willing to work for low wages, women were the preferred workers in this type of operation. Malaysia also had a large reserve of unutilized female labor in the 1970s.

In the 1970s there was some criticism of women's taking up paid employment based on the allegation that they would "deprive men of jobs." According to the author, there is little justification for such criticism, since the jobs created were in fact gender specific. Work conditions and the level of pay were not attractive to male workers and the availability of work was heavily dependent on fluctuations in the world market.

The present industrialization policy of Malaysia is geared toward upgrading the industrial structure. This may jeopardize the jobs of women due to increasing use of automated machines and also due to the fact that technically trained workers are mostly male.

Jane Richardson and Paul Riethmuller analyze the socioeconomic status of Japanese women, particularly from the point of view of their increasing participation in the paid workforce. In general Japanese women traditionally have been rather "invisible" outside the home, although they have always played an important indirect role in economic affairs. During and after the World War II it became more common for women to take on jobs, albeit mostly part-time work demanding little skill.

The postwar constitution formally established equal rights between men and women and women became entitled to vote. This, and the introduction of compulsory education for all, has gradually led to major changes in the status of women in Japan. The role of women in the workplace continued to be subordinate, however, as it was generally expected that a woman quit working when she got married.

The progress in education of women has been very rapid after the war. By now over 40 percent of an age group advances to tertiary education. A majority of the women attend junior colleges, though, contrary to their male counterparts, a fact that limits their access to the government bureaucracy or the big corporations.

Women workers offered a way out for the seriously labor-strapped Japanese industry after 1965. The pattern of labor force participation for women in Japan resembles an M, that is, the peaks are found for young and middle-aged women, while the participation rate is markedly lower between 25 and 40 years of age, when women often have young children to tend to. All in all, women now comprise over 50 percent of the workforce.

The Japanese system of lifetime employment where the salary is based on seniority was not extended to women until very recently, as they were regarded as temporary workers, not worthwhile to invest in. Even starting wages were lower for women than for men, and the gap widened over time. In 1992 Japanese women received on average only 60 percent of what men were paid, which is the largest pay differential in the OECD.

The situation for women in the labor market has improved after 1985, due to changes in labor legislation. In many firms two different employment streams are now offered to women, depending on their attitude to career and family responsibilities. Other changes in the recruitment policies of firms, usually from a men-only policy to recruitment of both sexes, can be observed as well. Despite this it is still unusual to see women in senior positions, and women are still sometimes hired only to contribute favorably to a company's public image. Moreover, at times of economic crisis, as in the early 1990s, the system tends to fall back into traditional roles where women are considered a secondary source of labor.

Contrary to their status in public life, the Japanese women have traditionally had a very strong position at home, including also the running of the economic affairs of the household. Allowing the husband to concentrate on work alone, the indirect contribution of women to the economic development of Japan has been very significant. The break-up process of the traditional Japanese family structure is now changing the role of genders in the household, too, but traditional roles are still perceived by women to be a major obstacle to equality at work.

In their chapter on South Asia, Kartik Roy and Clem Tisdell conclude that the socioeconomic status of women in India is higher than in Afghanistan, Bangladesh, Bhutan, and Nepal but lower than in Sri Lanka and China. In India the antifemale bias is related to the extent that women's work is socially visible and recognized as valuable. Hence, household work and other engagement in nonmarket activities is usually regarded as being of secondary value. However, access to land is limited for women, not least due to prevailing customary law, and even when this is not the case, women face difficulties trying to participate in socially visible activities. On the bottom of the social structure are the landless female laborers. Not only are they less paid than men, but their choice as far as employment opportunities is far more restricted.

Women are discriminated against within the family as well. Among other things, women tend to use a much larger part of their income on common family needs while at the same time receiving less food, in terms of both calories and nutritional value, than the male members of the household.

Among the modes of discrimination the custom of dowry is one of the major problems. This custom has gradually spread to all social classes and now often involves a continuous obligation of the natal family of a bride. Apart from being an excessive economic burden for this family, the custom has led to widespread abuse of daughters-in-law in their new families. Furthermore, dowry is frequently a reason for discrimination of women, not only by men, but by other women as well.

Employment is a way of achieving economic independence for women, while education is a means of obtaining and staying in employment. Enrollment in education has increased steadily for girls in India since independence, but the rate is still not impressive. The expansion of the educational system has been strongest at the higher levels, however. Less emphasis has been placed on primary and vocational education, which are the most important levels from a development point of view. Apart from improvements in education, indicators of health show considerable improvement since the early 1950s. Despite this, the figures are still modest in international comparison and the differences between different states are large.

Female workforce participation increased during the 1980s in the country as a whole. The number of marginal workers also increased, however, and unemployment is higher for women than for men. Household studies conducted by the authors indicated that women, on the whole, had gained from employment possibilities created by recent technological changes. Remarkably enough, high-caste women had not been able to benefit as much as others due to cultural restrictions, however. Environmental degradation, on the other hand, had aggravated the situation of women, and there are no signs that their work burden has decreased as a result of technological change. In urban areas the role of women is also changing, as economic necessities and various sociopsychological needs force educated women to take up paid work besides their traditional housekeeping role. Whether this puts more strain on women than before is a moot point, however, according to a recent study by the Indian Statistical Institute.

Felix Mlay, Kartik Roy, and Clem Tisdell scrutinize women's situation in Sub-Saharan Africa, especially in Tanzania. Historically, subsistence agriculture was the realm of women in Africa. The emergence of, first, animal husbandry and, later, cash cropping shifted the gender balance toward men, who also were able to enter the monetary economy earlier than women due to the paid work opportunities available to them. Women ended up in a situation where the products of their labor were considered inferior and where they lacked access to the resources of society. As a result, most African women are dependent on a male family member, both legally and practically. This dependent status is reinforced by many customary values of the society. For example, women in Africa cannot usually inherit land and may not have legal entitlement to productive resources while their men are alive. From this it follows also that women have difficulties in obtaining credit from banks and other "formal" institutions.

Women's role in politics and working life is very subordinate in Africa. Even highly educated women are subject to discrimination. As girls have a value partly as unpaid labor and partly because of the dowry they fetch, the education of girls is often neglected. Even if the effects of agricultural modernization on women is a matter of some controversy, it seems likely that women have been adversely affected by the process, especially when it involves mechanization and use of fertilizers and pesticides. The problem is exacerbated by environmental degradation, related or not to the modernization of agriculture.

The discussion on equality that took place in Tanzania after independence tended to be blind for gender differences. National policy took for granted that general programs would benefit all, including women. The National Women Organization, which is the main channel for communicating women's issues, is ill funded and does not reach out to the grass-roots level. Recently the low status of women in Tanzania has been increasingly recognized, however, and steps have been taken to encourage, for example, the education of girls. Primary education has for long been compulsory for all. Hence, girls comprise 48 percent of primary school students. The situation is much worse at higher levels, however. Only 20 percent of secondary school students and 15 percent of university students are female.

The socialist rhetoric of the government has done little to improve the situation for women, since actual policies have not addressed the factors that contributed to class and gender imbalances. The crucial issue here is the decision-making process and control of productive resources, which is necessary for other social and economic activities. Even the nationalization of land has not led to equal access to land for women and men. On the contrary, the establishment of "Ujamaa" villages on balance made the women worse off since their traditional land rights were not taken into account when the new communities were formed.

The structural adjustment programs imposed at the initiative of the International Monetary Fund (IMF) and the World Bank have caused some undesired side effects as far as women are concerned. Due to falling real income in rural areas, immigration to the cities has been surging, leaving more agricultural work to women than before. The relative profitability of cash crops as compared to basic foodstuffs—for which the women are responsible—has improved and, hence, the nutritional status of the population has declined. In its effort to cut down on government expenses, health care, and education have suffered, and in both cases women have been hurt more than men.

Harriet Silius deals with the situation of women in Finland, starting out from the concept of (implicit) gender contract. This concept describes institutions and practices that organize the relations between women and men and is used as a device for explanation of women's subordinate position in the labor market, and their primary responsibilities in the realm of reproduction and care, in advanced "welfare states."

The rural community, comprising small, independent farms, was dominant in Finland until recently. The upper and middle classes were small. In such a society both men and women had to work hard in order to survive. However, the society was much more equal than in most countries in continental Europe. Men and women mostly performed different tasks but women could take over the men's work should the men be absent for some reason.

The economic and social changes from the 1960s on as regards industrial structure and urbanization were both rapid and fundamental. The women mostly remained part of the labor force as the incentive structure of the Finnish society was geared toward dual-earner families. Labor force participation of Finnish women is among the highest in the world. A special feature of the Finnish labor market is the low prevalence of part-time work among women, compared to the other Nordic countries and most other European countries as well. Hence, most mothers of young children work full time in Finland; in fact, they did so even before public daycare facilities were made available (in the 1970s).

Extensive maternity care and other services facilitating the life of working mothers were made available starting from 1944, including paid maternity leave, child allowance, and free school lunch. In the private sphere, however, mothers still do considerably more unpaid homework related to childcare than men and also tend to be the ones who organize workable daily routines for families with two working parents.

Gender segregation of the labor market is characteristic for Finland, as well as in all other developed countries, and segregation is upheld by education patterns. On average, women earn 20 percent less than their male colleagues. Affirmative action programs do not exist and there are signs that the Equality Act has not improved the situation of the underprivileged gender but rather has enhanced the status of men in female-dominated workplaces.

The Nordic welfare state seems to a great extent to be built on underpaid female labor. According to Silius, the gender contract in the context of the welfare state comprises the right for women to work and a certain independence from individual men, as long as they go on taking responsibility for the caring functions in society. This gender contract was made between women, leaving the role of men virtually unchanged. The contract between men and women, on the other hand, seems to imply that women's quest for equality should be carried out in a way that goes unnoticed by men.

In his chapter on women in the European Union, Hans C. Blomqvist deals, on the one hand, with the measures taken by the Union to order to enhance equality and, on the other hand, with the reality of the socioeconomic situation of women in Europe. By and large, one can conclude that the situation of women has improved during the last few decades, a development that is due partly to deliberate measures but perhaps even more to the structural change of the economies in question.

Important issues remain unsolved, however. Women still earn less than men in all member countries, a fact that mainly seems to be a result of segregated labor markets. Due to missing or deficient social services, women are still frequently constrained in their ability to engage themselves wholeheartedly in paid work. Despite this, the unemployment rate for women is often higher than that of men. Safety regulations, often de facto, work to the disadvantage of women. Finally, the role of women in politics and other public affairs is much smaller than their share of the population would lead us to expect. This is obvious also in the administration of the Union itself—even if women represent about half of the employees, their share of the senior staff is very small.

In their chapter on the status of women in the United States, Cal and Janet Clark start out from the fact that women often enjoy a standard of living and equal gender status far above that of most women in the world. Despite this, there are problems, and as a matter of fact, the high level of development tends to create new ones.

Although the United States has had a very dynamic economy for most of the last 150 years there are now signs that this dynamism is faltering, creating increasing social stress as a result. The outcome of these developments, as far as women are concerned, is rather mixed. In the early days, the combination of individualism and availability of mass education most probably enhanced the status of women as compared to other countries. The rapid expansion of work opportunities in the nineteenth and early twentieth centuries was conducive to gender emancipation, especially as work opportunities in white collar occupations increased rapidly as compared to blue collar jobs. This development reached its final stage in the 1970s when large numbers of married women entered the labor force. The participation rate for women rose from 30 percent in 1950 to 58 percent in 1992.

While these developments have been predominantly positive, several problems have become apparent. Furthermore, in some respects the situation has been deteriorating rather than improving during the last few decades. Gender segregation of workplaces is still very much prevalent, not least in the white collar occupations, to the disadvantage of women. Equality in education has not translated into equality on the labor market. Presently, the average weekly pay of a woman is only about 75 percent of that of a man, despite a positive trend in the 1980s.

Social development has weakened the family ties and the lack of social security has made women vulnerable to the vagaries of a market economy. In fact, several indicators of women's status indicate that the United States ranks quite low among developed countries. Divorce rates and the numbers of unmarried mothers surged in the 1970s, creating a growing group of poor women. Then, in the 1980s, the welfare spending of the government was cut back by the conservative Reagan administration, further aggravating the situation. In 1991 almost half of female-headed households with children lived in poverty, compared to 8 percent of married couples with children.

Evidently due to the changing position of American women in society, their political values have recently come to differ considerably from those of men. Women's representation in politics is still rather low in the United States, however, even if their activity has been on the rise recently. Compared to the situation in other developed countries, the United States does not rate well as far as the share of women in the legislature is concerned. The main reason for this is likely to be the electoral system in the country, as the system of single member districts probably works in favor of men. On a more positive note, the last few administrations have been much more willing to appoint women to high positions than earlier administrations.

Helen Safa and María de los Angeles Crummett deal with the development of women's situation in Latin America against the backdrop of the recent emphasis on market forces and downplaying of government intervention in the region. The chapter focuses on three main topics: the increasing female labor force participation; the consequent effects on family structure, especially the growth of female-headed households and the growing contribution of women to the household economy; and the increasing participation of women in various social movements.

The authors conclude that recent changes in gender roles in Latin America have been conducive to promoting greater gender consciousness. The educational level of women has risen faster than that of men, and women's role as members of the paid labor force has become increasingly important. Still women encounter discrimination in the form of segregation of the labor market and lower earnings than men.

The problems inherent in poverty and inequality on the labor market are partly caused and certainly exacerbated by an ideology that identifies the role of women with that of a wife and a mother. This justifies treating women as secondary labor who can be paid less and segregated into less attractive jobs. In order to eliminate this problem, the myth of the dependent woman has to be replaced by a more egalitarian way of thinking, in which women are regarded as equals. The resistance from a male-dominated society which profits from the subordination of women tends to be strong, however.

In Australia, here covered by Sukhan Jackson, women's participation in the paid labor force has been on the increase during the last few decades both in absolute numbers and in terms of participation rate. The latter was 45.8 percent in 1993. The increase is due to the fact that more married women have recently joined the labor force. Important determinants of this trend are the increasing relative wage rate for women, declining fertility rates, higher education level for women, and changing social attitudes.

The Australian labor market is characterized by a high degree of segregation. Seventy-eight percent of working women are to be found in only five industrial sectors: community services; wholesale and retail trade; finance, property, and business services; recreation and personal services; and manufacturing. Even there women usually occupy the lower echelons. Women are overrepresented especially in the service sector. Also occupation-wise the degree of segregation is high in Australia compared to other OECD countries. A very high percentage of the working women in the country are part timers, holding jobs that offer low wages, little training, and poor prospects for promotion. Women's careers are negatively affected also by prolonged absence from the labor market due to, for example, childbearing. Even in full-time work women earn less than men: In the early 1970s the average relative wage of a woman was about 60 percent of that of a man. The gap has been diminishing, however, and the corresponding figure is now about 90 percent. (This comparatively high figure may be misleading, though, as it captures only the minimum wage rate enforceable by law.)

In the chapter the reasons for gender-based differences in pay are also discussed, from an Australian point of view. The author finds that the human capital theory of pay differences is not relevant for Australia, inasmuch as education is concerned, while the broken record of employment, typical for many women, may be more important. As to the demand-based theories of discrimination, the so-called distaste model is not relevant for Australia, whereas the theories of statistical discrimination and monopsonic discrimination seem to be more useful. Also the radical theories of labor market segregation and the concept of internal labor markets seem to have some explanatory value.

In order to overcome the discrimination problem, legislation on equality has been passed, although this was resorted to relatively late, starting from 1984. (The principle of equal pay was adopted during 1969–1972, however.) There are signs suggesting that this legislation has had the intended effect in the sense that a slow breakdown in gender segregation can be discerned.

The socioeconomic status of women is multidimensional, and economic development can improve the status of women in some respects and cause it to deteriorate in other respects. Because of this multidimensional aspect, there can be ambivalence about how the socioeconomic status of women overall has changed as a result of economic development. The contributions in this book explore how individual dimensions of the socioeconomic situation of women have altered in many different countries and continents and each arrives at an overall assessment for the areas concerned. In general, they provide some support for Tisdell's U-shaped relationship, namely, that in the early stages of development, the impact of economic development on the overall socioeconomic status of women is liable to be negative but becomes positive once development proceeds sufficiently. A variety of factors may give rise to this relationship, of which changes in the nature of the family from an extended to nuclear one, as mentioned by several contributors, is one. At the end of this development apparent tendencies to dissolution of the traditional core family seem to be creating new problems, however.

## ISSUES DISCUSSED

Contributions in this book examine the socioeconomic status of women on five continents, giving particular attention to social and economic discrimination against women and to changes in their status. Unfortunately, social and economic discrimination in terms of gender, race, or similar characteristics is mutually reinforcing. These aspects together create a social and economic trap for the victims of discrimination from which it is hard or even impossible for them to escape by means of their individual effort. Questions to be addressed in this volume include the following: What constitutes economic discrimination, how is it generated and sustained, and what impact does it have on economic efficiency? Why does it continue even in relatively developed and competitive market systems? How has economic development and the development of the market system altered the status of women? How can the position of women be improved harmoniously and in desirable ways by economic development? What role do women play in the development process and how can this be strengthened? Should the contribution of women to development planning and to social choice about the economic future be strengthened? How might this be achieved?

The influence of women on the economic and environmental future is very great, but their participation in public fora and decision making about these matters has been severely curtailed everywhere. This is so even in relation to the formulation of population policies, a subject on which women should at least have an equal voice to men. Issues in this respect are both specific and general, for example, the rights of women to choose their family sizes, choice about contraception and abortion, and at a more general level, the implications of population growth for sustainable development and environmental conservation. The issues outlined in this chapter are relevant not only to women but also to mankind at large.

During the last two decades, the increasing awareness in the world community of the very close link between women and the environment has helped raise in the international forum the visibility of issues affecting women's development. Researchers in women's issues, NGOs, the World Bank, and the international media have played important roles in lifting women's issues to the same stature as those of the environment. Consequently, while some of the barriers to women's progress have been dismantled, many such barriers still remain. Greater efforts by national governments, national and international NGOs, multilateral agencies such as the World Bank and the U. N., and the international women's groups are necessary to make significant progress toward dismantling social, legal, and institutional barriers to women's development. However, greater involvement of women as active participants in the whole process is also vital to the success of any effort to improve women's socioeconomic status. But, in the final analysis, it is the political commitment of governments at all levels which will stand between the success and failure of any effort to improve women's status in the world community.

# 2

## Discrimination and Changes in the Status of Women with Economic Development: General Views and Theories

### Clement A. Tisdell

### INTRODUCTION

The purpose of this chapter is to discuss general views and theories about how the socioeconomic status of women changes or might be expected to alter as economic development proceeds. However, this begs the question of what exactly is economic development and how does one judge socioeconomic status. Despite the fact that most economists recognize economic development as consisting of multiple attributes, possibly the majority persist in using GDP per capita as its prime indicator. In general, most economists associate a higher GDP per capita with greater economic development and it is an important, widely accepted indicator of economic development even though it is apparent from natural resource and environmental accounting (El Serafy 1989; Repetto et al. 1989; Young 1992) and development indices (Doessel and Gounder 1991) that it has shortcomings. As for the relative socioeconomic status of women, it is difficult to measure, and often measurement such as gender-gap analysis is limited to the type of statistical data that is readily and widely available, such as that used in the type of data contained in the UNDP, *Human Development Report 1993*.

Economic development and expansion in the use of the market system are commonly believed to go hand in hand. Historically there appears to be a positive correlation between these two attributes. The economic growth of high-income countries has over the long sweep of their history been associated with greater use of free-market systems, for example, the industrial revolution in Britain was associated with an expansion of free trade and a gradual dismantling of the mercantilist system. More recently the planned economies associated with the former Soviet

Union began to show poor economic performance and growth, and this was a major factor leading to the collapse of the communist government in these countries in the early 1990s. By contrast, China has made rapid economic growth following its market reforms, and the Chinese Communist Party has managed to remain in power. Of course, it is difficult to know to what extent economic growth is the cause of market expansion or to what extent the "causal" relationship is reversed. However, it seems clear that a full-blown relatively free market system on its own is not sufficient to ensure economic growth and that while the market system has its advantages, it is not an unmitigated blessing.

The above matter is of interest to us because it raises the question of how the market influences the socioeconomic situation of women. Does the market system ensure women of reduced inequality in relation to men in terms of income, job opportunities, access to resources, and so on? These particular questions are considered as well as the general influence of a widespread market system on discrimination against women.

## PESSIMISTIC VIEWS ABOUT HOW WOMEN FARE AS A RESULT OF ECONOMIC DEVELOPMENT AND THE SPREAD OF THE MARKET SYSTEM

Engels (1972, see also Ch. 9) believed that the socioeconomic status of women deteriorated with the advent of capitalism because men became the principal owners of capital and property. It certainly appears to be the case that gender ownership of resources influences the relative power of males and females. On the other hand, it is doubtful if capitalism per se determines the rules of property ownership and inheritance. Nevertheless, it is apparent that it was in patriarchal European communities that capitalism obtained its major flowering and it is not surprising that many of the existing paternalistic customs came to be originally embedded in the capitalist systems which grew up.

According to many Marxists, it is basically the spread of capitalistic market systems throughout the world that has led to women being subjugated to an inferior economic status. It is theorized that most "primitive" societies lived in an Eden-like communal state of egalitarianism and resource sharing that also involved equality between the sexes. These Rousseau-ideal societies were shattered by Western capitalist-inspired colonialism and imperialism commencing in the 1500s. It imposed similar systems of property rights in these societies and rights of access to markets and economic freedom to those existing in Europe which enshrined male dominance.

There are really two points to consider here: (1) Was it the case that egalitarianism was a quality of "primitive" societies? (2) Did European colonial powers impose systems of property rights and access to economic resources which favored males relative to females?

As for the first point, historical evidence indicates that it was by no means true that gender equality existed in all non-European or "primitive" societies prior to

European contact and imperialism. It is possible that in the remote prehistoric past, resources were so abundant that conflicts about resource use were not a major issue. This may have been made for relative equality. However, these circumstances (if they were ever that ideal) disappeared in Europe during the Neolithic Age, which began about 10,000 B.C. (Mithen 1994: 79) and presumably would have also disappeared in Africa by then. Mithen (1994: 79) claims that in Europe at the end of the Pleistocene (10,000 B.C.) people were living in a manner that had not changed radically for 20,000 years: "They were characterized by the egalitarian social organization and highly mobile lifestyles." Within 5,000 years the situation changed greatly: Ranked societies appeared, agriculture was introduced, and man dramatically altered natural environments.

Prior to Western European colonialism in Sub-Saharan Africa discrimination against women was already practiced by a number of tribal groups (see Ch. 8). It appears likely that in most non-European societies patriarchal rather than matri-archal systems existed prior to the colonial expansion of Western Europe. This is not to say that no matriarchal societies existed. It seems, for example, that in southern China matriarchal societies existed even though these were eventually re-placed mainly by Han patriarchal systems with the spread of the Han Chinese and possibly even prior to this. "Clan society became widely spread and flourished in China about 5,000–8,000 years ago. The matriarchal society practised communal marriage. The child saw only the mother but not the father. Therefore, women were put in a dominant position in the clan" (*Guanming Daily* 1988: 2). These relationships have been inferred from finds at Yangshao village, Henan, from the Hemudu site on the Quiantang River at the Banpo Village site at Xian. Further-more, it is clear that members of the Yangshao culture, as this group in the Yellow River region have been called, practiced animal husbandry and agriculture. Thus, these activities in themselves did not result in a paternalistic society as suggested by Engels (1972).

However, about 5,000 years ago the Longshan culture replaced the Yangshao culture in the Yellow River basin and spread to the Yangste, thereby ushering in a patriarchal clan society. The change, however, was gradual. It is suggested that "the transition from a matriarchal clan society to a patriarchal clan society was, in the main, due to the development of productive forces. As men played a leading role in agriculture and animal husbandry, they had a greater say and dominant power" (*Guanming Daily* 1988: 3). Communal marriage gave way to monogyny or polyandry. As a result, the child saw both his or her mother and father. Inheritance came to be according to the patriarchal line. Men became the main "producers" and controllers of wealth in society and so increased their power relative to females (*Guanming Daily* 1988: 3–4), a process not unlike that suggested by Engels (1972).

Matriarchal societies continued to exist in the far south of China for a consid-erable time. Some still exist in the North-East Frontier of India for example. For instance, it is reported that "the people around Shillong, the Khasias, are matri-lineal, passing down property and wealth through the female rather than the male line" (Crowther et al. 1990: 398).

The prevalence of patriarchal societies may have its roots in the relative physical strength of males, and sociologists have suggested this dominance may have psychological roots. In the latter respect, Chodorow (1978) provides a theory of the psychodynamic processes that result in males wanting to dominate. In outlining this theory Paula England and Lauri McCreary (1987: 163) state:

When women are the child rearers, girls are raised by the same-sex person, whereas boys are raised by a person of the opposite sex. As a result males become more individuated than females because defining themselves as a male requires separation from, rather than identification with their caretaker. Since male role models are relatively remote for a small boy surrounded by women, he may come to define maleness as the opposite of femaleness, producing the psychological roots of disdain for females.

Girls of course do not face the same problem.

The second question is whether Western European colonialism reduced the economic power and status of women in the countries colonized. On the whole this appears to have happened. Land titles were as a rule given to men and men in Africa were the ones employed in the cash economy, mines, and so on. Consequently men gained in relative economic power, a process described by Boserup (1970), and women became increasingly marginalized. They tended to be locked out of the market economy and be left with the activities of child raising, home duties, and subsistence farming using property and resources owned by men.

Ward (1988: 21–22) points out:

The colonial officials automatically assumed that men were the agricultural producers, because in England and other core countries, men controlled agriculture (Boserup 1970; Seidman 1981; Tinker 1976). Further the arrival of land reform often meant the displacement of women from the land. The colonial officials gave the ownership of property and land to men instead of the women who were working the land (Blumberg 1981; Boserup 1970). Even though women have produced most of the food, men controlled the distribution of the food or the profits from selling/trading the food (Blumberg 1981; Sanday 1974, 1981). Thus because of the patriarchal structures and their interaction with the world-system, women once again had little control over the products of their agricultural labor.

In addition, Ward (1988) contends that colonialism and the world trading systems in Africa, the Caribbean, and many parts of Asia have displaced women as traditional major traders. She says, "With the advance of the world system and the arrival of colonial administrations and trading companies men gained access to and control over international and national trading routes. Meanwhile, colonial officials, who ignored women's long-standing roles in trade, restricted women to regional and urban enclaves (Boserup 1970, Mintz 1971; Papanek 1975; Simms and Dunar 1976–1977)" (Ward 1988: 23). She quotes examples from Africa.

Certainly there is little to suggest that Western colonialism improved the socioeconomic status of women in colonial countries. In fact the evidence points on the whole to a deterioration. But it could be argued that this colonial era is no longer relevant and that capitalism has passed through its imperialistic stage.

Nevertheless, Ward (1988) argues that the capitalist world system (described by some neo-Marxists as the neocolonial system) has resulted in the economic status of women stagnating relative to that for men. She argues this, making use of the center-periphery paradigm of development and underdevelopment. Her basic thesis is that "general inequality increases when the processes of the capitalist world-system and underdevelopment interact with local forms of male dominance over women" (Ward 1988: 18).

Ward's argument proceeds mainly by use of examples. However, she also uses (Ward 1988: 35) some International Labor Organization (ILO) statistics to indicate that the increased *share of* women in the labor force in peripheral countries has been negligible and that their gains have mainly been in the service sector. She maintains that while some women may obtain increased employment through transnational corporations or in the service sector as a result of expansion of the global economic system, this employment is mostly low paid and insecure. She sees women as being displaced in employment in traditional sectors in peripheral economies as a result of "de-development" (induced backwardness) of these countries due to the growth of the global economy. Women are frequently forced to seek informal employment where their conditions of employment are even worse than before. She argues (Ward 1988: 33) that this has important consequences for the fertility and nursing behavior of women. In general, a lowering in the income of females is associated with higher fertility, especially if females are household heads. Women perceive an economic advantage to children when they are poor because children are a source of income through work in the informal sector. Furthermore, "women who are household heads are more likely to end their breast-feeding early, thereby, in the absence of contraception, shortening the birth interval and raising fertility" (Ward 1988: 33). A high proportion of households globally are in fact headed by women—those widowed, divorced, and abandoned. Ward suggests that globally about one-fourth or more of all households are headed by women. The incidence of poverty in such households tends to be much higher than in male-headed households. All in all, her argument indicates a deteriorating socioeconomic situation for women with the global spread of capitalism and the market system.

The view that economic developments such as the Green Revolution may have helped to marginalize women is expressed in Roy (1994a) and by Clark and Clark (1994). Clark and Clark (1994: 80) suggests that women in developing countries may face "a fairly unhappy set of alternatives in continuing their subordinate status in patriarchal cultures or facing the considerable chance of having their position eroded, not enhanced, by conventional development programmes."

Clark and Clark (1994) outline "feminist theory" which suggests that modernization rather than enhancing the status of women, may reduce it. Much of this theory, which stems from the pioneering work of Ester Boserup (1970), is similar to that outlined by Ward (1988). This is usually argued on the basis of anthropological and historical evidence, and Clark and Clark (1994: 83) summarize the suggested negative impacts on women's status as follows:

Changes in agriculture, especially the introduction of more advanced technology and the transformation from subsistence to cash crop production, undermined women's production role by decreasing their participation in actual agricultural work. After the advent of industrialization women's role in the "modern sector" was "marginalized" in the sense that they were generally confined to unstable, low-paying jobs, unskilled manufacturing jobs. Furthermore, their traditional roles and status, and support from kinship networks was substantially eroded (Anker and Hein 1986; Boserup 1970; Jaquette 1982; Leahy 1986; Nash and Fernandez-Keller 1983; Rogers 1979; Tinker 1990; Tinker and Bremsen 1976; *Women and National Development* 1977).

The exact position of Clark and Clark (1994) is a little difficult to garner. The empirical results which they provide about the ratio of females to males enrolled at school indicate that this ratio tends to rise with gross national product (GNP) per capita. However, it appears that taking all factors into account, they believe that the relative socioeconomic status of women has a U-shaped relationship with GNP per capita. It tends to decline at first with "modernization" and then to improve if GNP per capita rises sufficiently. Consequently there is a parallel with Kuznet's (1963, 1973) theory that the relationship between GNP per capita and inequality of income is of an "inverted U-shape" (cf. Clark and Clark 1994: 104).

It might be noted here that socioeconomic status depends upon many variables and its interpretation does allow a considerable degree of subjectivity. There is clearly an index problem if one indicator of socioeconomic status improves and another declines.

A number of institutionalists and neo-Marxists also argue on theoretical grounds that the extension of the market system and the development of capitalism disadvantage women because actual market systems do not satisfy the conditions postulated by neoclassical economists for a perfectly competitive "ideal." A substantial group believes that labor markets become segmented and that women become crowded into low-skill, unstable, and insecure employment possibilities with economic development and the extension of the market system. Hence, these developments do not reduce income differentials between males and females. These changes may very well increase differentials.

Crowding of women into a limited number of job markets may occur for a number of reasons. Acculturalization may play a part. Females are cast by society into particular roles; stratification may become widely accepted and be transmitted by parents and the educational system. Given decision making under uncertainty, employers may also downgrade their predictions of average productivity of females in particular types of occupations, so adding to segregation.

Some neo-Marxists suggest that the process arises from or is reinforced by class conspiracy. Male workers conspire or cooperate with capitalists to exploit females and push them into marginal occupations and insecure job positions so that females come to constitute the bulk of Marx's reserve army of workers, thereby signaling one of the later stages of capitalism, foreshadowing its collapse and replacement by socialism. However, it is far from clear that this scenario is being played out in more developed countries. There is, for example, a good deal of evidence that females are tending to replace males in middle-level work positions. Furthermore optimistic scenarios exist as far as economic development, the spread of markets, and the status women are concerned.

## OPTIMISTIC VIEWS ABOUT HOW WOMEN FARE AS A RESULT OF ECONOMIC DEVELOPMENT

The optimistic view is that the spread of markets and economic growth provide powerful forces for improvement in the relative socioeconomic status of women. Most subsistence economies are patriarchal and females are enslaved within male-dominated households with little or no possibility to escape and no means to obtain independent access to and control over resources. In the absence of economic growth and the spread of the market system, they cannot gain independent power and so there is no scope for them to improve their economic status.

With the growth of the market system specialization in production and employment is fostered, job opportunities open up for females outside the household, and eventually the relative economic power of males is reduced. In addition, the optimistic school believes that market competition will tend to ensure that there is no economic discrimination against females in conditions of employment. Competition will ensure that women are paid the value of their marginal product.

Proponents of this view argue that in a competitive market system discrimination against women and minorities in employment will not persist. If these groups are being offered less than the value of their marginal product, profit-maximizing employers will increase their demand to employ such labor, thereby forcing up the market wage rate or improving the conditions offered for employment of women and minorities. However, as noted earlier, this view has not gone unchallenged, for example, by those who argue that labor markets tend to be segmented and that women are crowded into a limited number of labor markets.

A second strand of optimistic theories is based on the view that economic growth results in the greater supply of educational opportunities, health services, and so on. Females as a result tend to benefit relatively more than males because their relative level of access to such services is very low when GNP per capita is very low. There is strong empirical evidence that the relative access of females in comparison to males to education rises as GNP per capita increases. The correlation is not perfect but it is significantly positive (Clark and Clark 1994; see also Ch. 8).

A rise in the educational level of women improves their employment opportunities and appears to lead to smaller sized families. These factors help to break poverty cycles and help to sustain further economic development.

On the basis of most available indicators of female-male socioeconomic gaps, it is clear that on average these gaps are much greater in low-income countries than in industrialized high-income countries (e.g., see Ch. 8). It is, however, possible that some of the gaps between these two sets of countries are not quite as great as indicated by the estimated figures. For example, the life expectancy gap is a possible case. For an equal increase in satisfaction of economic needs, the expected life of females may increase by a larger absolute amount than for males. Under relatively ideal conditions the expected life of females is higher than for males. In a comparatively ideal situation this does not imply discrimination in favor of females. Consequently, using gap analysis for this characteristic could tend to exaggerate the degree of discrimination against women if the female-male ratio for industrialized countries is used as the basis for comparison.

## TO WHAT EXTENT IS THERE ECONOMIC DISCRIMINATION AGAINST WOMEN IN HIGH-INCOME MARKET ECONOMIES?

There is considerable evidence that despite equal-pay legislation in most high-income countries, on average females receive less pay than men and that even within the same occupation their average pay tends to be less than males. For example, Mancke (1971: 316) observed:

It is widely recognised that women receive, on average, only one-half or two-thirds of the pay of men. Many empirical studies suggest for the United States at least, the two proximate causes of this phenomenon are: (1) in many occupations women typically receive lower wages than men holding the same or equivalent jobs and (2) women are systematically relegated to the lowest paying jobs.

There has been considerable argument about whether such differences indicate discrimination against women. A popular explanation is that sex-related economic discrimination is in fact occurring. While neo-Marxists are not unsympathetic to this view, they would add that women provide the bulk of the marginal labor force necessary to sustain capitalism. On the other hand, several neoclassical economists have argued that such differentials do not necessarily constitute economic discrimination against females.

Mincer and Polachek (1974), for example, contend, on the basis of human capital theory, that it is on the whole economically rational for women on average to be paid less than men because they generally have less continuous services in any occupation and therefore lower work-related skills. This is because it is still the case in developed countries that most women leave the workforce while they are child bearing and remain out of it while their children are young and growing up. This means that the skills which women have built up in earlier years through on-the-job work experience depreciate, they may forget knowledge previously learned, and they may be out of contact with the most recent technologies. Furthermore, on reentering the workforce after a break they have to learn about the organizational structure in the organization which they join. This takes time. Such factors help to explain the lower incomes on average of females in later life compared to males even when they are in the same occupation and have a similar amount of education.

In addition, Mincer and Polachek (1974) suggest, on the basis of the above pattern, that on average females will obtain a lower return from education than males. Consequently, it will be less profitable for them to invest in their education and they are liable on average to want less education than males. This further reinforces differences in income levels between females and males.

Not only are female incomes less than males in later life but their starting salaries on average are less than for males in developing countries even when they have the same level of education (Mancke 1971). Mancke argues that this is because employers base their employment decisions on the assumption that on average a woman is less likely to remain with the firm as long as an equally productive man. Consequently he argues, "(1) in those occupations where wages are negotiable women will earn lower wages on average than equally productive men, and (2) men will tend to be employed in those occupations where women receive the same wages as equally productive men" (Mancke 1971: 32). He provides evidence which supports this hypothesis.

However, even given such evidence it is quite possible that human capital theories do not provide the full story. Some discrimination could be present. To determine to what extent differences in conditions of work are due to economic factors and to discrimination is not an easy task. Economists have tried to use residual methodology to measure job discrimination. For example, as Hoffman (1991: 1–2) points out, "any wage gap not due to legitimate productivity-related variables such as education, experience and occupation is attributed to discrimination. It is difficult for economists to both reach consensus on the legitimate determinants of wage differentials and be able to measure these." Furthermore discrimination may occur in nonwage areas such as hiring, retention, training, and promotion and this adds to the complexity of measuring the residual which may be attributed to discrimination.

As far as economic development is concerned, there is one optimistic note regarding discrimination in job markets against women: The likelihood and the length of time for which women "quit" the workforce tend to decline with economic growth. This is because (1) family size tends to decline, (2) the real costs may decline and opportunities may increase for putting children into paid day care, and (3) social attitudes to women returning to work soon after the birth of their children may become more permissive or supportive. In these circumstances, one might expect male and female wages to move closer together.

Women suffer in paid employment in market economies because they are traditionally cast in the role of carers of the family. For sociologists, this role has been a matter of debate. Why is it that men have not played a larger role in that respect? The basis of role differentiation does not appear to be entirely biological but up to a point at least is socially influenced. As economic growth occurs and women spend more time in the marketplace workforce, changing circumstance and social attitudes may result in men making a greater relative contribution to the care of the family and the home. At the same time one might expect pressures to increase for substitution of new technology in the home for women power, for example, dishwashers, and greater buying in of services, for example, take-away meals, prepared products, housecleaning and other services. So there may be a tendency for the services provided traditionally by females in the home as part of their duties to be increasingly supplied by marketplace substitutes. In turn, this results in a change in family structure. With the growth of the market and economic development, family structures change from extended family systems to nuclear ones, and subsequently further fragmentation may occur with the degree of independence of individual numbers in nuclear families increasing.

It has been said that neoclassical economists are reluctant to accept the probability that discrimination exists in the workplace but that sociologists have little difficulty in accepting its existence (England and McCreary 1987). Economists have argued that under perfect competition job discrimination will not persist (Arrow 1972) and suggests that if it does occur imperfect competition may be present. In that case, the recipe for ending discrimination is to increase market competition and extend markets widely. In a different context, this argument was used by a set of neoclassical economists for favoring increasing trade with South Africa during its period of apartheid and encouraging South Africa to increase market competition. Their prediction was that in the end it would bring racial discrimination in South Africa to an end.

If imperfect competition is the sole or main source of economic discrimination against women, then how they will fare with economic development will depend on likely trends in the extent of competition in the economies concerned. If there is increasing market concentration with economic growth, then it is possible that discrimination could increase. Thus if capitalist economies are headed to a phase of monopoly capitalism, as some Marxists and neo-Marxists believe, then increased discrimination could arise. However, in practice it seems that while market concentration has increased nationally in many industries the size of markets has increased internationally and so economically significant concentration may not have occurred internationally. On the other hand, writers like Ward (1988) argue that with the increased internationalization of capitalism, discrimination has not been reduced but may very well have increased in relation to women. However, there is reason to be wary of Ward's hypothesis. It is based on limited data and examples. It is also at variance with findings on racial differences of income in the United States. Wohlstetter and Coleman (1972) found that nonwhite income in the United States rose relative to white income from the late 1940s to the mid-1960s and concluded: "Nonwhite income has plainly improved more than white income. That, however, hardly means that the problem of race discrimination in income will soon be solved" (Wohlstetter and Coleman 1972: 40).

England and McCreary (1987: 153) point out that human capital theory has been used to explain market segregation of males and females. Polachek (1979, 1981, 1985) argues that women who plan intermittent employment choose occupations with low depreciation penalties and that this leads to gender differences in job choices and so to segregation. Contrary to this theory, however, neither cross-sectional (England 1982, 1984) nor longitudinal (Corcoran, Duncan, and Ponza 1984) analyses have found that the amount of wage depreciation suffered by women while out of the labor force is greater in occupation containing mostly men than in occupations containing mostly women (England and McCreary 1987: 153).

Other reasons have been put forward by economists as to why gender discrimination in work might continue in high-income market economies. These include tastes, errors of judgment, statistical generalizations, and group monopolies. Becker (1957) suggests that some employers may engage in "taste discrimination," preferring to hire males or individuals of a particular category because it will make for more harmonious, work relations. This type of discrimination may in fact be necessary to maximize the profit of a business, given the prevailing social sentiments of its workforce (cf. Bergmann and Darity 1981). If greater social tolerance tends to occur with economic development (as is possible), then this factor will decrease in importance.

Concerning errors of judgment about productivity of females made by individual employers, these will be of little moment in a competitive market because employers who consistently underestimate the productivity of females in relation to rival employers will lose economic ground. However, when widespread statistical discrimination or generalization occurs, it may persist because of the costs of screening potential employees of differing gender. Whether or not screening becomes more or less difficult with economic development and the spread of markets is unclear. Historically it is possible that signaling improves which would reduce statistical discrimination, but it is not entirely clear that greater separation of potential employees in terms of potential productivity will occur.

The matter of "group monopolies" has already been discussed to some extent. These theories assume conspiracy or collusion among groups to exploit females from an economic viewpoint. As England and McCreary (1987: 158) mention, "Madden's (1973) model as well as Hartmann's (1976) and Strober's (1984) theories of patriarchy see women as being kept out of good jobs by collusion among men—as husbands, employers, legislators, and workers." However, if this does occur, it would have to be implicit rather than explicit collusion because of the large numbers involved. It is conceivable that social conditioning could result in group discrimination which if *uniform* could persist under competitive market conditions. However, social attitudes are liable to change with economic development and the spread of the market system. In Western countries, at least social discrimination against women appears to have declined in recent decades, and this decline has been correlated with economic growth.

## CONCLUDING COMMENTS

In this chapter, several theories have been considered of how the relative socioeconomic status of women is liable to alter with economic development. It has been seen that these theories and their predictions can be quite divergent. Nevertheless, it seems likely that the socioeconomic status of women may at first decline with economic growth and subsequently improve. In my view, the evidence does not support the contention that the socioeconomic status of women continuously declines with economic growth and development. Eventually an improvement seems to occur which may in part be correlated with reduced demand for manual work as technological progress proceeds. Nevertheless women as child bearers and as principal child carers remain at considerable socioeconomic disadvantage compared to men in high-income countries. In such a case, further improvement in the socioseconomic status of women depends on males playing a larger role in caring for and raising children and accepting more duties in relation to the household. In part this will require changes in social conditioning.

# 3

# Women and Development in Taiwan: The Importance of the Institutional Context

*Cal Clark, Janet Clark, and Bih-er Chou*

## INTRODUCTION

The impact of development upon the status of women seemingly gives rise to a cruel paradox. Most traditional cultures and societies are patriarchal ones which accord women only a secondary and subordinate status. Thus, the socioeconomic changes that development brings should, in theory, act as a force for improving the status of women by undercutting patriarchal norms. In advanced Western societies, for example, women's increasing movement from the home into the "public sphere" of the workplace and higher education is widely credited with making them more independent both financially and psychologically, stimulating the Women's Movement, and creating political pressure to improve their status (Klein 1984; Sinclair 1983). Similarly, one might expect that agricultural modernization and industrialization should provide opportunities and, indeed, force women to sunder some of their traditional bonds within the extended kinship systems that are prevalent in economies at low levels of development.

Yet, development's impact upon the status of women turns out to be quite problematic. Changes in agriculture, especially the introduction of more advanced technology and the transformation from subsistence to cash-crop production, undermined women's production role by decreasing their participation in actual agricultural work. After industrialization commenced, women's role in the "modern sector" was "marginalized" in the sense that they were generally confined to unstable, low-paying, unskilled manufacturing jobs. Furthermore, their traditional roles and statuses and support from kinship networks were substantially eroded (Anker and Hein 1986; Boserup 1970; Jaquette 1982; Leahy 1986; Nash and Fernandez-Kelly 1983; Rogers 1979; Roy 1994b; Saffioti 1983; Tiano 1987; Tinker 1990;

Tinker and Bramsen 1976; Wellesley Editorial Committee 1977). These processes, thus, may well present women in developing societies with a paradoxical and fairly unhappy set of alternatives—continuing their subordinate status in patriarchal cultures or facing the considerable chance of having their status eroded, not enhanced, by the conventional sequence of development.

Empirical tests of this so-called female marginalization thesis have produced inconsistent results with partial but far from complete support for its hypotheses (Cho and Koo 1983; Chou et al. 1990; Greenhalgh 1985; Humphrey 1984; Scott 1986). A principal reason for this almost certainly is that the impact of development on women's status varies by class. That is, while upper class women have expanded opportunities, women from poorer and lower classes, especially those in the agricultural sector, suffer at the onset of industrialization (Saffoti 1983; Wellesley Editorial Committee 1977). The idea that the social changes accompanying development may have differential impacts on women implies, furthermore, that some national development strategies and patterns may be more conducive to promoting the status of women than others.

This chapter, therefore, presents a case study of Taiwan to examine women's status in one very rapidly developing society. Taiwan presents an excellent case study for this purpose for several important reasons. First, Taiwan has a Chinese Confucian culture that is highly patriarchal. Women, therefore, might be expected to face particularly strong barriers to socioeconomic advancement which would make any observed progress particularly meaningful. Second, it has experienced extremely rapid growth during the entire postwar period and has completed the transition from a primarily agricultural to a primarily industrial economy. For example, GNP per capita has risen well over fiftyfold from $150 in 1952 to $1,500 in 1978 to $6,000 in 1988 to $10,000 in 1993, bringing the country to the very edge of being an advanced industrial society (Chan and Clark 1992; Li 1988; Ranis 1992). Thus, it provides a good context for assessing the impact of major social change since the effects of agricultural modernization, early industrialization, and the creation of a broad middle class should all be visible. Third, rapid growth and economic transformation in Taiwan, in addition, differed from many other developing societies in that they were not accompanied by growing inequality and poverty but, in fact, improved the quality of life for most of the population (Chan and Clark 1992; Fei et al. 1979). Given the distinctiveness of this pattern of development, therefore, there is some reason to suspect that factors mitigating women's marginalization may have been generated.

## WOMEN'S STATUS IN TAIWAN: IS THE LEVEL HALF FULL OR HALF EMPTY?

Assessing women's status is a somewhat problematic endeavor because it is hard to say with absolute certainty what measures necessarily show a "good" or "bad" position in society. Here, we will begin with a brief international comparison to suggest how women in Taiwan have fared relative to those in other nations. Then, much more detailed data on women's employment status will be presented to test whether or not they appear to have been marginalized. As will be seen, women in Taiwan appear to be doing quite well in terms of international comparisons. When their absolute position in the country's economy and society is examined, however, both positive and negative aspects are easy to discern, leading to the question of whether women's status there is a bottle which should be regarded as "half full" or "half empty."

While the theory of female marginalization suggests that women may have a poor or undesirable status in most parts of the world, it certainly makes sense to ask whether women's position in a particular country (i.e., Taiwan) is better or worse than might be expected. Since national social conditions and quality of life are highly dependent upon development level, moreover, it is valuable to control for development context in any such assessment. A common method for assessing the social conditions or economic performance of a nation relative to its affluence or level of development is to use regression analysis of data on nation states to calculate what these conditions would be like normally for a country with its GNP per capita. If social conditions are better than this predicted or expected level, the nation would be an "overachiever" that is doing a good job; conversely if they are worse, the country is an underachiever (Chan 1987/1988; Chan and Clark 1992; Clark and Roy 1995).

Table 3.1 presents such an analysis for three central indicators of women's quality of life and overall social conditions—(1) the fertility rate, (2) the infant mortality rate, and (3) women's life expectancy. Obviously, low fertility and infant mortality rates are desirable, as is a longer life expectancy. Analyses were carried out for both 1965, when Taiwan's prolonged growth spurt was first taking off, and 1989, when the island had clearly moved into the ranks of the upper middle-income nations. The temporal patterns for each of these three indicators differ slightly, but the results are clear, consistent, and convincing. In 1965, Taiwan's fertility rate was about 15 percent lower than normal for a nation with its GNP per capita, suggesting that women were a little better off than might have been expected. The "demographic transition" then occurred in earnest over the next twenty-five years, so that in 1989 the fertility rate of 1.9 was only two-thirds of what would have been expected for the considerably more developed island that Taiwan had become. In terms of infant mortality, Taiwan's record is almost stunning, as its fatality rate was less than a quarter of predicted levels in both 1965 and 1989. Finally, Taiwan's women lived far longer than "normal" in 1965, although this advantage had vanished by 1989. In short, women on Taiwan appear quite advantaged in terms of international comparisons.

The fact that social conditions for women in Taiwan appear good compared to other parts of the world does not, of course, mean that women's status there is necessarily good, nor that women have escaped marginalization—they might simply be less marginalized, subordinated, or exploited than in other nations. To get a more accurate picture of how women have fared, hence, we now turn to data on their economic participation, which is often used as the central measure of their status.

Table 3.1
Taiwan's Performance on Fertility and Infant Mortality

| | Taiwan's Rate | Rate for Taiwan Predicted from GNP per Capita* | Ratio of Actual Rate to Predicted Rate |
|---|---|---|---|
| **Fertility** | | | |
| 1965 | 4.8 | 5.7 | 0.84 |
| 1989 | 1.9 | 2.8 | 0.68 |
| **Infant Mortality** | | | |
| 1965 | 24 | 114 | 0.21 |
| 1989 | 5 | 23 | 0.22 |
| **Female Life Expectancy** | | | |
| 1965 | 70 | 54 | 1.30 |
| 1989 | 76 | 76 | 1.00 |

* Computed from regressions using the log of GNP per capita for the relevant year to explain fertility ($r = -.71$ in 1965 and $-.75$ in 1989), infant mortality ($r = -.83$ for 1965 and $-.82$ for 1989), and women's life expectancy ($r = .87$ for both 1965 and 1989) for the 124 countries included in the 1991 World Bank tables plus Taiwan.

*Sources:* Adapted from *Social Indicators in Taiwan Area of the Republic of China, 1988.* Taipei 1989: 24, 155, 159. World Bank. *World Development Report, 1991.* New York 1991: 256–259, 266–267.

The data on labor force participation rates in Table 3.2 show that rapid development in Taiwan has acted to bring a considerable number of women into the formal labor market. The proportion of women over fifteen years old who were employed rose from 36 percent in 1961 to 46 percent in 1988. The ratio of this compared to men's rate jumped more impressively, though, from 41 percent to 61 percent (an aging population and expanding higher education system over this time would have normally acted to reduce labor force participation). These data, hence, strongly suggest that most women were no longer solely tied to home and hearth (even if their employment responsibilities constitute an onerous "second shift" for many working women). Whether or not such movement from the "private" world to the "public" one acted to liberate women in Taiwan is an open question, however. The theory of female marginalization, for instance, predicts that women would be concentrated in the least desirable and remunerated positions, which would very probably create additional burdens and bondage for them.

    The data for a preliminary and aggregate assessment of whether women were segregated into marginal and undesirable occupations are presented in Table 3.3. This table contains the percentage of all employed men and all employed women

Table 3.2
Taiwan's Labor Force Participation Rates (for population over 15)

| | Total | Men | Women | Ratio of Women's Rate to Men's Rate |
|---|---|---|---|---|
| 1961 | 61.8% | 86.4% | 35.8% | 0.41 |
| 1965 | 58.2% | 82.6% | 33.1% | 0.40 |
| 1970 | 57.3% | 78.9% | 35.5% | 0.45 |
| 1975 | 58.2% | 77.6% | 38.6% | 0.50 |
| 1980 | 58.3% | 77.1% | 39.3% | 0.51 |
| 1985 | 59.5% | 75.5% | 43.5% | 0.58 |
| 1988 | 60.2% | 74.8% | 45.6% | 0.61 |

*Source:* Adapted from *Social Indicators in Taiwan Area of the Republic of China, 1988.* Taipei 1989: 62.

Table 3.3
Percentage of All Employed Men or Women at Specific Levels of Occupational Hierarchy*

| | 1966 | | 1986 | |
|---|---|---|---|---|
| | Men | Women | Men | Women |
| Managerial & Adm. | 4.4% | 1.4% | 1.2% | 0.2% |
| Professional | 4.6% | 5.8% | 6.0% | 6.7% |
| Clerical | 7.3% | 6.1% | 11.2% | 18.0% |
| Sales | 10.4% | 12.4% | 13.3% | 13.7% |
| Production | 20.2% | 16.6% | 42.6% | 36.2% |
| Agriculture | 42.4% | 46.6% | 18.5% | 14.2% |

* Columns sum to only about 90% because some jobs cannot be classified in this hierarchy.

*Source:* Adapted from *Annual Report of Labor Statistics 1996 & 1986.* Taipei, 1966, 1986—in Chinese.

with jobs in six broad categories of the occupational hierarchy (managerial, professional, clerical, sales, production, and agriculture). The top of the occupational hierarchy in Taiwan, as in almost any nation, is composed of those in managerial positions; and professional and technical occupations rank a clear second. Moving down the occupational status hierarchy, clerical and sales jobs come next in the occupational hierarchy. They have considerably lower pay and social status than managerial and professional occupations. Yet, the economic boom in Taiwan has made many who hold such positions prosperous enough to acquire middle class tastes, values, and styles of living. Finally, agriculture clearly ranks at the bottom of the occupation hierarchy in Taiwan; and work in direct production (industry) ranks between agriculture and clerical-sales occupation in terms of status and income.

There are two ways to evaluate women's marginalization—one vis-à-vis men and one in absolute terms for themselves. The first way would ask whether women (compared to their male colleagues) were disproportionately concentrated in low-status occupations and excluded from high-status ones. The second would ask what types of jobs most women held, regardless of how this distribution compared to men's. The answers to these two questions turn out to be quite different.

With the very glaring exception of the very top occupational stratum of managerial and administrative jobs from which they remained largely excluded even in 1986, women were not especially disadvantaged in this gross occupational hierarchy. Surprisingly, women gained "equal representation" in the professional occupations throughout this period in the sense that a slightly larger proportion of employed women than of employed men held professional positions. Thus, women have gained surprisingly equal access to many middle-class occupations and even to some upper middle class ones. In the middle of the job hierarchy, women did extremely well in gaining the rapidly expanding number of clerical positions between the mid-1960s and the mid-1980s, becoming well overrepresented in this category in the process, while the proportion of both men and women working in sales stayed approximately the same throughout the period. Women were not disproportionately concentrated at the bottom of the occupational ladder either. Throughout these two decades, women were slightly underrepresented among production workers; and women went from being slightly overrepresented in agriculture in 1966 to slightly underrepresented in 1986.

In terms of their comparative job distribution, therefore, women do not appear to have been marginalized in Taiwan's economy to any great extent. However, when one looks at how many women are in desirable jobs, a much different picture emerges. Only a tiny minority of women (about 7 percent in both 1966 and 1986) were able to enter professional and managerial positions, while many if not most (60 percent in 1966 and 50 percent in 1986) remained on the two bottom rungs of the ladder. Moreover, women suffered from decided wage discrimination as well. In the mid 1980s, for example, women earned only two-thirds of the salaries paid to men with comparable education with the gap being inversely related to level of education, that is, it is widest among those in the least prestigious and most marginalized occupations (Chiang and Ku 1985). Focusing our lens from this different angle, therefore, certainly implies that while women in Taiwan may have come "a long way," they still have a long way to go.

Furthermore, the aggregate data in Table 3.3 may well understate women's economic marginalization considerably because they gloss over differences in gender status within these broad occupational groups. It is very significant, for

**Table 3.4**
**Percentage of All Men and Women Employed with Specific Types of Employment Status**

|  | 1966 | | 1986 | |
|---|---|---|---|---|
|  | *Men* | *Women* | *Men* | *Women* |
| **IN COMMERCE** | | | | |
| Employer | 5.6 | 1.5 | 10.6 | 2.4 |
| Self-Employed | 57.7 | 34.6 | 46.6 | 23.1 |
| Employee | 28.4 | 22.3 | 36.2 | 38.3 |
| Unpaid Family Help | 8.3 | 41.6 | 6.6 | 36.3 |
| **IN AGRICULTURE** | | | | |
| Employer | 0.9 | 0.3 | 1.8 | 0.5 |
| Self-Employed | 51.8 | 9.4 | 67.6 | 20.4 |
| Employee | 18.6 | 15.5 | 14.1 | 11.8 |
| Unpaid Family Help | 28.7 | 74.9 | 16.5 | 67.3 |

*Source:* Adapted from *Annual Report of Labor Statistics 1996 & 1986.* Taipei, 1966, 1986—in Chinese.

example, that production now accounts for by far the largest amount of female employment (36 percent in 1986, twice the share of any other category). Women's participation in the industrial labor force is clearly of a "second-rate" nature. For example, women form a disproportionate number of the "part-time proletariat" who work in factories before marriage, rank at the bottom of pay and status among manufacturing employees, have almost no opportunity for advancement, and for the most part continue to be subordinated within traditional family structures (Gates 1979; Greenhalgh 1985; Kung 1981, 1983).

Women are especially disadvantaged in commerce and agriculture where, as demonstrated by the data in Table 3.4, most workers fall into the self-employed and unpaid family help categories, demonstrating the small-scale and perhaps marginal nature of these activities in Taiwan. Women's very unfavorable position in commerce is readily demonstrated by the fact that they were five to six times as likely as men to be unpaid family help (42 percent to 8 percent in 1966 and 36 percent to 7 percent in 1986). Thus, a large proportion of women in this area were in by far the least desirable job status, while only a small percentage of men were, indicating a substantial degree of vertical gender segregation.

If anything, an even bleaker situation exists in agriculture. The glaring problem of vertical segregation is sharply reflected in the data on the lowest employment status of unpaid family help. Three-quarters of the women working in agriculture were unpaid family help in 1966; and this only decreased to two-thirds in 1986—

approximately three times the percentage for men in the former year and four times in the latter. Superficially, the figures for self-employed farmers look better for women. The percentage of female workers who described themselves as self-employed doubled from 9 percent to 20 percent over the 1966–1986 period. What this denotes, however, is women running their own small farms. Especially since agriculture is a declining sector, this probably represents an important aspect of the "feminization" of agriculture in Taiwan that the broader aggregate data discussed above did not uncover. An examination of the impact of rapid growth and industrialization upon women's status in Taiwan, therefore, indicates that women have made considerable progress but that facets of continued marginalization and subordination are easy to find. Compared to the "cross-national norms" for the improvement of social conditions as GNP per capita rises, women in Taiwan appear to have done quite well. Their general economic role has both advantages and shortcomings; and whether this represents a glass that is half full or half empty probably depends more on an observer's values than objective facts. Still, it is hard to gainsay the progress that has been made which, in turn, raises the obvious question—Why were a significant number of women able to improve their status?

## INSTITUTIONAL INFLUENCES ON WOMEN'S STATUS IN TAIWAN

An approach called "historical institutionalism" provides an interesting framework for trying to answer the question of why development seemingly benefited more women in Taiwan than it did in many places elsewhere in the Third World. In essence, this theoretical paradigm presumes that social, economic, and political institutions evolve historically which, in turn, shape socioeconomic conditions and policy responses to them. There are two very different types of institutions. First are permanent arrangements for conducting affairs, such as family structures or government organizations; second are long-standing policies which influence social and economic decision making. Historical institutionalism, then, centers its analysis on the institutions that exist in a nation and the causes and consequences that flow into and from them (Thelen and Steinmo 1992).

In Taiwan, several such institutional explanations for the partial improvement in women's status can be adduced both for creating opportunities for women to make social progress and for permitting a significant number of women to take advantage of these opportunities. In particular, opportunities were created by the special nature of agricultural and industrial development in Taiwan. The radical land reform program structured agricultural modernization in such a way as to minimize the dangers of "female marginalization" that usually accompany the Green Revolution; and Taiwan's particular pattern of industrialization helped to maximize mobility opportunities. Taiwan's women were able to take advantage of these opportunities, moreover, because of a policy of universal primary education. None of the fundamental policies involved here, however, were explicitly targeted at women. Thus, when their consequences for some groups of women turned negative, there was no effective remedy, thereby explaining the partial nature of women's status improvement.

Taiwan's early postwar development was dominated by its massive land reform program. Landlords were forced to sell agricultural holdings over about three hectares (depending upon the quality of land) at below-market prices to the government, which then resold the land to tenant farmers at the same price, repayable over a ten-year period. This established a small-holder agriculture system, created incentives for increased agricultural production that helped finance industrialization, reduced income inequality substantially, and drastically changed the social hierarchy in the countryside. Overall, Taiwan's Land-to-the-Tiller program is usually judged a huge success, although by the 1970s agriculture had become a declining and relatively ignored sector (Ho 1978; Lee 1971; Yang 1970).

Taiwan's pattern of industrialization is noteworthy too. It was geographically dispersed, at least until recently, and small, often family-owned firms played a leading role, particularly in the vital export sector. Consequently, the industrial transformation involved less disruption of the society. For example, family ties remained strong; and rural families could participate in both agricultural and industrial activities simultaneously. Taiwan also experienced very rapid industrialization, both in terms of aggregate growth and of moving rapidly into increasingly more sophisticated types of production (Chan and Clark 1992; Ho 1979; Lam and Lee 1992; Ranis 1979), thereby opening and maintaining broad routes for upward mobility.

The implications of land reform for rural women were significant. For the 1950s and 1960s, these effects were clearly positive. Because of small plots, large-scale mechanization was limited, thereby curbing the pressures for a gender-based division of labor in which men monopolize the new, much more productive technologies. Thus, women shared the benefits of vastly increased ownership and somewhat increased productivity with men without facing the negative spinoffs that the Green Revolution can produce for the status of women. In addition, the growth of nearby factories minimized the disruption to traditional ties and support systems that industrialization inevitably generates. The way that this system worked for women changed drastically in the 1970s and 1980s, however. The ease with which families and even individuals could split their efforts between agriculture and industry resulted, as we saw in the preceding section, in the growing "feminization of agricultural" which became a "feminization of poverty" as agriculture declined.

The impact of industrialization upon the status of women was quite variegated as well, with the temporal trend being the exact opposite of conditions in agriculture—over time, women's status improved rather than declined. Initially, women flowed into labor-intensive assembly operations, often seeing factory work as a temporary interval before marriage. While there is some evidence that moving into factory dormitories made women slightly more independent and interested in gaining further education, their status as a "part-time proletariat" created generally subordinated and exploitative working conditions (Gallin 1984; Gates 1979, 1987;

Greenhalgh 1985; Kung 1981, 1983). Rapid industrialization brought some significant benefits, though. By the early 1970s, essentially full employment was reached which helped improve wages and working conditions for even unskilled labor. More importantly, many more jobs opened for more sophisticated production operations, "pink collar" service activities, and professional occupations. As the last section showed, considerable numbers of women were able to move into all of these better jobs with the exception of top-level managerial ones. Taiwan's successful climb up the "international product cycle" was not an unmitigated benefit for women, though. The rapid movement of low-tech assembly operations off-shore that began in the late 1980s, in fact, threatened to leave many unskilled women workers behind with few alternatives for improving their status, analogously to the feminization of agriculture.

The economic institutions in Taiwan's agricultural and industrial sector, then, created the opportunity for many women to improve their status, but women in most traditional societies would probably need help to take advantage of such opportunities. In Taiwan, such help came in the early 1950s in the form of a universal program in basic primary education and literacy that was gradually expanded as Taiwan become more prosperous and industrially sophisticated. Taiwan's strong investment in education is usually credited with developing the "human capital" that undergirded the Republic of China's "economic miracle" (Huang 1984). The central question for the status of women, of course, is the degree of access that women had to these expanding educational opportunities, especially given the traditional reluctance of Chinese to invest in education for their daughters, who are regarded as "spilled water" because they leave the family upon marriage. The key factors of Taiwan's education program, then, were that it was compulsory and paid for by the government, thus obviating cultural opposition to educating women.

The data in Table 3.5 on enrollment ratios by age from the late 1960s certainly indicate that women have indeed benefited both from the rapidly rising levels of education in Taiwan and from a narrowing in the years of schooling afforded women and men. In 1951, access to education was extremely limited and manifested a pronounced gender imbalance as the average man had attended school for four years and the average woman one and a half (Chiang and Ku 1985: 5). The dramatic change that the mass education program brought is obvious in Table 3.5. By 1968, almost all six-to-eleven-year-olds were in school, but the enrollment ratios fell sharply to about two-thirds of children twelve to fourteen and one-third of those fifteen to seventeen. Over the next two decades, these percentages jumped substantially to 90 percent and 75 percent, respectively.

The expansion of educational opportunity in general was also accompanied by a narrowing of the differential education afforded to girls and boys. In 1968, boys and girls only had equal enrollment in the youngest group of six-to-eleven-year-olds. By the 1980s there was little gender difference in enrollment ratios, although this does not necessarily mean that the two sexes were enrolled in equally prestigious or advanced schools. Thus, while women have not achieved total educational equality, many women receive substantial secondary and higher education which

**Table 3.5**
**Percentage of Age Group Attending School**

|  | 1969 | 1975 | 1980 | 1988 |
|---|---|---|---|---|
| **Age 6–11** |  |  |  |  |
| Male | 98 | 99 | 99 | 99 |
| Female | 97 | 99 | 99 | 99 |
| **Age 12–14** |  |  |  |  |
| Male | 70 | 85 | 89 | 91 |
| Female | 54 | 75 | 86 | 90 |
| **Age 15–17** |  |  |  |  |
| Male | 43 | 54 | 57 | 73 |
| Female | 31 | 44 | 56 | 80 |
| **Age 18–21** |  |  |  |  |
| Male | 20 | 25 | 23 | 29 |
| Female | 15 | 23 | 23 | 33 |
| **Age 22–24** |  |  |  |  |
| Male | 7 | 7 | 6 | 8 |
| Female | 3 | 4 | 5 | 8 |

*Source:* Adapted from *Social Welfare Indicators, Republic of
China, 1989.* Taipei, 1989: 25.

should qualify them for professional jobs and public service because of Taiwan's
open public education. Clearly, they are no longer treated as spilled water who are
denied education because their families fear their "loss" to their husband's family.

If education has opened doors for many women in Taiwan, however, the absence
of education has closed most possible doors for many others, especially those employed in agricultural and unskilled industrial production. Several broader sociological studies of women's status in Taiwan have found that there are important
rural-urban and class differences in how development has affected the status of
women in Taiwan. Thus, while rural, uneducated, and older women have suffered a loss of status during industrialization, urban, better educated, and younger
women appear to have benefited from the opportunities generated by economic
development (Farris 1986; Gallin 1984; Kung 1981; Tsui 1987). This picture
of partially successful modernization and continuing significant marginalization
indicates the need to manage the developmental processes to help shape social
change. Several of the most important avenues of progress were created by specific governmental policies regarding land reform and education. Yet, none of
these policies were specifically aimed at women. However, the success of education policy suggests that the state might well be able do something for the women
who have been marginalized (i.e., young girl factory workers in the "part-time

proletariat" and older, uneducated women in agriculture). What would be needed is for the government and the society to recognize explicitly the harm done by marginalizing and subordinating women. Here, there is a cruel irony about the impact of culture on the status of women. Women were the indirect beneficiaries of Confucian regard for and emphasis upon education, but the patriarchal nature of Confucianism inhibits the supplementing of these indirect effects with more direct and targeted policies.

Studies of development are increasingly finding that the development of human capital is central to economic performance (Clark and Roy 1995; Moon 1991). From this perspective, the marginalization of women (approximately half the population) may create a substantial cost in terms of developmental potential (Clark and Clark 1994), suggesting a strong need for much greater efforts for "bringing women in" the developmental processes (Kardam 1991; Leahy 1986). The results from Taiwan suggest that nations undergoing development need to follow a two-pronged strategy in regard to protecting and promoting the status of women. First, policies must be devised to prevent agricultural modernization from "marginalizing" large numbers of women. Second, as the transformation to secondary and tertiary activities progresses, educational and labor policies should be used to ensure that women benefit from the expanding socioeconomic horizon.

*Who will care for children?*

*Household?*

*lowering fertility = < children to care for about Someone entirely.*

*Still Must Care farther*

*Household — structural change? less importance?*

*where to go? We can't just all go to work as is, we value "home!"*

# 4

# The Socioeconomic Status of Today's Chinese Women

## Gao Kun

Chinese women, representing a quarter of the world's female population, were for a long period subjected to oppression, humiliation, and destruction during China's feudal period that lasted thousands of years and its semicolonial and semifeudal period that lasted more than a century. With the founding of the People's Republic of China, Chinese women have won liberation and, in principle, achieved equal rights with men in such aspects as politics, economics, culture, society, and family life, thus emerging as a vital new force propelling the society forward. As China is still a developing country and restricted by the level of social development as well as influenced by old concepts and ideas, Chinese women still have a long way to go and need to make arduous efforts in order to win emancipation and to develop their status.

This chapter gives a brief account of issues concerning Chinese women's participation in government and political affairs, their employment situation, their education, and finally, theoretical research being done about women's problems.

## CHINESE WOMEN'S PARTICIPATION IN GOVERNMENT AND POLITICAL AFFAIRS

Statistics show that there were 147 women deputies attending the First All China National People's Congress, accounting for 12 percent of the total number of deputies, whereas at the eighth session of the National People's Congress the total number of the deputies rose to 626, accounting for 21 percent of the total number (*Statistical Yearbook of China* 1993: 805). Among the delegates attending CPPCC (The Chinese People's Political Consultative Conference) in 1949, women delegates accounted for 6.6 percent of the total, while at the eighth session of the CPPCC in 1993, women delegates accounted for 13.52 percent.

In 1994, there were 16 women ministers and vice-ministers in the various ministries and commissions under the State Council and 18 women governors or vice governors of provinces nationwide. In the 517 cities all over the country, there are over 300 female mayoresses and deputy mayoresses. In 1993, women government officials constituted 32.44 percent of the total (*China Women's State Affairs*, June 1994). During the country-level change-over election (Sept. 1989–Apr. 1991), 1,238 women leading officials at the county level were elected, and 7,510 female leading officials at both township and village level were elected (*China Women's News*, May 10, 1991). In 1989, among the division-level officials, department chiefs, and ministerial-level officials throughout the country, women officials accounted for 8.12 percent, 6.58 percent, and 6.18 percent of the total, respectively (*Work for Women*, ninth issue 1990).

According to Wang Weidong at Jilin University, Chinese women have six different channels for participating in politics: first, participating in social management by way of exercising a citizen's political right; second, exercising any employee's right as an equal member of her work unit to take part in management work; third, by way of participating in democratic management, control, and political consultation through the democratic parties of which she is a member; fourth, as a member of a governmental organization, business enterprise, or public service unit she is required to participate in state administrative work; fifth, elected into state organizations of various levels as a woman representative she is able directly to exercise power regarding political decisions on state management; and sixth, participating in management and supervision upon the recommendation of a nongovernment organization of which she is a member.

## SOME PROBLEMS AFFECTING WOMEN'S PARTICIPATION IN POLITICS

The Chinese women's participation in politics is the result of a long and tedious historical process. Those Chinese women who aim at full participation in politics will not only be restricted by the level of social development but also by the political system that awaits reforming. Moreover they will be checked by the huge ineptness generated by the old Chinese cultural heritage as well as by their own awareness and their diathesis, which is kept on a low key and is determined by various factors, subjectively or objectively. All these are manifested in the following:

1. Women's organizations fall short of the practical needs. Although Chinese women have their own national association, the All-China Women's Federation, which in its full capacity of a mass organization is invested with every feature of an authentic administrative body, it lacks any administrative power. Taking a look at its inner structure, it is obvious that it is hierarchically divided according to the nation's administrative hierarchy into the All-China Women's Federation, then the Provincial Women's Federation, City Women's Federation, District Women's Federation, and finally County Women's Federation. However, in large factories, schools, hospitals, and such service units and enterprises where women form the

bulk of the workforce, there are generally no women's organizations but trade union organizations instead. Women's organizations and trade unions are of course two different and independent mass set-ups and therefore it is hard for women's units to establish direct contacts with and gain a timely understanding of the needs and voices of the women at the grass-roots level.

2. The greatest problem confronting the women in their drive to participate in politics is the unadaptability of their innermost psychology. Li Xiaojiang from Zhengzhou University estimates that this unadaptability is derived from three contradictions, namely, first, between historical and actual circumstances; second, between individual and social interests; and third, between career and family interests.

These three contradictions and contention at work often cause extreme confusion in the minds of the broad women cadres, which is hard for their male counterparts to comprehend.

3. The nonconformity between the social, political, and economic development and women's possibilities of participation in political life: The phenomenon of competition that came into being along with the socialist reform and opening policy has brought forth even deeper and broader participation in production and social life on the part of Chinese women, and as a result, women have shown a higher degree of creativeness and initiative in managing state affairs and there has emerged a whole group of women entrepreneurs. On the other hand, there are enterprise leaders who out of their anxiety to satisfy immediate interests tend to adopt a discriminatory attitude against women in respect to enrollment, employment, and promotion, making things difficult for women. The broad mass of women, on the other hand, earnestly wish to have women take part in the management and decision-making process on their behalf.

4. Research on women's participation in government and political affairs: In the 1980s, a drastic and sudden change emerged in women's power and rights which stemmed from social, political, and economic changes that happened in China which gave rise to strong social and psychological shocks and a series of repercussions in the society. All this drew a lot of public attention. In the mid-80s women of China initiated the role of mass media with *China's Women News* and the pictorial, *The Women of China* while *The People's Daily* and *The Worker's Daily* published articles on women's issues regarding women's participation in government and political affairs and also comprised reportage and special features pertaining to problems arising from the way women's political participation was organized. *The Contemporary Women* (from Gansu Province), *Women's Life,* (Henan Province), and *Bosom Friend* (from Hubei Province) published numerous articles. The Provincial China Women Federation of Henan and Shanxi organized symposia in April 1989 and in January 1990, respectively. The symposia discussed questions like "The connotation of and significance for women's political participation"; "Past and Present Situation for Women's Political Participation"; "The Law Governing the Growth of Women Cadres"; and "What Are the Necessary Qualifications for Any Woman to Practice Political Participation?" The discussions that

took place have effectively enhanced theoretical studies on women's participation in government and political affairs.

## THE EMPLOYMENT SITUATION FOR CHINESE WOMEN

Looking at the total number of employed women, we will see that the People's Republic of China is founded on a extremely large basis in terms of production power. In 1949, the total number of women employees was 0.6 million, comprising 7 percent of the total workforce. In 1992, the total number of women workers reached 55 million and 860 thousand (*Statistical Yearbook of China* 1993: 116). Besides, to be added to that figure were women workers working in the village factories or as individual laborers scattered in villages and towns. So the total number of women workers throughout the country was 291 million and 14 thousand, which was 485 times more than the total number in 1949, accounting for 45 percent of the total workforce (*Census Yearbook of China* 1993: 16), excluding a considerable part of women farmers in the countryside. The employment rate for Chinese women was, in fact, relatively higher than in the rest of the world.

Regarding the type of employment, the All-China Trade Union conducted a survey in 1986 on the employment situation and competence of a sample comprising 247,000 Chinese women workers. Likewise, the All-China Women's Federation also conducted a sample survey on the Chinese women workers and employees. The findings were as follows:

1. Women employees' level of education showed a remarkable increase; for instance, first, women workers had generally obtained secondary education level, which forms and reinforces the basic structure of their educational background; second, the women employees' educational foundation was a little lower but close to that of the male employees and the extent women obtain education before taking on jobs was similar to that of the male employees; third, 80.7 percent of the women employees who entered the workforce after 1966 were brought up after the liberation of the Republic and had become a new generation of workforce with secondary education or above.

2. Women employees' vocational and technical education level was raised, which was manifested in the following way: First, middle-level or middle-lower-level women cadres and women technicians had increased in number; second, the technical skill of women employees was increased; but third, on the whole and as compared to male employees, women workers' technical competence still lagged behind that of the male employees.

3. How were the women employees doing in terms of industrial participation? In 1992, the number of women employees working in the primary, the secondary, and the tertiary sectors were 2.91 million, 29.50 million, and 23.45 million, respectively (these data refer to state-owned work units only). The proportion of women government workers and white collar women technicians working in various fields of occupations in those three industries constituted 18.7 percent of the total number of women employees (*Statistical Yearbook of China* 1993: 116).

As far as women's freedom of employment is concerned, we may note the following:

1. Job expectations: Chinese women have high expectations as far as their job is concerned. The overwhelming majority of women desire to have a life-long job, which is in line with China's employment policy and our present economic development level.

2. Job motivation: According to the two large-scale surveys conducted by the All-China Trade Union and the All-China Women's Federation, the main motive for Chinese women to obtain jobs is the economic factor, and to break it down, the family economy plus health insurance and social security constitute the factors prompting women to enter paid employment. Apart from those factors, there are political and social factors which also play a certain role. Many a woman wishes to achieve economic independence by way of work and contribute to the prosperity of the nation by displaying her own talent and enriching her own life. With the country's open-door policy and the accompanying fast economic growth, these factors, be it economic, political, or social ones, pertaining to women's job motivation have become, to varying degrees, more important and more interdependent.

3. Job selection and job mobility: When the job-hunting women make a choice about work unit, the nature of ownership, and type of work, they will find the job offers and opportunities far from satisfactory. The current employment system can in no way satisfy the working women in terms of opportunities for rational selection and job mobility. The reform policy has prompted a trend to switch jobs more frequently. This is the case for job-hunting women who tend to weigh pros and cons regarding income level, job intensity, personal benefit, and chances of displaying one's talent. This goes also for women already at work who would consider job location, for example, husband and wife working in two distant places, income, working conditions, personal fulfillment, and even pregnancy and birth-delivery.

Over the past few years, the reforms in China have affected working women greatly. For one thing, the reforms have provided women with new job opportunities and broadened the spectrum of occupations. Furthermore, they have enhanced their sense of competition, the concept of efficiency, the concept of economizing, and such modern concepts as self-awareness and self-evaluation, thus greatly raising their working competence and giving full display to their talents in the development of the economy. On the other hand, reform broke their "iron bowl," leaving them in a whirl of competition to face a series of new problems and new challenges.

Here we would like to mention how reform has affected the masses of village women. Beginning in 1979, and acting in accordance with the actual circumstances in the rural areas, the Chinese government has adopted flexible rural economic policies. The responsibility system being carried out in the rural areas on a large scale has motivated the farmers highly, resulting in rising labor productivity and releasing much of the surplus labor, which has paved the way for further development in rural industry, trade, services, and transportation. In turn, the development of rural enterprises has opened up new horizons for emancipation of women in general and for providing new job opportunities for women in particular.

Among 0.35 billion Chinese laborers, women laborers constitute 42.3 percent of the total and are becoming the main workforce propelling the rural industrialization. According to a survey conducted by Duan Daohuai, Associate Professor of the Information Department of the China Academy of Agricultural Science, women have constituted 75 to 85 percent of the total workforce serving in the light-industry type rural enterprises such as the textile, garment, electronics, knitting, and processing sectors, 50 percent of the total laborers in other manufacturing, and 25 percent in the construction sector. The proportion of women securing jobs in the rural enterprises is higher than that of women working in the state-owned enterprises. Here is a picture of the age groups of women laborers working in the rural enterprises: 60 percent of the women workforce is aged from 18 to 25, 30 percent from 26 to 36, and 10 percent from 36 and above. Hence, one can see that young and well-educated rural women have become the backbone of the workforce in the rural enterprises. In 1992, China's gross national industrial product was valued at 3,706.571 billion yuan (*Statistical Yearbook of China* 1993: 412) out of which 1,797.54 billion yuan was derived from the gross product of the rural enterprises in China (*Statistical Yearbook of China* 1993: 396), which thus produced 48.5 percent of the total national industrial product. In addition, the rural agricultural gross product was valued at 908.471 billion yuan (*Statistical Yearbook of China* 1993: 355). Those figures show that China's rural workforce has already played a decisive role in China's national economic construction and, at the same time, the development of the rural enterprises not only have played an important role in propelling China's rural development and the nation's industrialization, but also in enhancing women's emancipation.

## THE EDUCATIONAL ISSUES

Over the past decade the education of women in China witnessed an upsurge and has contributed greatly to cultivating and bringing up thousands upon thousands of women laborers and contributed to raising their ideological and technical knowledge. Nevertheless, one should not nurture any unrealistic optimism about the education of women. The average duration of education for women is markedly shorter than that of their countrymen. Women's educational rights are often violated; instances of school girls being obliged to discontinue or drop out from education are common, and women college students cannot easily find jobs after finishing their education, although they are a small proportion of the total women workforce. With these problems unsettled, Chinese women are faced with serious and acute challenges in the field of education.

In 1993, the total working population of various trades amounted to 647.2447 million, of which 291.0145 million were women. Of that figure, women B.A. holders were 1,128.7 thousand; associate degree holders were 2,377.1 thousand; secondary occupational degree holders were 5,309.1 thousand; junior middle school degree holders were 77.7823 million; primary school graduates were 113.1695 million; and illiterate and semi-illiterate people were 69.64 million (*Census Yearbook of China* 1993: 62–109).

In 1992, the total number of women students at regular schools at various levels was 80.85 million and among them 736 thousand students were higher learning institutions, accounting for 33.7 percent of the total number of students at that level: 1.111 million were secondary technical school students, accounting for 46.1 percent of the total: 20.565 million were ordinary secondary school students, accounting for 43.1 percent of the total; 1.582 million were agriculture and professionally oriented secondary school students, accounting for 46.1 percent of the total; 56.856 million were primary school pupils, accounting for 46.6 percent of the total primary school pupils (*Statistical Yearbook of China* 1993: 228).

In the following some problems and targets of women education are presented. For the sake of clarity, we classify the target groups into one regular education group and one adult education group, which is to be further divided into two categories: the employee education type and the village education type.

1. The regular educational group: Ever since the proclamation and implementation of the Compulsory Education Law in 1986, the urban and the rural environment enrollment rate, taken together, rose from 49.2 percent for the year of 1952 to 97.8 percent for the year 1990. However, in accordance with the fourth national census, at present there are still 33.739 million school-aged children ranging from six to fourteen years of age who are kept absent from school, which accounts for 19.07 percent of the total number of children aged six to fourteen and among which 19.036 million were female, accounting for 56.42 percent of the total. In the countryside, there were 28.30 million people kept away from school, a figure which was 83.88 percent higher than the similar type of absenteeism in the urban areas. The problem was especially serious in provinces in the northwest and southwest of China (*Census Yearbook of China* 1993: 273).

The deprivation and discontinuation of education among middle and primary school students have drawn the attention of the government as well as of social groups. The Youth Development Research Center sponsored a large-scale donation campaign within and outside the country, named the Hope Project. Among its many activities there is one called the Buddy System, inviting households to sponsor one student to go to school; another type of activity is called "pairing-off," requiring one school in a developed area to help another in a poor area. The whole project has collected a fund amounting to 0.201 billion yuan donated by individuals, groups, and overseas Chinese from the year 1989–1993. The money helped 549 thousand students to resume their studies in a thousand counties or so in the nation's 26 provinces by setting up 204 "Hope" primary schools. Under this project, the government leaders, the central government organizations, and 33 government ministries or commissions donated 880 thousand yuan, and with that amount of money, they set up Yanan "Hope" primary school. Sixteen Beijing middle schools entered into pairing-off partnership with sixteen Yanan middle schools in order to promote education.

In order to cut down on students' expenditure, the government reformed the tuition procedure by cutting down on unnecessary tuition, at the same time increasing the educational funding to improve conditions.

In the realm of higher learning, women candidates in the process of application, affected by notions of "difficult enrollment" and "difficult employment," are constantly subjected to confusion as to selecting the "right" major, with the risk of being diverted to some favored courses, such as liberal arts and pedagogical subjects, thus further limiting themselves in development and job selection in the long run.

There are two reasons why women graduates find it hard to obtain jobs; first, there is the old custom of "preferring boys to girls" which is due to general prejudice against women's talents; second, some objective prevailing conditions tend to work against the employment of women as well. For instance, one thing that is most likely to interrupt a woman's career is pregnancy and maternity leave. As the service facilities in China are still few and inadequate, all this would mean running of nurseries and loss of working hours, thus seriously impairing work and management efficiency for the enterprises. Women are generally absent for three to four years and, moreover, women retire five years earlier than men. All this means a loss of ten years of effective working time for women, reducing their possibilities to compete with the men in the society.

Modern women shoulder the double burden of both career and family and these burdens naturally affect their upward mobility at work. Faced with this situation, leaders of various enterprises and units are compelled to make a choice of some kind when they select college graduates.

2. The Adult Education Group: The nation's adult women education is facing many practical problems. According to an article written by Xu Ming and entitled "The Problems Confronting China's Adult Women's Education and Their Countermeasures," at the present stage, there are four problems: First, the ambitious objectives of the adult women education cannot be properly dealt with by existing educational facilities, nor can the system be expected to cope with the overall planning and strategic planning to be carried out by any adult women educational set-up, which is an inseparable part of the state educational system. Second, the old idea of "male superiority to female" remains an obstacle in the development of women's talents. Third, the excessive economic burden and family chores have made it hard for women to enroll in education. Fourth, many problems emanating from the rapid growth of the education of adult women since the period of reform started are still waiting to be settled (*Beijing Adult Education* 1985). On the other hand, over the past decade, the party, the government, and women's organizations have stressed the need of raising women workers' professional competence. The studies carried out on feminine talent have played a role of cultivating feminine quality and women's quality awareness.

As far as the education of employees is concerned, the following observations can be made: As reflected in the first national survey conducted by the All-China Women's Federation in 1990, the urban women are taking up or have taken up

39.1 percent of the total amount of the adult education, of which 6.1 percent was for higher education, 7.2 percent for secondary vocational education, 7.7 percent for general subjects, 6.4 percent for professional advancement, 9.1 percent for technical and skill study, 1.5 percent for special courses of interest, and 1.1 percent for other adult education subjects.

Regarding education in the rural areas, there has emerged a fresh prospect and new hope following the reforms and opening up of the economy. These are manifested in the following: First, the party and government organs concerned have endeavored to collect information and make summaries based on experiences and then in turn use the information and experience in reforming the teaching practice at the grass-roots level. Over recent years, conferences organized by women federations have emphasized the need to organize women in their efforts to study culture, science, and technology and in their joining the building of the economy. Second, the strategy of upgrading agriculture by means of science and technology laid down by the Party Central Committee has offered new approaches in solving the problems regarding rural women's education, that is, to incorporate the government and private sector initiatives to run schools utilizing the zeal for education displayed by rural women. Past years' experience as shown in the first nationwide sample survey conducted by the All-China Women Federation in 1990 illustrates that Chinese rural women who are engaged or have been engaged in studies accounted for 25.45 percent of the total amount of adult educational volume.

## THEORETICAL RESEARCH INSTITUTIONS ON WOMEN'S ISSUES

As far as theoretical research institutions attached to the Women's Federation System are concerned, the following observations can be made: In 1979, the All-China Women Federation set up its research division on the history of the women's movement. Afterward, by the end of 1989, women research agencies had been set up by various women federations of various levels stationed in every province, autonomous district, and city directly under the jurisdiction of the central government. On the basis of all this, family education research agencies have been established in 297 districts (including cities), 127 counties, and 7,584 villages and towns.

Research agencies on women's issues incorporated in the institutions and universities have been established. According to an incomplete estimation, by the end of May 1994, teaching and research agencies on women's issues have been set up in twenty-seven women administration cadre institutes; a women research center has been set up at the Beijing University; a women research and a venereology institute has been set up at the People's University; a women science institute has been established at Beijing Foreign Language Institute; a women's issues seminar has been organized at the Central Party Academy; a feminine study institute has been set up at the China Institute of Management Science in Beijing; there is a study group on women's past and present at Tianjin Normal University; a women research group has been set up at Shanghai Fu Dan University; a Shanghai women salon has been established at Shanghai Academy of Social Science; there is a China's Women study center at the Zhengzhou University; and a female talent study group has been established at the Chongqing Normal Institute.

Since 1979, the Women's Federation and popular women's academic groups have set up broad contacts among themselves. Women workers engaged in women affairs together with scholars, and academic experts devoted to the study of women's issues have established a study network of numerous researchers and carried out various kinds of research work.

Theoretical research on China's women involves the following subjects: feminine anthropology, feminine population study, feminine ethics, feminine literature, feminine talent study, feminine sociology, feminine psychology, the law of feminine science, the law of science governing women's profession, marriage and family affairs, feminism and aesthetics, feminism and feminine character study, and theory on Chinese women, which involves the following: employment problems for Chinese women, women's participation in political affairs, women's education, marriage and family, prostitution and visiting prostitutes, feminine culture, problems for rural women, medical security for pregnant women, and labor protection for working women.

The theoretical studies take the following forms: convening of theoretical symposium seminars, information exchange meetings, special subject studies, publication of periodicals, and compiling of documents and treatises.

# 5

# Economic Development, Industrial Trends, and Women Workers in Malaysia

## Jamilah Ariffin

## INTRODUCTION

Industrialization has often been valued by many Third World countries as a development strategy to generate rapid economic growth, create employment opportunities, and help solve several societal problems. This strategy has always been apparent in Malaysia's development planning programs.[1] Even prior to her political independence from the British colonial rule (1876–1957), the need for vocational training to prepare the nation for industrial development was highlighted by foreign experts to the Malaysian government, as emphasised in the International Bank for Reconstruction and Development (IBRD) Mission report in 1955. The industrial development strategy considered then was the classical pattern of an import substitution industrialization (ISI) with tariff barriers and fiscal incentives, and this was implemented by the government from the late 1950s until the first half of the 1960s. A significant feature of these import substitution industries was that they were small-scale enterprises employing less than 50 workers and were mostly owned by locals (*First Malaysia Plan* 1967: 124). Similar to the experience in other Third World countries, the limitations and inadequacies of import-substitution strategy were becoming apparent by the 1960s and hence a reformulation of development strategies was undertaken (Lim, D. 1973: 109–113). As will be explained in the second part of this paper, Malaysia, in following the example set by other Third World countries (and notably by her neighbor, Singapore), began to emphasize export-oriented industrialization (EOI) as the engine of economic growth and this strategy was vigorously pursued from the 1970s to the mid-1980s. Export-oriented industrialization, besides creating vast employment opportunities, ensured the possibility that the industrial sector could grow faster and thus earn valuable foreign exchange. This was confirmed by an economic assessment study in 1992 which showed that export-oriented industries which have a lower capital-labor ratio performed better than import substitution industries in terms of employment creation (Mahani 1992).

At present the Malaysian government now aims to move into a new stage of industrialization and to achieve the status of "newly industrialized country" (NIC) by the year 2020. Thus, the government is laying a strong foundation for its entry into the third and final stage of industrial development which involves technologically intensive industries. As such the industrial policies for the 1990s are geared toward capital-intensive technology and skill-intensive industries. Besides large multinational corporations and large local enterprise, the role of small- and medium-scale industries is emphasized in the development plans of the 1990s. For example, one of the development strategies in the Sixth Malaysian Plan is "to encourage technological upgrading, diversify the industrial base, and promote industrial restructuring and modernization especially among small and medium scale industries" (*Sixth Malaysia Plan* 1991: 41). A major review of development strategies has been made and steps to implement the objectives of the new Industrial Master Plan (IMP) have begun.[2]

The aim of this chapter is twofold. First, it seeks to inform readers about the direct correlation between the economic development process of Malaysia, premised on export-oriented industrialization and Malaysian women's entry into industrial employment. Second, it aims to show that this correlation can be understood in the context of gender issues and economic development.

With these objectives in mind, the chapter is organized into three parts. The first part begins by providing the general context for a discourse on the direct relationship between the economic development process and women's gendered participation in industrial employment. It then focuses on Malaysia and specifically on the issue of Malaysian women's participation in the manufacturing sector for the period 1957–1990. The second part is a further elaboration on this issue, that is, the factors explaining women's massive entry into the manufacturing sector's labor force during the export-oriented industrialization era. It then discusses the implication of this phenomenon in the context of gender and development. The third part reports on changing economic trends in Malaysia and the government's new industrial strategy for the 1980s and 1990s with the aim of highlighting its implications for women workers.[3]

## ECONOMIC DEVELOPMENT AND WOMEN'S PARTICIPATION IN INDUSTRIAL EMPLOYMENT

The economic development of any nation usually entails changes which are characterized by a relative decline in the contribution of agriculture to the gross domestic product (GDP) and employment and simultaneously a relative increase in the contribution of the industrial and services sector. According to development economics literature, the development process involves a structural transformation whereby the economy changes from one with a predominant rural and agricultural base to one which is predominantly urban-industrial and services oriented. On the basis of the knowledge cited above, the following hypothesis on the relationship between development and women's participation in industrial employment can be made:

Other than in certain countries where women are deliberately prohibited from entering into paid formal employment, the normal course of economic development and structural transformation process of a nation will therefore inevitably encourage the entry of women (and men) in increasing numbers into the industrial and services sector.

This has been the experience in the industrialized Western countries where women have become a permanent feature of the industrial sector's labor since the dawn of the twentieth century.

Malaysia has been undergoing significant economic structural transformation since the 1960s when the importance of agriculture to the economy started to decline at a fairly steady rate while the contribution of the manufacturing sector increased steadily.[4]

Since Malaysia is experiencing rapid economic structural transformation, and since Malaysian women are not faced with serious sociocultural norms prohibiting them from participating in paid employment,[5] it can therefore be expected of them to participate increasingly in urban-industrial employment. Available information does indicate an increasing trend. For example, in 1957, female employment in the manufacturing industries was estimated to be 22,500. This number increased to 73,000 in 1970, 290,000 in 1979, 212,634 in 1985, and by 1990 it had increased to 428,311 (Department of Statistics, *Industrial Surveys*, 1957–1990). In terms of total female labor force, government statistics indicate that, in 1947, 6 percent of the women in the labor force were in the manufacturing sector. This increased to 6.9 percent in 1962, 8.1 percent in 1970, and 16.3 percent in 1980. Within two decades, that is, during the NEP (New Economic Policy) period (1970–1990), this percentage tripled, and by 1990, the manufacturing sector in this country provided employment for 24 percent of the female workforce as compared to only 15 percent of the male workforce. These figures are shown in Table 5.1.

In terms of the male-female composition of the manufacturing sector's labor force, government statistics indicate that, since 1970, the female's rate of increase has been faster than the male's due to the more rapid intake of women into the workforce. As a consequence, while prior to 1970 the male's share of the manufacturing sector's labor force was very much larger than the female's share, this has changed since then. Consequently in 1988, the composition of the workforce began to display characteristics of gender equality, where the percentage of female workers employed equaled that of male workers. By 1990, the female share was larger than the male's, that is, 50.7 percent were females as compared to 49.3 percent males. These figures are shown in Table 5.2.

The predominance of female workers in export-oriented manufacturing firms is most evident, for example, in 1970. There were then only about 41 manufacturing

**Table 5.1**
**Employment Distribution by Industry and Sex, 1970–1990**

| Industry | 1970 | | 1980 | | 1985 | | 1990 | |
|---|---|---|---|---|---|---|---|---|
| | Male | Female | Male | Female | Male | Female | Male | Female |
| Agriculture & Forestry | 49.6 | 67.9 | 37.5 | 49.3 | 28.6 | 33.7 | 28.9 | 28.2 |
| Mining & Quarrying | 2.3 | 0.7 | 1.4 | 0.3 | 1.1 | 0.2 | 0.7 | 0.2 |
| Manufacturing | 9.3 | 8.1 | 11.8 | 16.3 | 13.0 | 18.9 | 15.2 | 24.3 |
| Electricity, Gas & Water | 1.0 | 0.1 | 0.2 | 0.1 | 0.8 | 0.5 | 0.9 | 0.1 |
| Construction | 3.1 | 0.5 | 6.4 | 1.0 | 10.7 | 1.2 | 8.7 | 0.7 |
| Wholesale & Retail Trade, Hotels & Restaurants | 11.6 | 5.8 | 13.1 | 11.2 | 16.8 | 19.1 | 16.9 | 19.7 |
| Transport, Storage & Communications | 5.0 | 0.5 | 5.0 | 0.7 | 5.9 | 1.3 | 5.9 | 3.9 |
| Finance, Insurance Real Estate & Business Services | — | — | 1.9 | 1.6 | 3.8 | 3.9 | 4.0 | 3.9 |
| Community, Social & Peronal Services | 18.1 | 16.4 | 22.7 | 19.5 | 19.3 | 21.2 | 18.8 | 21.4 |
| Total | 100.0 | 100.0 | 100.0 | 100.0 | 100.0 | 100.0 | 100.0 | 100.0 |

*Source:* Government of Malaysia. *Sixth Malaysia Plan, 1991–1995,* Table 16.1, p. 415.

firms employing a total of 3,200 workers and, of this, 99 percent of the production workforce were females. This figure increased to 138 firms in 1976 employing 47,000 workers. Other examples of this rapid expansion are as follows.

In 1985, the electronics and electrical industry was the single largest employer of industrial workers, employing 81,432 workers, and of this, 74 percent were females. By 1990, these figures have more than doubled, whereby there were 422 firms in this industrial group employing a total of 216,528 workers, and of this total, 163,807 (or 76 percent) were female workers.

Besides the electronics and electrical industry, the garment industry is the second major employer of female workers in Malaysia. The garment industry employed 31,094 workers in 1985 and this doubled to 64,157 workers in 1990. This is another industry where females constituted about 85 percent of the workforce. A similar pattern is prevalent in the textile industry where women constituted more than 50 percent of the workforce. Gender is clearly a determining factor in this emerging industrial scenario. The reasons for this will now be deliberated in the light of two probing questions.

First, is the trend of women's increasing participation in industrial employment in Malaysia just a logical consequence and part of the normal course of the eco-

**Table 5.2**
**Percentage Distribution of Employed Persons by Sex in the Manufacturing Sector**

| Year | Male | Female | Total |
|------|------|--------|-------|
| 1957 | 83.0 | 17.0 | 100.00 |
| 1970 | 71.0 | 29.0 | 100.00 |
| 1974 | 60.3 | 39.7 | 100.00 |
| 1975 | 60.7 | 39.3 | 100.00 |
| 1979 | 61.2 | 38.8 | 100.00 |
| 1980 | 60.5 | 39.5 | 100.00 |
| 1981 | 58.4 | 41.6 | 100.00 |
| 1982 | 55.5 | 44.5 | 100.00 |
| 1983 | 55.4 | 44.6 | 100.00 |
| 1984 | 56.0 | 44.0 | 100.00 |
| 1985 | 55.4 | 44.6 | 100.00 |
| 1986 | 53.3 | 46.7 | 100.00 |
| 1987 | 51.8 | 48.2 | 100.00 |
| 1988 | 50.0 | 50.0 | 100.00 |
| 1989 | 49.6 | 50.4 | 100.00 |
| 1990 | 49.3 | 50.7 | 100.00 |

*Source:* Compiled from unpublished data from the Statistics Department of Malaysia (1957–1979), and *Industrial Surveys*, 1980–1990, Department of Statistics, Malaysia.

nomic development process as hypothesized earlier or is gender the determining factor? Second, what are the factors which can explain the massive increase in women's labor force participation in the manufacturing sector, which has recorded female labor growth rates that have exceeded the male participation rates? The next section will attempt to provide the answers to these questions.

## EXPORT-ORIENTED INDUSTRIALIZATION AND FEMALE EMPLOYMENT

It can be stated at the outset that Malaysian women's increased participation in industrial employment in the 1970s not only was due to the normal process of economic development but also was augmented by new developments in the world economy which have a significant link with export-oriented industrialization activities in Malaysia. As will be elaborated hereafter, these factors, combined, have created a sudden demand for female workers. In addition, there was also a coincidental ready supply of women job seekers in the labor market in Malaysia at that time. Let us look at each of these factors in turn.

## Demand Forces for Women Industrial Workers

One new feature which emerged in the world economy in the late 1960s and 1970s was the growing internationalization of productive activity. This was characterized by the export of capital from the "growth centers" of the First World to offshore factories of transnational corporations in the Third World. This new pattern, which developed in the mid-1960s, replaced the classic scenario of an international division of labor where Third World countries were integrated into the world economy on the basis of exporters of raw primary commodities and cheap labor for industries located in the industrializing West. Through the expansion of activities of Western-owned multinational corporations (MNCs), some Third World countries have become industrial sites for MNC factories. The MNCs established their subsidiaries in low-wage countries to carry out labor-intensive assembly and/or processing of industrial goods. In some cases, the MNCs subcontract parts of the production process to local businessmen and industrialists. The industrial goods are then reexported from the Third World countries back to the MNCs' home countries for their markets or the components are assembled into finished products and sold to other Third World countries.

The Southeast Asian countries became the target for "offshore-sourcing" activities because of the intense "cost-cut" competition faced by the electronics industry following the "electronic revolution" and trade union demands. Therefore in their pursuit to secure cheap and productive workers so as to retain their competitive edge in the world market, they had to look for new locations.

In an attempt to speed up economic growth, a number of Third World countries, including Malaysia, were eager to participate in the internationalization of production and offered free-trade and production zone facilities to foreign investors and cooperated to develop export-oriented industries. Consequently, in 1970, Malaysia embarked on its export-oriented industrialization program. The government designated the electronics industry as a "priority industry" and pioneer industrial status together with investment incentives were given to these foreign companies. Malaysia has become a favored location for multinational electronic firms. Among the factors which attracted MNCs to establish their plants here are the stable poltical climate, good infrastructure, and cheap trainable labor with an ability to comprehend the English language, the main *lingua franca* of the MNCs.

By the 1960s, many Third World countries were absorbed into the internationalization of production by their involvement in labor-intensive manufacturing for export with direct foreign participation of MNCs from the developed countries of Europe, United States, and Japan. In the early 1960s, Korea and Taiwan were already participating with the MNCs, and by the late 1960s, countries such as Indonesia, Singapore, and Australia followed suit. Today, we not only have a wide spectrum of MNCs establishing their operations in Malaysia but also increasing numbers of small- and medium-sized companies from Japan, Taiwan, and Europe. One outstanding feature of export-oriented industrialization is that they are located in free-trade zones, which are also known as export processing zones. In these free-trade zones, where only manufacturing activities are allowed to be carried out, foreign companies enjoy minimum customs control together with duty-free import of raw materials, component parts, and all machinery which are required directly for the manufacturing process.[6]

The establishment of world market factories throughout the Third World in general and Malaysia in particular was stimulated by both the demand of the MNCs for cheap labor and the desire of Third World countries to achieve economic development through export-oriented industrialization. In their effort to attract MNCs and to ensure the success of export-oriented industrialization strategies, host countries of "offshore-sourcing" areas have imposed strict control on wages and the trade union movement.

## The Impact of World Market Factories on Gender Composition of the Workforce

Before 1970 and prior to the introduction of export-oriented industrialization and the establishment of free-trade zones, the structure of the Malaysian industrial labor force showed two distinct features. First, it was male dominated. Second, in terms of its racial composition, the majority of the workers were from the Chinese ethnic group.

This scenario changed significantly after the government embarked on its export-industrialization program which coincided with its new economic policy (NEP) in 1970, which was designed so that the intake of workers should reflect the racial composition of the country. In keeping with this policy requirement, all new establishments had to abide with the employment quota for the indigenous people who comprised more than 50 percent of the Malaysian society. Consequently, more Malays began to be employed in the manufacturing sector and most of them were rural migrants.

Another notable feature was the significant increase in the entry of women into the manufacturing sector, particularly as production workers. This is a direct feature of export-oriented industrialization in Malaysia which is labor intensive and cost conscious. Hence many industries preferred to employ female workers, who, unlike male workers, were willing to accept low wages.

Hence the employment structure which had emerged in the export processing zones by the late 1970s was characterized by the following features. First, industrial production was confined to a few highly specialized labor-intensive manufacturing processes, namely, inputs imported from outside the country were worked on by the local labor force in "world market factories" (for example, sewing, soldering, assembly, and testing) and then exported in their processed form. Second, the work opportunities were given mainly to young single females since the majority of the production processes located in the world market factories required cheap labor who could perform tasks with dexterity and patience. Third, investment per workplace was on average relatively low and there were no significant linkages with local industries nor major utilization of local resources other than labor (Frobel et al. 1980).

Gender has become a feature of investment strategies; for instance, in an endeavor to pursue export-oriented industrialization as a development strategy, the Malaysian government embarked on various ambitious and aggressive trade missions in the 1970s in which gender was used as an attraction. Although this is denied by government planners and administrators (who claimed that their strategies have not and need not be "gender specific"), it was proven by researchers that during these trade missions abroad, the gender assets of the "fast fingered," dextrous, highly productive, and trainable Malaysian female workers were widely published in order to attract MNCs to establish their factories in Malaysia.[7] To ensure an industrial environment conductive to foreign investors, legislative measures which affected women workers were also introduced. For example, legislative regulations prohibiting night shift work for women were relaxed (Jamilah Ariffin 1984b: 75). The formation of an electronics industrial union was also prohibited. Only "in-house" unions are allowed.

With direct reference to development planning, it is pertinent to ask these questions: First, "Was it also only incidental that the industries designated by the government as 'priority industries' in the export-oriented program were mainly the female-dominated labor-intensive industries, namely, the electronics, clothing, and textile industries?" and second, "Were government planners not aware then of the gender-related implications of such industries and the need to assess their impact in terms of gender-sensitive analysis?"

Notwithstanding the professed "genderless" approach taken by Malaysian planners, the establishment of export-oriented industries in the 1970s has in fact created more job opportunities for women than for men. The electronics industry, for example, besides being the largest exporter of manufactured products (and the main foreign exchange earner), has become the largest employer in the manufacturing sector with women comprising over 75 percent of its workforce. As shown by the figures in Table 5.3, the growth of this female workforce in the export-oriented industries, namely, the electronics, textiles, garments, pharmaceuticals, and food industries, is phenomenal. Such a situation could never be anticipated nor explained simply by the traditional "economic-development process" logic. It can be explained only in terms of the new international division of labor in the internationalization of labor in the world economy which has created a sudden and large demand for female workers.

### Supply of Female Labor for the Manufacturing Sector

With reference again to the Malaysian government's stand on the "unnecessity of gender specificities in development planning" we may ask whether it was only fortuitous that the program of export-oriented industrialization was launched at a time when a large supply of women job seekers was also emerging and which suited the demand requirements of the MNCs. This sudden supply can be explained in

Table 5.3
Distribution of Employed Persons in Manufacturing Industries in Malaysia*

| | | 1985 | | | 1990 | | |
|---|---|---|---|---|---|---|---|
| Code No. | Industry | Males | Females | Total | Males | Females | Total |
| 311–312 | Food Manufacture | 41,130 [67%] | 20,173 [33%] | 61,303 | 47,794 [65%] | 25,492 [35%] | 73,286 |
| 313 | Beverage Industries | 3,909 [69%] | 1,727 [31%] | 5,636 | 2,999 [66%] | 1,527 [34%] | 4,526 |
| 314 | Tobacco Manufacture | 2,446 [54%] | 2,089 [46%] | 4,535 | 2,287 [45%] | 2,852 [55%] | 5,139 |
| 321 | Textile Manufacture | 9,772 [36%] | 17,433 [64%] | 27,205 | 15,894 [42%] | 21,693 [58%] | 37,857 |
| 322 | Manufacture of Wearing Apparel [Clothing] | 3,301 [11%] | 27,793 [89%] | 31,094 | 9,457 [15%] | 55,118 [85%] | 64,575 |
| 323 | Manufacture of Leather Products | 261 [42%] | 356 [58%] | 617 | 719 [36%] | 1,273 [64%] | 1,992 |
| 324 | Manufacture of Footwear | 425 [45%] | 520 [55%] | 945 | 471 [46%] | 550 [54%] | 1,021 |
| 331 | Manufacture of Wood Products | 38,255 [75%] | 12,926 [25%] | 51,181 | 58,395 [72%] | 22,564 [28%] | 80,959 |
| 332 | Manufacture of Furniture | 6,725 [74%] | 2,336 [26%] | 9,061 | 10,605 [70%] | 4,473 [30%] | 15,078 |
| 341 | Manufacture of Paper | 4,303 [61%] | 2,702 [39%] | 7,005 | 9,053 [67%] | 4,410 [33%] | 13,463 |
| 342 | Printing & Publishing Industries | 12,658 [61%] | 8,017 [39%] | 20,675 | 13,097 [59%] | 9,269 [41%] | 22,366 |
| 351 | Manufacture of Industrial Chemical | 5,174 [84%] | 993 [16%] | 6,167 | 8,204 [84%] | 1,554 [16%] | 9,758 |
| 352 | Manufacture of Other Chemicals | 5,623 [57%] | 4,188 [43%] | 9,811 | 7,235 [59%] | 5,095 [41%] | 12,330 |
| 353 | Petroleum Refineries | 1,284 [93%] | 101 [7%] | 1,385 | 1,023 [91%] | 107 [9%] | 1,130 |
| 354 | Manufacture of Other Petroleum Refineries | 918 [86%] | 148 [14%] | 1,066 | 824 [84%] | 162 [16%] | 986 |
| 355 | Manufacture of Rubber Products | 16,219 [58%] | 11,670 [42%] | 27,889 | 29,260 [50%] | 29,681 [50%] | 58,941 |

Table 5.3 (continued)

| | | 1985 | | | 1990 | | |
|---|---|---|---|---|---|---|---|
| Code No. | Industry | Males | Females | Total | Males | Females | Total |
| 356 | Manufacture of Plastic Products | 6,957 [46%] | 8,221 [54%] | 15,178 | 16,909 [46%] | 19,523 [54%] | 36,432 |
| 361 | Manufacture of Pottery | 1,035 [45%] | 1,282 [55%] | 2,317 | 2,990 [40%] | 4,487 [60%] | 7,477 |
| 362 | Manufacture of Glass Products | 1,986 [85%] | 338 [15%] | 2,324 | 2,854 [86%] | 464 [14%] | 3,318 |
| 369 | Manufacture of Nonmetallic Products | 17,123 [78%] | 4,821 [22%] | 21,944 | 19,839 [80%] | 4,908 [20%] | 24,747 |
| 371 | Iron & Steel Basic Industries | 9,213 [87%] | 1,366 [13%] | 10,579 | 12,126 [89%] | 1,568 [11%] | 13,694 |
| 372 | Nonferrous Metal Basic Industries | 2,563 [84%] | 486 [16%] | 3,049 | 3,961 [83%] | 801 [17%] | 4,762 |
| 381 | Manufacture of Fabricated Metal Products | 13,676 [69%] | 6,183 [31%] | 19,859 | 22,565 [69%] | 10,314 [31%] | 32,879 |
| 382 | Manufacture of Machinery | 11,267 [83%] | 2,243 [17%] | 13,510 | 19,813 [75%] | 6,747 [25%] | 26,560 |
| 383 | Manufacture of Electrical Machinery, Apparatus & Appliances | 21,242 [26%] | 60,190 [74%] | 81,432 | 52,721 [24%] | 163,807 [76%] | 216,528 |
| 384 | Manufacture of Transport Equipment | 15,125 [80%] | 3,798 [20%] | 18,923 | 19,882 [79%] | 5,425 [21%] | 25,307 |
| 385 | Manufacture of Professional & Scientific Equipment | 1,642 [29%] | 4,077 [71%] | 5,719 | 4,032 [27%] | 10,679 [73%] | 14,711 |
| 390 | Other manufacturing Industries | 2,439 [30%] | 5,758 [70%] | 8,197 | 6,692 [37%] | 11,546 [63%] | 18,238 |
| Total | | 256,671 [54.8%] | 211,935 [45.2%] | 468,606 [100%] | 401,701 [48.5%] | 426,359 [51.5%] | 828,060 [100%] |

* The figures are only for Malaysians. Non-Malaysians are not included. Figures in brackets show percentage.

Source: Compiled from unpublished data from the Department of Statistics, Malaysia (1985–1990).

the following way: Due to the demography and age structure of the Malaysian female population, the number of females in the fifteen to twenty-four age group increased more rapidly than any other group in the last fifteen years (i.e., for the period 1962–1977). This resulted in a ready supply of young female job seekers in the labor market. In addition, this was also the cohort of women who had been given greater access and opportunities by the government in the postindependence era to obtain formal education, unlike the situation of women belonging to the earlier generation. As such, by the 1970s, most of the present generation of females had received at least middle-level education. However, by this time it was more difficult for them to obtain jobs in the preferred "feminine" occupations like nursing, teaching, and government clerical professions. Given the recent industrial development where factory jobs were in abundance and female labor was needed, it was therefore not surprising for these women to take on factory work in the manufacturing sector.

In a nutshell, the supply of middle-level, educated, young, single women in the Malaysian labor market in the 1970s has colluded with the labor demands of "offshore sourcing" activities of the MNCs. This was also the time when the new economic policy (which emphasized racial equity) was implemented, hence encouraging the urban-ward migration of young, educated, rural Malay women and their rapid absorption into the manufacturing sector's labor force. The state has also helped the MNCs to obtain female workers from the rural villages, as exemplified by the role played by the ruling party, that is, the United Malay National Organisation (UMNO), in recruiting women from the East Coast for the urban-based factories (Jamilah Ariffin 1984b: 75).

## Gender and Development Issues Pertaining to Women in the Manufacturing Sector

It was obvious in the 1970s that the sudden presence of thousands of rural female factory workers in the urban-industrial areas was regarded with antagonism by several quarters in Malaysian society (for details see Jamilah Ariffin 1978). Some Malaysian academics alleged that this antagonism can be explained by the "fact" that Malaysian men (and other patriarchal-minded people) were generally envious of these women because of the new employment opportunities open to them. Such a view was echoed by other quarters also. For example, during the beginning of Islamic fundamentalism in Malaysia in the 1970s, it was also common to hear Muslim student activists proclaiming that women should not work because, by doing so, they would be depriving men of jobs. A similar stand was voiced by some Malaysian public figures in the 1980s.[8] There is little truth in this allegation. Wide-ranging studies conducted by the HAWA Project at the University of Malaya and other similar studies on export-oriented industrialization in Malaysia show that men expressed sympathy for women workers' conditions of work characterized by lower pay, long hours, and tedious work, and they would not want to compete for such jobs (HAWA 1981).

Other in-depth studies conducted in other countries on the labor requirements of the export-oriented industries in which women workers predominate also prove that there is no basis for competition between men and women for these factory jobs due to the fact that these jobs are gender specific. This is because the nature and demands of the production process in these industries are more easily fulfilled by women than by men workers because of certain gender-related abilities such as manual dexterity, the patience to sit for long hours on the factory bench, ability to do intricate work, and the willingness to work under strict supervision. Studies have shown that under these job requirements, women's productivity has always been higher than men's.

Studies have also shown that the reason why MNCs prefer women workers to men workers is because women are more willing to accept lower wages (see, for example, Lim 1978). Management also tends to capitalize on the traditional viewpoint that women workers are "secondary income earners" who work for "pin-money," hence providing the rationality of paying lower wages to women workers. By the same logic, it was also not inhuman of these industrial firms to retrench these women workers during periods of slack demand. Female workers are therefore preferred by any volatile industry, such as the electronics industry, which needs cheap, disposable labor for its survival in the competitive market. Due to gendered socialization practices and girls' upbringing patterns, women workers tend to be more docile and less daring than men to organize collectively against management. For these reasons alone, the industrial capitalists prefer female workers since they are more suited to the production process. Women also tolerate employment conditions where workers rights and interests are not sufficiently protected.[9]

The aim of the above discussion is to establish the fact that Malaysian men are not competing against their women for industrial jobs because work conditions in the electronics and garment factories are not sufficiently attractive to them. The issue of sex discrimination cannot therefore be made a "bone of contention" between gender, especially in the capitalist world of industrial development.

Rather than harping on the sex discrimination issue, what people-oriented studies should rightfully stress is the unfair deal that women are getting from their participation in industrial development, that is, the position of women in these industries; the *quality* and implications of these new forms of employment for them must be seriously assessed. Although thousands of women gained entry into the manufacturing sector's labor force, the majority of them occupy the lowest echelon of the occupational hierarchy. As indicated by the figures in Table 5.4, the women's share in the production laborers' category is consistently higher than men's, whereas men's share is higher in the professional and managerial categories. In 1985, government statistics revealed that the number of female workers in the semiskilled and unskilled category constituted 40 percent of the total female labor force. But by 1990, this figure has increased significantly to 50 percent.[10] (Refer to Table 5.5.)

Table 5.4
Employment Distribution by Occupation and Sex, 1970–1990, %

|  | 1970 | | 1980 | | 1985 | | 1990 | |
|---|---|---|---|---|---|---|---|---|
| Occupational Category | *Male* | *Female* | *Male* | *Female* | *Male* | *Female* | *Male* | *Female* |
| Professional, Technical & Related Workers | 4.6 | 5.3 | 6.4 | 8.5 | 6.8 | 9.1 | 6.4 | 9.4 |
| Administrative & Managerial Workers | 1.0 | 0.1 | 1.4 | 0.3 | 3.2 | 0.6 | 2.8 | 0.6 |
| Clerical & Related Workers | 5.4 | 4.1 | 6.8 | 11.1 | 7.4 | 14.2 | 7.0 | 14.1 |
| Sales & Related Workers | 9.8 | 4.9 | 10.3 | 7.2 | 11.1 | 11.0 | 11.4 | 11.4 |
| Service Workers | 8.1 | 8.4 | 9.0 | 9.0 | 10.1 | 13.7 | 9.9 | 14.1 |
| Agricultural Workers | 47.6 | 66.8 | 35.9 | 46.3 | 28.7 | 33.7 | 29.4 | 28.1 |
| Production & Related Workers | 23.5 | 10.4 | 30.3 | 17.6 | 32.7 | 17.7 | 33.1 | 22.3 |
| Total | 100.0 | 100.0 | 100.0 | 100.0 | 100.0 | 100.0 | 100.0 | 100.0 |

*Source:* Government of Malaysia, *Sixth Malaysia Plan, 1991–1995.*

## CHANGING ECONOMIC CONDITIONS AND ITS IMPLICATIONS FOR WOMEN WORKERS

Although it enjoyed rapid economic growth rates in the late 1970s and early 1980s, the Malaysian economy experienced a short period of recession from 1982 to 1986. This is because, as an open economy, Malaysia was adversely affected by the world recession. The worst year was in 1985 when the economy registered a negative growth rate of $-1.5$ percent (Kamal Salih 1987: 5). Due to this bad experience the government planners became more aware of several structural weaknesses in the Malaysian economy. Some of these are:

1. overdependency on primary exports;
2. a narrow industrial base which comprised mainly electronics and textiles and the lack of a sufficiently developed small- and medium-scale industrial sector;
3. a large oversubsidized public sector and an overregulated economy; and
4. a shortage of skilled workers (Kamal Salih 1987).

It was also obvious to the government that the present form of export-oriented industrialization has other undesirable effects since it is constantly subjected to the vicissitudes of world demands. As a consequence, several thousands of Malaysian workers would be retrenched whenever a downturn in demand occurs.[11]

In taking stock of the recession and the factors as cited above, the Malaysian government started to implement various structural adjustment measures in mid-1982. Among other things, public sector spending on most development items (other than health and education) was cut, and the consolidation and rational-

Table 5.5
Distribution of Employed Persons by Occupation and Sex*

| Occupation | 1985 | | 1990 | |
|---|---|---|---|---|
| | *Male* | *Female* | *Male* | *Female* |
| Total Working Proprietors | 2,599 | 398 | 2,481 | 471 |
| & Unpaid Family Workers | [1%] | [0.2%] | [1%] | [0.1%] |
| Managerial & Professional | 18,092 | 1,960 | 25,009 | 3,779 |
| | [7%] | [0.9%] | [6%] | [0.9%] |
| Technical & Supervisory | 35,347 | 6,753 | 57,153 | 13,811 |
| | [14%] | [3.2%] | [14%] | [3%] |
| Clerical & Related Workers | 18,341 | 23,090 | 21,073 | 34,198 |
| | [7%] | [11%] | [5%] | [8%] |
| General Workers | 20,629 | 5,321 | 26,141 | 6,842 |
| | [8%] | [2.5%] | [7%] | [2%] |
| **Other Directly Employed Workers** | | | | |
| Skilled | 50,519 | 70,583 | 72,983 | 123,591 |
| | [20%] | [33.3%] | [18%] | [30%] |
| Semi-skilled | 28,650 | 19,102 | 50,669 | 60,868 |
| | [11%] | [9%] | [13%] | [14%] |
| Unskilled | 52,002 | 66,434 | 99,683 | 154,548 |
| | [20%] | [31.3%] | [25%] | [36%] |
| Contract Workers | 26,784 | 15,344 | 41,255 | 23,144 |
| | [10%] | [7.2%] | [10%] | [5%] |
| Total Paid Employees | 3,708 | 2,950 | 5,254 | 5,107 |
| [Part Time] | [2%] | [1.4%] | [1%] | [1%] |
| Total | 256,671 | 211,935 | 401,701 | 426,359 |
| | [100%] | [100%] | [100%] | [100%] |

* The figures are only for Malaysians. Non-Malaysians are not included. Figures in brackets show percentage.

*Source:* Compiled from unpublished data from the Department of Statistics, Malaysia (1985, 1990).

ization of activities of non-profit-making public sector enterprises (NFPEs) were undertaken. A more aggressive strategy to promote private investment, both from local and international sources, was implemented. Various types of relaxation of regulations on direct foreign participation and ownership were introduced. Sectoral policies on agriculture, manufacturing, and services were also undertaken (Chung and De 1988).

In line with this realization, the trend with regard to the industrial policy today is toward "industrial deepening" with an emphasis on heavy and resource-based industries. In an attempt to achieve the status of a "newly industrialized country," the government is also encouraging the entry of higher technology industries in Malaysia, especially those with higher value-added content and more forward and backward linkages with the local economy (Annuar Ali 1988).

It must however be stated here that even before the government was considering this change in industrial strategy, the MNC industrial companies were already undergoing an industrial restructuring process. This was motivated by various forces in the world market such as the ever-increasing stiff competition among the industrial companies. This influenced the trend for MNCs to implant higher technology production process in their "offshore" locations, as well as to introduce more automated machines. To keep up with the level of technology and the new labor skills required by the higher technology industries, the skills of the Malaysian workforce too have to be upgraded. By this reasoning, it must be realized that when previously the type of workers demanded by the MNCs was mainly unskilled women workers, there is now a change, that is, the new demand is for highly skilled, technically trained workers (Jamilah Ariffin 1984a).

What are the implications of these changes for women workers in the manufacturing sector? This issue can be analyzed in terms of three major situations confronting women workers in the industrial sector. To recapitulate, these are:

1. The position of the electronics industry in Malaysia: This industry will still be given priority status despite the change in industrial strategy. Since it will continually be subjected to the vagaries of world demand, women workers in this industry will continue to be subjected to the threat of retrenchment.

2. The challenges posed by the process of industrial restructuring, whereby higher technology production processes will be located in Malaysia, hence needing more technically trained and skilled workers.

3. The change in the government's industrial strategy, that is, from export-oriented industrialization dependent on female labor-intensive industries to a more broad base and diversified industrialization.

Two sets of implications for women can be observed at the present time:

First, due to upgrading of the production process in several existing industries, the factories of women workers will either have to adapt to the changing situation by learning to handle more automated machines or be shed off. Due to the more capital intensive and automated structure, less workers will be needed in each production line. Under these new circumstances women workers will face the constant threat of retrenchment due to displacement by new technological upgrading as well as the effects arising from usual vagaries in the world market. However, preliminary research findings by the writer indicate that in the present situations of expansion by the existing industrial companies in Malaysia due to increasing demand for electronics products in the world market, several firms in

Malaysia are refraining from dismissing their workers but prefer to transfer them to the additional production lines. Another factor for retaining workers is because the management realizes that, despite the trend toward automation, there still remain some tasks in the production process which are dependent on manual labor and human discretion (Jamilah Ariffin 1984b).

Second, in taking stock of the situation as a whole (where the trend now is for the entry of higher technology industries which require more skilled and technically trained workers), the implications for women in terms of job opportunities are not as favorable as before. This is because unlike in the past when the nature of the production process favored women workers, now most of the machines can be easily handled by men. When previously the industries located in "offshore-sourcing" areas were mainly labor intensive, hence requiring a large supply of workers, now the trend is for more capital intensive industries requiring less workers, hence providing less opportunities for unskilled women job seekers. Studies conducted in Singapore (where the trend toward industrial restructuring and entry of higher technology industries had started earlier than in Malaysia) indicate that the ratio of women to men workers in the electronics industry has declined (Jamilah Ariffin 1984a). This is because with the shift to higher technology, more technicians, engineers, and skilled workers, rather than unskilled workers, are required. Even if we overlook the fact that several firms have a male bias, that is, they prefer to employ men rather than women for supervisory and technical positions, there are definitely more qualified male than female technicians available in the market. Under the prevailing circumstances, most of the new positions in the higher technology industries are therefore filled by men.

## CONCLUSION

Despite rapid changes in its industrial strategy, Malaysia will continue to emphasize the role of the manufacturing sector as the main engine of growth. It will be expected to remain the major foreign exchange earner and generator of employment. In this line, the electronics and the electrical industries which have contributed so significantly, especially in terms of employment creation for many women in Malaysia, are likely to expand and be given preferential treatment. However, the type of labor that they need now will not be in the favor of unskilled women workers since a demand for a more skilled workforce can be envisaged. It is in this changing scenario that a new discourse on the new dimension of "gender and work" must be developed.

## ACKNOWLEDGMENT

I would like to formally acknowledge the contribution of Geetha Subramaniam, my·Master of Economics student for her assistance in updating the data cited in this chapter. A broader version of it was written jointly with the title "Economic Development and Women in the Manufacturing Sector" and presented at the joint

HAWA/PSU/SAMA workshop "Malaysian Women Through Two Decades of Development," May 5–6, 1994, Kuala Lumpur, Malaysia.

## NOTES

1. Malaysia is a land of opportunities with abundant natural resources. Labor is cost-effective and industrial land ample. Its infrastructure is well developed, and the currency strong. All these assets have been utilized by the government to the nation's advantage as revealed in the steady rate of economic growth and sound social and infrastructural development.

Located in the tropics, Malaysia straddles the South China Sea and measures 329,758 $km^2$. It comprises three major territories, namely Peninsular Malaysia, Sabah, and Sarawak. Peninsular Malaysia is at the tip of Southeast Asia while the states of Sabah and Sarawak are on the island of Borneo. Malaysia was formerly under British colonial rule from 1876 to 1957. Today, it is a rapidly developing independent nation, governed as a parliamentary democracy with a constitutional monarchy. Latest figures on its population estimate that it has approximately 18.6 million people. This figure comprises the indigenous people (i.e., the Malays, Ibans, Kadazans, Orang Asli, etc.) who form about 50 percent of the population, and those of migrant origin, mainly Chinese and Indians, who first came to peninsular Malaya as laborers, artisans and businessmen during the British colonial period.

The Malay language is the national language but English is widely spoken. Islam is the state religion but there is complete freedom of worship.

Malaysia's per capita income is steadily rising. It was RM6206 in 1990 and this has risen to RM7554 in 1992. The inflation rate is less than 5 percent and has been at this level for the past seven years. The foreign exchange rate of the Malaysian currency, that is, Ringgit Malaysia (RM) in the international market in 1993 is about RM2.40 for one U.S. dollar and RM3.8 to one pound Sterling.

2. The Industrial Master Plan (IMP) was commissioned to expert consultants in 1984. The formulation of the IMP for the period 1986–1995 emphasises that one of the imperatives of future industrial development is to diversify away from overdependence on certain export-oriented industries and build up resource-based and high value-added industries and subsequently advance to a stage of higher-technology industries (see Annuar Ali 1988: 1–9).

3. This report is based on secondary data only. Data on manufacturing activities has been drawn primarily from the *Industrial Surveys* conducted annually by the Department of Statistics, Malaysia, the most recent of which was conducted in 1990. Data on labor is based on the *Labour Force Survey Reports* by the Department of Statistics.

Besides these statistical reports, other sources of data include:

(a) *Sixth Malaysia Plan*, 1991–1995;

(b) *Economic Reports*, Ministry of Finance;

(c) *Occupational Wages Survey in the Manufacturing Industries*, Ministry of Human Resources;

(d) Malaysian Industrial Development Authority (MIDA) *Annual Report*.

However, in tracing the growing participation of women in the labor force, we have drawn upon other sources of data such as undocumented material from MIDA, unpublished data from the Department of Statistics, recent case studies of female workers in the manufacturing sector, and so forth, so that the data presented is the most recent available.

4. At the end of the 1970s although agriculture was still the largest contributor to the GDP, its share of GDP declined from 38 percent in 1960 to 30.8 percent in 1970 and to 21.1 percent in 1988 and 16 percent in 1992. This sector also showed declining average annual growth rates, from 5.7 percent between 1971 and 1975 to 3.2 percent between 1981 and 1985. The economic recovery began in 1987 and the economy grew at 6–7 percent in 1988. Simultaneously, the contribution of the manufacturing sector to the GDP has been steadily exceeding that of agriculture. While in 1970 its share of GDP was only 13.4 percent, it increased to 24.1 percent in 1988, and this further increased to 26.9 percent in 1990. On the average, the annual growth rate of the manufacturing sector was 11.5 percent in the 1960s and 12.5 percent in the 1970s. However, due to the economic recession of the 1980s, its growth rate declined to 5.2 percent between 1981 and 1985. The other sector which has also seen rapid growth is the services sector (Annuar Ali 1988: 4–6; Chamhuri 1988: 5). It can be observed that the development process changed from one premised on agriculture to one characterized by an expansion of the manufacturing and services sectors.

5. For details on this aspect, please see Jamilah Ariffin, *Women and Development in Malaysia*, Ch. 1 and 2.

6. Free-trade zones were developed by the government under the Free Trade Zone Act of 1971, the purpose of which was to encourage the growth of export-oriented industries. They are actually a modernized version of the export enclave where all infrastructural facilities such as roads and buildings and amenities such as water and electricity are supplied by the host country. Besides minimum customs formalities, many incentives such as the five-year "tax-holiday" are enjoyed by these companies. The first of the many free-trade zones in Malaysia was established in 1972 at Bayan Lepas in Penang followed by four others. To date a total of twelve free-trade zones have been established in six states in Malaysia including the latest one in Sarawak. Most of the established trade zones are situated in the west coast states of Peninsular Malaysia where the infrastructural facilities are better than the ones on the east coast. In addition to free-trade zones, there are many companies designated as "Licensed Manufacturing Warehouse (LMW)". Similar to the facilities provided to companies located in free-trade zones, those with LMW status are allowed to import duty-free raw materials and capital equipment for their production process. Besides the establishment of free-trade zones, there were many other industrial incentives which favored foreign investment. For example, the Malaysian government ensured an industrial environment conductive to investors such as pioneer status and several legislative measures to protect the interests of the foreign investors.

7. See, for example, Government of Malaysia 1970–71, p. 12.

8. See, for example, the statement made by the (then) Vice-Chancellor of Universiti Teknologi Malaysia in 1987.

9. Until 1988, the Malaysian government prohibited the formation of unions in the electronics industry. It is only in June 1988 that the government agreed to the formation of "in-house" unions.

10. Calculated from unpublished data from the Department of Statistics, Kuala Lumpur, Malaysia.

11. Even though all sectors of the economy have suffered to some extent due to events in the world market (such as a fall on commodity prices, collapse of the international tin

market, downturn in world demand for industrial goods, introduction of various protectionist policies in the West, etc.), it is the manufacturing sector which accounted for the highest level of reported retrenchments. This is documented by the Ministry of Labour and Manpower in 1985 (Lockhead and Rohana-Ariffin 1986). According to a report from the Labor Ministry, the number of manufacturing sector workers retrenched in 1984 was 4,452 and this increased to 27,598 in 1985 (Jomo 1990: 121).

# 6

# Women in Japan

## Jane Richardson and Paul Riethmuller

Long inconspicuous as members of society, Japanese women have made a significant contribution to the development of one of the world's largest economies. Rarely seen as industrial or commercial leaders, the women of Japan have nevertheless been integral to the successful modernization of Japan throughout the history, but most particularly in the twentieth century as providers of important ancillary and support roles. While the women of Japan can be broadly described as "policy implementors" rather than "policy instigators," they can nevertheless lay claim to at least one third of the success of their nation's economy (Iwao 1993: 157).

## INTRODUCTION

One of the most significant economic and social developments to have occurred in Japan over the past decade has been the increased involvement of women in the workforce. About 39 percent of those employed in Japan's major industries in 1992 were women, an increase from 1975 when women represented 32 percent of those employed. According to the 1992 Employment Status survey conducted by the Management and Coordination Agency, the percentage of the female population engaged in "regular employment" (those in work for thirty days or more per year) exceeded 50 percent for the first time in Japan's postwar history in 1992 (*Ippan Joho Information Bulletin,* 1993).

In the less important industries such as agriculture, women are also a significant part of the workforce. This is particularly so on the small farms that have dominated the agricultural sector for much of the postwar period. Men in the younger age groups left these farms for the factories of the cities during the 1950s, leaving the farm work to women and older men (Fukutake 1980). However, unlike other high-income (Western) countries, few women in Japan have risen to senior management positions.

This chapter will describe and analyze female participation in the Japanese economy and the economic and social factors that have influenced this participation. Information will be presented on female workforce participation by industry and by job status. The chapter will give details of the education attained by women as well as information on female income. The social and legislative barriers to women's involvement in the workforce will be described along with any developments that may lead to some modification of these barriers.

## HISTORICAL OVERVIEW

The Portuguese "discovered" Japan in 1543 and soon introduced the country to Christianity, to the new technology of firearms, to foreign dress, and to travel and exploration. Spanish missionaries and traders followed the Portuguese. It was not long before the Japanese authorities began to tire of their presence. They brought down a number of edicts against the Christian missionaries, culminating in their expulsion in 1587. The persecution of Christians resulted in an exodus of Japanese Christians overseas.[1] Japan came under the political control of the Tokugawa Shogunate shortly after this, in 1603. Within forty years, the shogun had expelled the Portuguese from Japan and banned Christianity. Furthermore, the only Europeans permitted to remain in Japan were the Dutch. Even then, they were kept on a tiny island of about 1,000 m$^2$ called Deshima in Nagasaki harbor. At any time there were only about 20 Dutch present on the island but there was a Japanese bureaucracy to cater for their needs. This bureaucracy was paid for by the Dutch. The only Japanese permitted to visit Deshima were Japanese courtesans. The Dutch were a window to the West for the Japanese, in that they were required to provide information to the shogun on matters such as shipbuilding techniques, Western food, watchmaking, and weaponry. Japan's policy of isolation, which was pursued for around 250 years under a strict feudal system, was successful in that Western powers were unable to annex and colonize Japan as they had other parts of Asia.

The origins of the modern Japanese economy can be traced to the mid-nineteenth century when it was opened to the West. In 1853, the U.S. government sent Perry and his "black ships" to force Japan to open its economy to trade. A series of treaties were signed over the next few years and other countries—France, Britain, Russia, and Holland—also got involved. These treaties established the rights of foreign ships to call at Japanese ports and gave foreign diplomats the right to reside in Japan but not much else. The United States negotiated the first trade treaty with Japan in 1858. It was known in Japan as the "Unequal Treaty" since tariffs were set at very low rates, with the Japanese government having no say in their level. This made it difficult for Japan to protect its fledgling industries. The opening of Japan also meant the end of the Tokugawa shoguns because of domestic political strife. Some factions believed that Japan should have resisted the Western powers, while others argued that resistance was pointless. In the end, those favoring cooperation won the day and the imperial family was reinstated under Emperor Meiji in 1868. This marked the beginning of the Meiji era, which lasted until 1912.

It rapidly became apparent that the economic institutions that had served Japan well during her isolationist period were inadequate in the international context. Japan had traditionally been an agrarian economy operating at a subsistence level. Contact with the West highlighted the necessity for it to industrialize rapidly if it was to maintain its autonomy and establish itself as a modern, developed nation.

The period from 1868 to the turn of the century was a watershed in terms of laying the foundations for economic development. In the first two decades of the Meiji era, an economic infrastructure that included the following, was put in place (Nakamura and Grace 1985):

a national monetary system with the Bank of Japan as sole issuer of bank notes;

a fiscal system based on land tax;

expansion of infrastructure, including roads, railroads, and shipping;

a nationwide post and telegraph system;

adoption of the joint stock organization as the corporate form;

import of machinery and foreign engineers;

government-operated factories.

Japan's victory in the Russo-Japanese war of 1904–1905 was a significant event of the Meiji era. The reason for this was that it was the first time an Asian nation had defeated a European power. Japan's victory provided the impetus for the country to continue with industrial development and by World War I this had been achieved. By 1920, Japan had become a creditor nation (Nakamura and Grace 1985).

This prosperity was shortlived as the rest of the world entered the recessionary period of the 1930s. However, despite this setback, industrial income had overtaken income from other sectors of the economy by 1936, with heavy and chemical industries dominating. World War II, and the years leading up to it, further transformed Japan. All available resources were concentrated toward the war effort.

Postwar development was limited until the escalation of cold war hostilities and the threat of communist expansion in the region during the 1950s. The occupation forces and engineers of the postwar constitution pursued a policy of demilitarization and democratization in the Western sense of the word. This resulted in the virtual elimination of many of Japan's existing social, political, and economic structures. There was a shift back to the land, and Japan temporarily reverted to a subsistence-level, agrarian society striving to overcome the food shortages of the postwar period.

As global tensions mounted in the 1950s, the U.S. government increasingly came to view Japan in terms of a potential ally in its strategy to contain the spread of communism through Asia. Some features of the harsh postwar reconstruction policies were relaxed, and the United States began to actively pursue a policy that would allow Japan to develop as a strong democratic ally. This period presented Japan with many opportunities to expand and prosper.

Between 1953 and 1970, the Japanese economy grew at an annual rate of over 10 percent, while between 1970 and 1982, it grew at a rate of about 5 percent. In both periods, the rate of Japanese economic growth outstripped that of most other nations including the United States and Germany (Nakamura and Grace 1985). The benefits of this development—better health services, access to education, and stronger international understanding—have had a cumulative positive effect that has helped Japan's economic development to its present strong state.

## ROLE OF WOMEN

A popular Western view of Japan's economic success, particularly in the postwar era, is that it is attributable to the "overworked salary man" (ordinary male salaried worker) carefully executing the policies of economic planners and government agencies. While it is true that government and industry have had a close working relationship, it would be erroneous to assume that economic contributions are the sole domain of the male worker.

Japanese women have made contributions through providing valuable support systems in the workplace and outside it. Sometimes this support has been given in the face of tremendous social and legislative barriers. Moreover, since 1976, their rate of entry into the workforce has outstripped that of men (Ministry of Labour 1991). Recent legislative changes ensuring equality of opportunity in the workplace may allow women in the future to contribute at a level other than basic ancillary levels.

### Women in Meiji Japan (1868–1912)

With the commencement of the Meiji era and the subsequent drive to modernize, it became quite common for men and women to work outside the agrarian sector: "By the beginning of the Meiji period, national markets were already established in salt, cotton and cloth, and some 20–25% of farmers are thought to have had other jobs concurrently as artisans, carpenters, plasterers, barrel makers etc., and women jobs in spinning, and weaving" (Nakamura and Grace 1985: 28).

The nature of work carried out by women was dictated by their husbands, fathers, and families. At this time, the dominant Confucian ethic saw women's lives bound by "three obediences": obedience to fathers when young, to husbands when married, and to children in old age (Iwao 1993). As a result, there were constraints on the work done by women in this period, obliged as they were to attend to the needs of their families first. However, as economic necessity demanded, they took on jobs outside the home, but mainly on a part-time basis. Their inferior position was underlined by their omission from the constitution of the time, the Meiji civil code.

The pattern of working on the land and outside the home remained in place for women until the conclusion of the World War II. Attitudes to women remained largely unchanged throughout this period. However, as industry developed and all resources galvanized for the war effort, it became more common for women to take on part-time work outside the home. Nevertheless, the notion that a woman's loyalty should be to the home and family remained unchallenged.

### Post–World War II

The immediate postwar period and the massive social and legal changes that took place then laid the groundwork for a turn-around in the pattern of working women's lives. As part of their policy of "democratization" the occupying forces redrafted the constitution in November 1946 and put it into effect in 1947. The new constitution was a complete departure from the Meiji code and contained explicit references to equality between the sexes. The emperor was stripped of all power as the supreme head of state. This, along with specific articles abolishing peerage, meant the end of the social structure based on privilege and property ownership that had ensured the inferior status of women.

The new constitution also entitled women to vote. In the Meiji era, voting rights were determined by the amount of tax paid. The vote was extended to all males in 1925, but the franchise did not apply to men under twenty-five years of age or to women. This changed under the postwar constitution since it gave the right to vote to all men and women twenty years of age and older who had been residents of a given locality for at least three months. Further, any man or woman over twenty-five years could become a candidate for political office. Women are more inclined to exercise their right to vote than men. In 1990, almost 75 percent of women voted compared with 72 percent of men, continuing a trend going back to the late 1960s (*Economic Eye* 1992).

While these changes were important, perhaps most significantly, the new constitution said:

All of the people are equal under the law, and there shall be no discrimination in political, economic or social relationships because of race, creed, sex, social status or family origin. (Article 14)

All people shall have the right to receive an equal education correspondent to their ability as provided by law. All people shall be obligated to have all boys and girls under their protection receive ordinary education as provided for by law. Such compulsory education shall be free. (Article 26)

All people shall have the right and the obligation to work. Standards for wages, hours, rest and other working conditions shall be fixed by law. (Article 27)
(*Kodansha Encyclopedia* 1993: 229–230)

In this way, the constitution not only removed the old structures of the Empire of Japan, but also created and legislated for their replacement institutions and made way for the emergence of a new changed nation.

Japan did not change overnight of course. It took some time until the effects of the new constitution filtered through to exert an influence upon the everyday existence of the population. Nevertheless, free access to education and the right to work and equality caused changes to the way society and employers viewed women, at least in principle. Eventually, this led to changes in the way women viewed themselves.

The positions available for women in this period were concentrated in factories or offices as clerical workers. Few skills were required for this work, and the role of women was squarely to provide workplace support. This was due in large part to social mores still prevalent at the time which placed emphasis on a woman's domestic and family responsibilities. Even for young, single women, society's expectation was that they would work until marriage. Then their duty to their husband and family would eclipse any other commitments they might have.

Young single women in the workplace were often described as "business girls" or "workplace flowers" (*Shokuba no Hana*), indicating that their working lives would be short and their contributions small. Their main purpose was to make the workplace more aesthetically pleasing. While the women worked conscientiously, management assumed that they would only be a temporary feature of the workplace. Work experience for women was considered valuable in terms of allowing them to "study the world" (*shakai kengaku*). Nonetheless, it was seen largely as preparation for their main job, which was marriage and domestic management.

Despite the changes to the constitution, the old cultural ideals were slow to respond. This was particularly visible in the Labour Standards Law of 1947. The law set out specific wages and working conditions for all employees as well as containing a bill of rights for all workers. At the time of its enactment, most people saw it as a major victory for the labor movement since it improved conditions over those of the Meiji era.

However, the law also contained special protective clauses for women. In light of their child-bearing and family responsibilities, women were allocated monthly "menstrual leave." The law also banned them from carrying out work between the hours of 10 p.m. and 5 a.m. As well, it banned them from undertaking jobs which the authorities considered detrimental to their health. This meant they could not be employed in jobs that involved heavy lifting and the like. In principle, these provisions prevented the exploitation of female workers. However, they also prevented women from making greater contributions to the running and direction of their employing firms. Women's personal ambitions also suffered. The government did not revise or revoke the protective clauses until the mid-1980s.

During the early 1950s, the Japanese economy began to take off. By 1956, the government could declare that the postwar period of reconstruction was over. As a display of the nation's increased affluence, it became something of a fashion for women who had no need to work to drop out of the workforce entirely upon marriage. By doing this, they could devote themselves to being full-time wives and mothers.

Concurrent to this economic boom was an increase in access to educational opportunities. The so-called education revolution gained momentum in the 1960s. This resulted in increased retention rates for all levels of education, and most women could graduate with a minimum of their secondary schooling completed.

## Female advancement to tertiary institutions

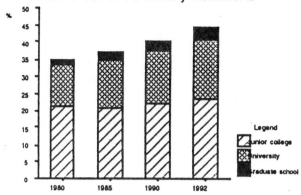

## Male advancement to tertiary institutions

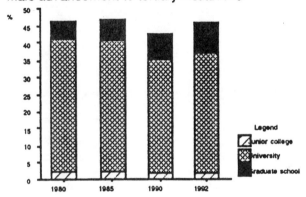

**Figure 1**
**Female and Male Advancement to Tertiary Institutions**

Of the first generation of postwar educated women (born between 1936 and 1945), 51 percent completed both primary and secondary education, with tertiary graduates comprising 9 percent. Of the second generation (born between 1946 and 1955), 57 percent had completed secondary education with 22 percent graduating from tertiary institutions, according to the 1990 census, while in the third generation (born between 1956 and 1964), 67 percent completed primary and secondary education with 26 percent completing tertiary studies. Since then, the trend has persisted, with an increasing proportion of women advancing to tertiary education (Figure 6.1). Unlike their male counterparts, about half the women undertaking tertiary study attended junior colleges. This would severely limit their opportunities to enter the bureaucracy or major Japanese corporations. They tend to recruit graduates only from the seven so-called Imperial universities and the prestigious private universities.

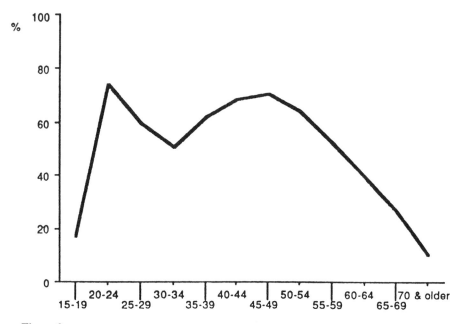

**Figure 2**
**Female Participation in the Labor Force, by Age: Japan, 1990**

Because of the education boom, more Japanese entered the workforce at an older age. By 1965, there was an acute labor shortage in the secondary sector. Higher retention rates for school and the greater job expectations of female graduates, resulting from their education, were two of the reasons. Part-time workers helped alleviate this shortage. Many "career housewives" of the 1950s were finding they had extra time on their hands. This was the result of labor-saving devices in the home[2] and children going into the school system.

These women became temporary "pinch hitters" for the burgeoning Japanese economy and have remained a fairly permanent feature of the labor force since then. This pattern of leaving the workforce and returning later has seen the development of the "M-curve" for women's labor (Figure 6.2). After completing formal education, graduates enter the workforce until marriage, which forms the first peak of the curve. In line with social customs, women drop out of the workforce to attend to child rearing. They return in their mid-forties as "returnee part-time labor," represented by the dip and second peak of the curve. Over time, the M-curve has been moving upward as more women enter the workforce. According to the results of a survey conducted by the Prime Minister's office in 1989 and reported by Horiuchi (1992), 64 percent of women responding to the survey thought the M-curve pattern of employment was the best. The "returnee" is a valuable addition to a company's pay roll. Their attributes as employees were summarized by the

Ministry of Labor as follows (Japan Institute of Labor, *Japan Labour Bulletin*, 29 1990):

they have already received basic training as a wage earner when they entered the job market after completing their education;

they are well versed in social customs and practices;

they have sound sense in money-related matters as they are in a position to control the family purse strings;

they are able to take affectional response to people in disadvantageous situations, because they had learned the art of compassion through child bearing;

they know what is meant by "serving people" through preparing meals;

they know the value of being patient;

they are accustomed to making quick decisions through shopping experiences.

The returnee pattern also provides advantages for housewives, allowing them to supplement the household budget while also allowing them to fulfil other obligations. However, the protective provisions of the Labour Standards Law and the M-curve phenomenon have also brought with them disadvantages, particularly when looked at in conjunction with common employment practices. Salaries and conditions for women in the workforce are often worse than those received by male workers.

Japan's system of lifetime employment with pay scales based on seniority is a long established feature of the Japanese workforce, at least in the major corporations. Once employed, it is very rare for workers to change jobs, and a sort of patron-client relationship develops.[3] Workers devote their careers to the company, and in turn, the company rewards employees with continued employment and progressive salary increases.

There is a tendency, therefore, for companies to view their employees in terms of "human capital" to be nurtured, trained, and developed in order to increase their individual and collective productivity. Significant resources are channeled into the development of this human capital, with workers periodically being assigned to new areas of progressive difficulty to facilitate "multiskilling." Sometimes this may entail longer working hours and transfers, but as the workers move up the corporate ladder, they are rewarded with an increase in wages.

The perception of women as in need of protection and prohibited from performing certain tasks as contained in the Labour Standards Law, coupled with the expectation that they will be only temporary workers, has led employers to view female employees in a different light.

Given the high costs associated with continuous staff training and upgrading, most companies considered women as "bad investments" regardless of ability. Moreover, the provisions prohibiting night time and overtime work meant that it was impossible for women to work the same long hours as their male colleagues, which was vital to career success. For educated women who wished to pursue a career—particularly in the 1960s and 1970s when rapid industrialization and urbanization were taking place—the reality of the workplace situation did not en-

Table 6.1
Distribution of Female Employees by Type of Work, Japan, Selected Years

| Occupation | 1960 (%) | 1975 (%) | 1990 (%) |
|---|---|---|---|
| Professional & technical workers | 9.0 | 11.6 | 13.8 |
| Managerial & official employment | 0.3 | 0.9 | 1.0 |
| Clerical & related workers | 25.4 | 32.2 | 34.4 |
| Sales workers | 8.7 | 11.1 | 12.5 |
| Agricultural, forestry & fisheries | 3.6 | 0.8 | 0.6 |
| Mining | 0.7 | na | na |
| Transport & communications | 0.3 | 1.5 | 0.5 |
| Craftsmen & production process workers | 35.9 | 24.6 | 20.6 |
| Laborers | 0 | 3.7 | 5.6 |
| Protective service workers & service workers | 16.1 | 13.7 | 10.7 |
| Total[a] | 100.0 | 100.0 | 100.0 |

Notes: na not available; [a] total may not add to 100 because of rounding.

Source: Japan Institute of Labor, Japanese Working Life Profile, 1991.

gender tremendous optimism. Starting wage levels were always lower than male wage rates and the gap widened as the males moved through the ranks of the company.

For the middle-aged returnee, the situation was more difficult, as pay rates depend upon seniority. Such a system is biased against those who do not follow a pattern of continuous service. As recently as 1992, it was estimated that, on average, Japanese women received approximately 60 percent of the equivalent male wage. This made Japan the OECD country with the highest disparity in wage levels between the sexes. More is said later in this chapter about wage differentials between the sexes. In terms of career advancement, also, Japan's record is quite poor. In 1990, women held only 1 percent of Japan's managerial posts. By way of comparison, in 1984 women held 34 percent of such positions in the United States and 21 percent in Sweden. Table 6.1 shows that Japan's female workforce has been mainly employed in clerical positions, with relatively few finding employment in the professions.

## United Nations Decade for Women (1975–1985) and the Enactment of the Equal Employment Opportunity Law (1986)

The turning point for Japan's female workforce came as a result of the United Nations Decade for Women (1975–1985) and subsequent changes to labor legislation.

In 1985, Japan ratified the U.N. Convention on the Elimination of All Forms of Discrimination Against Women and in 1986 introduced the Equal Employment Opportunity Law (EEOL). Japan's parliament also revised the Labor Standards Law and amended or removed those protective provisions that it deemed discriminatory. Monthly menstrual leave was abolished and reclassified as sick leave (Japan Institute of Labour, *Japan Labour Bulletin* 1986).

The EEOL sought to ensure that, irrespective of gender, all members of the workforce were granted equality of opportunity and treatment in the workplace. Under it, employers were asked to make their best efforts to ensure that there was no unfair bias in the treatment of women in recruiting practices. They were also asked that women be given equivalent treatment in job assignment, promotion, and training. However, unlike other countries with this type of legislation, such as France, Germany, and the United States, there are no penalties for lawbreakers, only that employers do their best.

As a response to the law, many large firms but particularly trading firms, banks, and life insurance companies, now offer two employment streams for women entering the workforce (Mori 1992). Which stream the woman enters is contingent upon her attitude and desires in terms of career development and family obligations. These streams are the managerial employee track and the clerical employee track. Key features of the two employment streams are shown in Table 6.2.

Entrance to the managerial track for women is by examination or interview. The opportunity for entering only arises after they have been in the clerical track for between two and five years. For men, entrance to the managerial track is automatic. This system has drawn criticism from many sides, with perhaps the sharpest being

**Table 6.2**
**Features of Employment Streams Available to Japanese Women**

| Managerial Employee Track | Clerical Employee Track |
| --- | --- |
| Jobs assigned in this track require complex judgement (business negotiations, personnel management, designing or developing products, planning of company policies or strategies). | Jobs are considered less complicated and more manual |
| Employees are subject to comprehensive job-rotation and transfers for career development and business necessities. | Job-rotation and transfers are carried out within a limited scope |
| No limit to promotion and employees can eventually become top-level managers or executives. | There is a formal limit to promotion. |

*Source:* Japan Institute of Labour, *Japan Labour Bulletin*, 1987.

made by Iwao (1993: 180): "men may earn the lowest score on the entrance examination, but are on this track by virtue of being male; only the brightest, most dedicated, career oriented superwomen are admitted to the integrated track." Nevertheless, the law has in principle provided female workers in Japan with greater opportunities to work than at any other time in the nation's history.

## WHAT HAS BEEN THE EFFECT OF THE EQUAL EMPLOYMENT OPPORTUNITY LAW?

While the EEOL did not have any specific provisions for ensuring compliance, in the period immediately after its enactment in 1986, it seemed that acceptance and implementation of the legislation was remarkably swift and wide ranging. A 1987 survey revealed that 51 percent of companies had shifted their recruitment policies from men only to both sexes. It also found that 79 percent of firms recruited college graduates of both sexes compared to a figure of only 37 percent in 1986. Seventy-two percent of job openings for this period were for both sexes. In 1986, this figure was only 32 percent.

However, these advances have been criticized by some economic observers as being of "more form than substance." Shitamori (1992), in discussing the experiences of women in the management track, claimed that many companies decided to use women "in highly visible positions where they could upgrade the company's image. They formed all-female project teams and assigned women to planning, public relations, and other glamour posts. These women were in effect no more than public attractions" (p. 13). Likewise, in a survey conducted in 1987 to ascertain the effectiveness of the new legislation, Professor Kazuo Sugeno of Tokyo University found:

In answering the survey questionnaire, firms tend to express their positive attitude toward hiring women. Yet in informal hearings conducted inside the Ministry of Labor, the author often encountered the testimony of college employment officers that even when they received job offers for "both sexes" firms often reveal their preferences for men in the process of screening (Japan Institute of Labor, *Japan Labour Bulletin* 1987: 5–8).

Similarly, in the recruitment period that occurred at the end of the 1993–1994 academic year, controversy arose when larger companies decided to recruit more males than females for entry and executive positions. Companies cited Japan's recessionary period as being behind this decision.[4] While the recruitment rate for male graduates was about 100 percent, the corresponding figure for female graduates was 60 percent. Most of the positions filled by women were clerical.

Earlier in this chapter it was pointed out that fewer women are employed in senior positions. Not surprisingly, therefore, substantial differences in the earnings of men and women existed in 1990. These differences increased with age and with years of experience (Table 6.3). This may reflect differences in education; earlier Figure 6.1 showed that more women went to junior colleges than men. Or it

Table 6.3
Average Differences in Contracted Earnings of a Standard Employee* by
Age and Sex, 1990

|  |  | Differential by age | | Differences by sex |
|---|---|---|---|---|
| Age | Years of service | Female | Male | (Male = 100) |
| 18–19 | 0 | 84.4 | 82.2 | 91.7 |
| 20–24 | 3–4 | 100.0 | 100.0 | 89.2 |
| 25–29 | 5–9 | 116.3 | 125.8 | 82.5 |
| 30–34 | 10–14 | 135.4 | 154.8 | 78.1 |
| 35–39 | 15–19 | 152.4 | 185.8 | 73.2 |
| 40–44 | 20–24 | 166.3 | 212.0 | 70.0 |
| 45–49 | 25–29 | 193.2 | 242.4 | 71.1 |
| 50–54 | 30 & over | 205.2 | 255.1 | 71.8 |

* A standard employee is one hired immediately after graduation and has worked continuously for the same enterprise.

Source: Japan Institute of Labor, Japanese Working Life Profile, 1991.

could reflect the fact that the legislative changes have only recently been made and therefore have not been fully reflected in women's wages.

According to Mori (1992), the differences in remuneration has led to dissatisfaction with the dual-track system for advancement. Clerical track women complain that although their work is not much lower than women on the management track, their wages are lower. Women on the management track object that although they are given the same tasks as men, they do not get the same pay.

## WOMEN AND JAPANESE FAMILY

Home and family have been the two spheres in which Japanese women have traditionally dominated. Child rearing, house maintenance, and the organization of household finances have often been viewed as women's tasks, and inside the home women have always been strong. It is fairly common procedure for working husbands to present their entire pay to their wives. Provided necessary payments are made, household affairs run smoothly, and a comfortable existence for all is maintained. Men have traditionally played a minimal, if not negligible, role in household affairs. So adept at running the household have women become that a "good husband" is one defined as "healthy and absent"—healthy, so they can continue to work and support their families, and absent, so as not to interfere with the running of the household.

The absence of responsibility in the home has allowed men freedom to devote their time completely to work and pursuits outside the home. Hence the comparatively longer hours worked by Japanese men in particular is a result of the traditional family structure and gender roles. Iwao (1993) believes that, by playing their traditional role and allowing removal of household responsibilities from men, women have indirectly made an even larger contribution to the economic development of Japan.

The traditional family structure consisted of husband and wife, two or three children, and the parents and unmarried siblings of usually the husband, but sometimes the wife. Marriage in traditional Japan did not necessarily mean the beginning of a new family, but rather the entry of one more member—the bride—into the husband's family (Fukutake 1980). This was a remnant of Japan's farming past, where families worked closely together in most aspects of their daily life. Today such family structures are still quite common in provincial areas, but in the more urbanized areas there has occurred a distinct change due to a number of factors. These include the high cost of living, the high cost of raising children, better health services and amenities for aging parents, and the practical difficulties associated with having a large family in a crowded city. A population imbalance between the sexes, with women being comparatively fewer, has also exerted an influence in this regard. For many women, living with the family of their spouse has often been fraught with difficulty, and it is not unusual for them to be treated somewhat badly by their relatives in the first years of marriage. Not only are they required to look after the needs of their husbands and children but an equivalent amount of care must also be given to their newly acquired relatives. Mothers who have experienced this have encouraged their daughters not to marry into such families, and so women have been demanding that their family structure in marriage be the nuclear family only. Such has been their bargaining power that there has been a shift to smaller family structures, as well as an increase in the number of Japanese men (usually farmers with large families) marrying non-Japanese women.

The average family size in Japan is decreasing while the number of households is increasing. In 1991, there were about 40 million households, with an average size of three people. Thirty-one years earlier, there were 22 million households, with an average household size of 4.14 people (Figure 6.3). Just after the end of the World War II, average household size was 4.9 people. To maintain Japan's 1992 population of 124 million, the birth rate would need to be 2.1. In recent years, however, it has been around 1.5, implying that the population will decline if these trends persist.

Up until the World War II, arranged marriages were more common than "love marriages." Around the 1960s, the custom of arranged marriages went into decline, and love and courtship began to play a greater role. Today, probably around 85 to 90 percent of couples would choose their own partners, although sometimes they may still be introduced by a third-party "go-between."[5] In rural areas, parents play a greater part in choosing marital partners (Fukutake 1980). Divorce is becoming more common in Japan, possibly reflecting the higher career aspirations for Japanese women and an increasingly westernized Japanese society. At the same time the number of marriages is declining and the average age at which couples

## Household characteristics

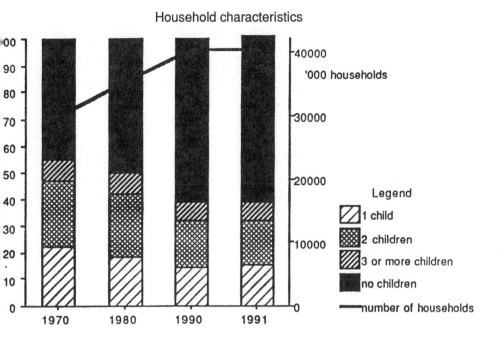

## Changes in household type

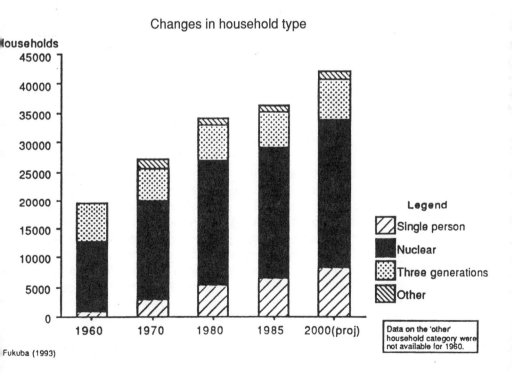

Fukuba (1993)

**Figure 3**
**Household Characteristics**

**Table 6.4**
**Marriage and Divorce in Japan, Selected Years**

| Item | 1970 | 1980 | 1990 | 1991 |
|------|------|------|------|------|
| Number of Marriages | 1,029,405 | 774,702 | 722,138 | 742,264 |
| Marriages between Japanese man & foreigner | 2,108 | 4,386 | 20,026 | 19,096 |
| Marriages between Japanese woman & foreigner | 3,438 | 2,875 | 5,600 | 6,063 |
| Age of husband first marriage | 27.6 | 28.7 | 29.7 | 29.6 |
| Age of wife first marriage | 24.6 | 25.9 | 26.9 | 26.9 |
| Divorces per 1,000 marriages | 0.93 | 1.22 | 1.28 | 1.37 |

*Source: Asahi Shimbun* 1993.

marry is increasing (Table 6.4). In 1990, 58.2 percent of women in the workforce were married, compared with 32.7 percent thirty years earlier.

Although women play a dominant role in Japanese families, Mori (1992) cites survey results that indicate that women feel that the burden of providing care to elderly relatives and to children and in managing the household are major factors hindering equality at work. Women felt that a cut in men's working hours so that the husband and wife shared more equally in household duties would help achieve workplace equality.

## CONCLUSION

The Japanese economy has been undergoing change almost continuously since the end of the World War II. These changes have resulted in dramatic increases in Japanese income levels and have helped Japan become one of the world's richest nations. Women have played a major, but often overlooked, role in the transformation of the Japanese economy. Relatively few women have achieved prominence in Japanese public life or in Japanese corporations. However, they have been an important pool of reserve labor and have played an important support role to their families. Women are active in their communities, working as volunteers in consumer organizations, recycling programs, and environmental protection campaigns. Unlike employment, these activities can be easily balanced with household responsibilities.

Women now comprise over 50 percent of the workforce, and the indications are that they will demand more prominent positions than in the past. Due to antidiscriminatory laws and a recognition and perception by women that they are indeed equal to male co-workers, there may be increasing numbers of women taking up positions of responsibility and power alongside men. Given Japan's propensity to continually reinvent itself at short notice, this would not be entirely impossible.

The only barrier to this may in fact be the attitudes and ideas about a woman's role in society and the home by older male members of society. Presently, these men still dominate in large companies and government and conceivably exert an influence over policy directions and hiring practices. Hiring practices in the spring 1994 have shown that in times of crisis the traditional pattern prevails and women are still seen as poor seconds to male labor.

However, as the men and women educated and raised in the postwar era of equality become the dominant part of Japanese society, it is possible that this too could die out. There is no doubt that women have been and still are integral to the success and smooth running of the economy of Japan, either as active members of the workforce or behind the scenes by ensuring the supply of healthy, long working labor to Japan's many industries. What remains to be seen is whether, given more liberal labor laws and the slowly changing structure of Japanese society in general, women can rise to more executive and high-profile positions.

## NOTES

1. Manila had about 3,000 Japanese by the early seventeenth century; there were also Japanese in what is now Vietnam, Macao, Jakarta, Thailand, and Taiwan. Nagasaki is the site of the martyrdom of six foreign missionaries and twenty Japanese Christians crucified in 1597 and canonized in 1862.

2. By the end of the 1950s, most Japanese families had the "three treasures"—washing machine, television set, and refrigerator.

3. The economic slowdown that hit the Japanese economy in the early 1990s has placed the system of lifetime employment and age-based salary increases under pressure. Forced to cut costs, some firms have shed labor. Other firms have avoided doing this only because of societal pressure.

4. For example, one of Japan's largest companies, Mitsubishi Shoji, decided against recruiting women completely during this period. According to newspaper reports, the company cited the recession as a major contributing factor (*Japan Times*, July 28, 1994: 1).

5. The idea of arranged marriages goes back to the warrior class of the medieval age. Marriages served to cement alliances between families. "Go betweens" played the role of ensuring that the alliance would be mutually beneficial. Although they have survived to the present, magazines and computer dating services now supplement the role of the go-between.

# 7

# Women in South Asia with Particular Reference to India

*Kartik C. Roy and Clement A. Tisdell*

## INTRODUCTION

Before 1947, the year in which the Indian subcontinent gained independence from British rule, South Asia comprised India, Sri Lanka and Nepal, Bhutan, and Afghanistan. At independence, the subcontinent was broken into two independent countries—India and Pakistan. In 1971 at the conclusion of the war between India and Pakistan, Pakistan lost its Eastern Province, which became the independent Republic of Bangladesh. Thus since 1971 the former Indian has consisted of three countries.

In mid-1993, South Asia's population reached close to 1.2 billion with India's population exceeding 900 million and accounting for slightly over 76 percent of total South Asian population. The population of Pakistan exceeded 10 percent of the total and that of Bangladesh reached nearly 10 percent. Since religion played a prominent part in the division of the subcontinent, Pakistan and, later, Bangladesh became predominantly Muslim countries and India a predominantly Hindu country. On the other hand the majority of the population in Sri Lanka are Buddhists and those in Nepal are Hindus. Of the total population of South Asia, 73.8 percent are rural and 26.2 percent are urban. Religion combined with state policy has shaped and classic patriarchy embodying purdah has dominated women's lives in both Pakistan and Bangladesh.

Historically before the Aryan invasion, the social structure in India was governed by matriarchal ideology. As Aryan control over India began to spread from the northwest through the center to Bengal in the east, some sections of the local population of these areas moved to the south where Dravidian culture was also influenced strongly by matriarchal ideology under which the dominance of females and their equal status with males in economic and social relations were recognized.

Since Dravidian culture was basically the tribal culture, those tribal members who lived in deep forests and escaped Aryan onslaught maintained their culture. Similarly in the northeastern frontier region, matriarchal ideology governed economic and social relations. However, in Aryan-dominated India, despite the presence of patriarchal ideology, women continued to enjoy very high status in social and economic spheres for thousands of years until about 1000 A.D. when Muslim invaders brought in and imposed "classic patriarchy" in the governance of social and economic relations. To safeguard the honor and chastity of girls, Hindus began to enforce and practice early marriage rules and the ideology of seclusion. In order for the young wife to be protected and well maintained by her husband, the system of "dowry" was introduced. Since only relatively well-off families could afford dowries, the ideology of seclusion was confined mostly to women of these families. However, Muslim families also began to practice the system of dowry in marriages. With the partition of India and the subsequent partition of Pakistan, the classic patriarchy and the system of purdah spread from Muslim-inhabited parts of India to Pakistan and Bangladesh.

With the spread of industrialization and economic development and the concomitant breakdown of joint family system, the need for women to contribute to the income of nuclear families began to grow. As a result, on the one hand, the forces of gender restriction on educated women in urban areas, particularly in India and Sri Lanka, began to weaken and, on the other hand, the adverse impacts of development may have strengthened the forces of these restrictions on women in rural areas in these countries.

An overview of the historical trend is necessary to view the socioeconomic status of women and discrimination against females in their Asian perspectives. For example, those socioeconomic practices which to rational economists may appear to be gender discrimination against females may not appear to be so to South Asian females due to the Asian sociocultural environment under which they have been brought up.

## SOCIOECONOMIC STATUS OF WOMEN AND DISCRIMINATION AGAINST FEMALES: CROSS-COUNTRY COMPARISONS ON THE INDIAN SUBCONTINENT

There are a number of difficulties in making comparisons of the socioeconomic status of women between countries. For instance, available data are usually not completely reliable because of sampling problems. Furthermore, figures for a country as a whole usually indicate the average situation in the country and deviations around it are normally not reported. In the case of females, their socioeconomic status can vary considerably between geographical areas of a country and between social groups. This tends to be the case on the Indian subcontinent, for example, within India. Nevertheless, broad or average figures do provide a reasonable basis for making qualitative comparisons between countries about the relative socioeconomic status of women. One way to make such comparisons is

Table 7.1
Female-Male Gap for Infant Mortality (mortality rate for children
under 5) in South Asian Countries, China, and Industrial Countries, 1991

| Country | Ratio × 100 | % of industrial |
|---|---|---|
| Afghanistan | na | na |
| Bangladesh | 101 | 112 |
| Nepal | 102 | 112 |
| Pakistan | 100 | 110 |
| India | 100 | 110 |
| Bhutan | 96 | 105.5 |
| China | 95 | 104.5 |
| Sri Lanka | 93.5 | 102.5 |
| Industrial Countries | 91 | 100 |

Source: Based on World Develpment Report 1993, Table 32.

by means of female-male gaps (*Human Development Report* 1993) based upon a number of socioeconomic indicators such as access to education, literacy rates, differences in degrees of infant mortality, length of life expectation, and so on. The United Nations Development Programme (*Human Development Report* 1993) has collected useful data in that regard which will be used in this section, supplemented by some World Bank (*World Development Report* 1993) data to make intercountry comparisons of the socioeconomic status of females on the Indian subcontinent.

First, consider the mortality rate among infants under five years of age, according to their gender, using the indicators of the female-male gap calculated as the ratio of females in the category times 100. Consequently, a figure of less than 100 indicates a smaller relative frequency of occurrence of characteristic among females than males. This may or may not indicate that females are disadvantaged. Possibly the most satisfactory guide to whether they are is to compare the situation (the gap) with that in industrial countries. For example, consider the infant mortality gap figures shown in Table 7.1. This indicates that the infant mortality rate among females is higher than for males in Bangladesh and Nepal and about the same in Pakistan and India for both sexes. The infant mortality rate is lower for females than male infants in Bhutan, China, Sri Lanka, and industrial countries. These figures suggest that female infants are particularly disadvantaged in relation to males in Bangladesh, Nepal, Pakistan, and India. They may be given less medical attention, care, and nourishment than male infants, thereby resulting in their greater rate of mortality. Consideration of female-to-male population ratios suggests that in most South Asian countries the relative socioeconomic deprivation of women results in higher rates of mortality among females than males, the ratio of females to males being below unity, significantly so in many cases. This ratio is significantly

Table 7.2
Female-Male Gaps for Population Composition and Life
Expectancy for South Asian Countries, China, and Industrial
Countries, 1990

| Country | Population | Life Expectancy |
|---|---|---|
| Pakistan | 92 | 100 |
| India | 93 | 101 |
| Bhutan | 93 | 97 |
| Bangladesh | 94 | 99 |
| Afghanistan | 94 | 102 |
| China | 94 | 105 |
| Nepal | 95 | 98 |
| Sri Lanka | 99 | 106 |
| Industrial Countries | 106 | 110 |

*Source:* Based on *Human Development Report 1993.*

lower for most South Asian countries than in industrial countries. Life expectancy gaps show a similar pattern (but not an identical pattern) to the population gaps (see Table 7.2).

Other indicators of the relative socioeconomic status of women are their literacy rates and the attendance of females at secondary school in comparison to males. Those are all relatively unfavorable for women in South Asia (with the exception of secondary enrollments in Sri Lanka). The situation is worse for women in South Asia than in China, except in the case of Sri Lanka. Serious disparities exist for females in relation to literacy and access to education in Bhutan, Nepal, Afghanistan, Bangladesh, and India with the disparities being of greater order for the first mentioned countries than for the latter ones (see Table 7.3).

Another possible indicator of socioeconomic bias against women is their relative employment in the labor force. This is extremely low in Bangladesh, Afghanistan, and Pakistan (predominantly Islamic countries), moderately low in India, and higher in Bhutan, Nepal, and Sri Lanka, even though lower than in China and industrial countries (see Table 7.4).

The above data suggest that, on the whole, females enjoy a higher socioeconomic status relative to males in India compared to Afghanistan, Bangladesh, Bhutan, and Nepal, but a lower socioeconomic status than in Sri Lanka and China. In terms of relative socioeconomic status, females in India still have a considerable way to go to achieve a comparable level of relative socioeconomic status to that of females in industrial countries.

It is worthwhile noting that the apparent relative socioeconomic status of women on the whole tends to increase with the GNP of countries and shows some positive correlation with the degree of urbanization of a country, for example, the proportion

Table 7.3
Female-Male Gaps in Secondary Enrollments (1988–1990)
and Literacy (1990) in South Asian Countries and China

| Country | Secondary Enrollments | Literacy |
|---|---|---|
| Bhutan | 29 | na |
| Nepal | 40 | 35 |
| Afghanistan | 45 | 32 |
| Pakistan | 45 | 45 |
| Bangladesh | 50 | 47 |
| India | 61 | 55 |
| China | 77 | 73 |
| Sri Lanka | 107 | 89 |

*Source:* Based on *Human Development Report 1993.*

Table 7.4
Female-Male Gaps in the Labor Force (1990) South
Asian Countries, China, and Industrial Countries

| Country | Ratio × 100 |
|---|---|
| Bangladesh | 7 |
| Afghanistan | 9 |
| Pakistan | 13 |
| India | 34 |
| Bhutan | 48 |
| Nepal | 57 |
| Sri Lanka | 59 |
| China | 76 |
| Industrial Countries | 77 |

*Source:* Based on *Human Development Report 1993.*

of females relative to males at secondary school tends to rise with the degree of urbanization of a country. There is also a relatively close positive association between the level of GNP per capita of countries and the proportion of females in their population.

It was mentioned earlier that aggregate figures often disguise significant interregional differences and differences between socioeconomic groups. This is confirmed by differences in female-to-male sex ratios in India. These ratios are higher for scheduled tribes and for scheduled castes than for nonscheduled components of the total population and lower on the whole in the northwest of India than elsewhere in India (Agnihotri 1994). Agnihotri (1994) suggests that these ratios are related to the social possibility of women being able to participate in the labor force and considers how these ratios have changed over time and how estimates can be affected by migration, for example, the outward migration of males from some regions. Where females are of little socioeconomic worth relative to males in a community, they tend to be neglected and suffer higher mortality than males, thus reducing the female-to-male sex ratio. According to Agnihotri (1994: 9), the most promising way to increase female-male ratios is by the "creation of opportunities for female participation in productive activities and ensuring the female's control over the income thus generated."

## INDIA'S EXPERIENCE

About 73 percent of total Indian population live in rural areas and about 48 percent of total population are females. Rate of illiteracy is significantly higher in rural areas than in urban areas. Also females constitute the overwhelming proportion of rural illiterates. Poverty is more widespread and pervasive in rural areas than in urban areas. Despite more than 40 years of planned development activities, the socioeconomic status of rural women does not appear to have improved by any measurable extent. Due to all these factors, gender restrictions are more widely enforced on rural women than on urban women.

### Female Cultivators, Female-Headed Households, and Landless Families

A large number of studies (Epstein 1973; Dandekar 1975; Saradamoni 1980; Horowitz and Kishwar 1982; Manimala 1983; Taylor and Faruque 1983; Sen and Sengupta 1983; Venkataramani 1986; Harris 1986; Dasgupta and Maity 1986; Kishwar 1987; Agarwal 1986, 1989; Duvvury 1989; Chen 1989; Bhalla 1989; Roy and Tisdell 1993a,b) on the economic development and socioeconomic status of women in rural India have found gender-based discrimination against women are practiced in many forms in rural India. While a smaller number of these studies tend to suggest that sex differentials by birth order are far stronger than by socioeconomic class, the majority of these studies suggest that the forces of discrimination based on gender which were primarily found in upper class families have become stronger due to increasing economic pressure and are now found also in lower class families. In dry-land agriculture, the low demand for labor combined with the exclusion of women in property rights and the high cost of marriage results in a preference for sons and a discrimination against daughters.

The degree of antifemale bias in poor families tends to be inversely related to females' effective contribution to the total family income and to the amount of dowry that the parent and other male members would be required to pay at the time of her marriage. Females' contribution is considered effective if their work is socially visible and socially recognized as valuable. Since agricultural field work and work using private-property resources (PPRs), which is more visible than home-based work and work which brings in earnings, which is economically more visible than collection of nonmarket goods from common-property resources (CPRs) and household duties, appear to be given a higher social valuation, greater gender discrimination against girls has been found among those landless families in which boys are involved in socially visible and recognized earning activities and girls are engaged in procuring goods from CPRs, although the total time spent in both activities does not differ much between the sexes. In South India, particularly in Karnataka, it was found that with improvements in economic condition in small peasant households, female members were withdrawn from productive field work. As a result, the marriage price of socially perceived unproductive female members increased, although they switched their work from the field to indoors. This increase in marriage price, as well as its replacement in many states by ever-escalating dowry, may have strengthened the antifemale bias within families across the country.

The preexisting antifemale bias in institutional arrangements has been further strengthened by changes in customs and conventions. Customary access to land has been largely confined to male household members, as noted in Agarwal's (1989) pioneering study of 145 village communities. Although under Hindu law, women are given a smaller share than males of the ancestral property, women of other religious communities do not even possess this right of inheritance. But the mere possession of right does not ensure the effective control over land as the control in most cases is vested with a male member (a practical manifestation of patriarchal ideology). As far as agricultural land is concerned, in most states in India, the religious law has been superseded by regionally prevailing customary law under which women have been typically excluded. With economic activities in the rural sector gaining momentum due to the adoption of Green Revolution technology in agriculture, the enforcement of such customary laws by male members gained strength as the surplus from agriculture began to increase. Furthermore, due to the growth of population, penetration of market forces, and the growth of commercialization in the rural sector, the demand for land increased greatly. As a result, the enforcement of patriarchal ideology with full force led women to lose even the traditional rights to an ancestral home and minimum security, let alone land ownership.

Even where women's inheritance right is legally recognized, customary practice links this right to the women staying in parents' home, thereby making it difficult for married women living with their husbands in distant villages to exercise this right. Even this limited right appears to be disappearing, particularly among northeastern hill tribes due, among other things, to changes in the mode of cultivation from shifting cultivation to settled agriculture, under which new technology and land privatization have led to the marginalization of female labor. There are also evidences, particularly in Bihar, of direct violence against single women to prevent them from exercising their customary rights and even filing their cases with legal authorities. In both Bihar and Rajasthan there are instances of land enforcement agents not implementing just laws in favor of women because of their traditional biases against them. Even assuming that women are able to exercise their customary rights to land, they still experience practical difficulties in engaging themselves in socially visible productive activities. The ideology of seclusion by restricting their interaction with male strangers makes it difficult for them to obtain information on agricultural practices. Social customs, prejudices, illiteracy and ignorance, and lack of collateral also prevent them from obtaining credit from village money lenders as well as from financial institutions located in distant towns. Even when both men and women did not have collateral, village money lenders refused to lend to women on the grounds that men could find wage work more easily than women and that men could repay the debt, if necessary, by migrating. Agarwal (1989) found this to be the case in Rajasthan. Furthermore, gender biases in extension services limit their access to information and other kinds of help and social taboos prevent their effective participation in agricultural work. Dasgupta and Maity (1986) observed that due to the long-held belief of the Oraon tribes of Bihar that plowing the field by a woman would cause drought and natural calamities, those who had plowed family land had been severely punished.

Thus compared with male cultivators, land-poor female cultivators experience such difficulties in managing their farms as lack of credit and risk-bearing capacity to invest in high-yielding varieties (HYVs); lack of crop insurance; poor quality of land; inadequate agricultural infrastructure for inputs, extension, and credit; inadequate markets for purchasing inputs and selling produce; limited knowledge of crop varieties and cropping choices; neglect by agricultural research and extension due to the presence of male bias in mainstream agriculture and male bias in traditional patterns of ownership and control (Chen 1989).

Female-headed households are further disadvantaged by gender biases in employment and wages and, in general, are found to have significantly less access to and control over land, greater dependence on wage labor for employment, a higher incidence of involuntary unemployment, and a lower level of education and literacy than male-headed households.

Landless female laborers are the largest and most visible section of India's female labor force. They come from poor rural households and more often than not from scheduled, backward, or tribal castes. They work for very low wages, quite often, in stereotyped jobs and suffer major disadvantages relative to men in their search for employment opportunities. Although often primary bread earners, they are more disadvantaged than men in their access to opportunities for employment and earnings than men due to (a) less job mobility resulting from their vulnerability to class- or caste-related sex abuse, ideology of seclusion and responsibility for child care; (b) more limited access than men to information on job opportunities due to lower literacy rate, less contact with the marketplace and access to mass media; (c) confinement to casual work in agriculture; (d) lower payment than males receive often for the same work performed; (e) lack of access to training to operate productivity-increasing equipment (Agarwal 1989); and (f) the mode of wage payment to females which excludes wage provisions (Ryan and Wallace 1985). Alarming decline in the supply of CPRs and minor forest produce (MFP) has greatly reduced the availability of such goods to poor women, especially tribal members as well as increased their work burden.

## Intrahousehold Discrimination Against Females

While it is expected that irrespective of the socioeconomic status of households, the total income generated by a family and the assets owned by it would be shared equally by all members of the family, Agarwal's study (1989) indicates the presence of (i) gender-based inequalities in the distribution of resources for fulfilling the basic needs; (ii) differences in household spending patterns, with women's earnings much more than men's in poor households going toward the family's basic needs; and (iii) a strong link in poor households between the nutritional status of children and mother's earnings.

Most rural health surveys record a much higher incidence of illness among women. It has been further noted that when women became ill, they do not receive medical treatment as men receive during their illness. More females than males receive no treatment (Dandekar 1975) and fewer girls than boys receive aid in the first twenty-four hours of their terminal illness (Taylor and Faruque 1983). A study (Harris 1986) on intrahousehold food allocation found that adult females, adolescent girls, and small female children receive less vitamins and minerals through food allocations in both north and south India and also receive less calories and proteins in parts of north India than their male counterparts.

Although landless poor women encounter greater difficulties in obtaining paid employment, they spend a much larger proportion of their income on their families' maintenance than men. Furthermore, goods collected by women from CPRs and forests are also used for the family's sustenance. In general, compared with males, females spend a very small proportion of their income on their personal consumption.

## Other Kinds of Discrimination

The type of agricultural work undertaken by women also exposes them to greater health risk than men. For example, rice planting is usually done by women. However, since this task is performed in the rainy season, women tend to suffer from intestinal infections, arthritis, rheumatic joints, leech bites (Mencher and Saradamoni 1982), and gynecological infections. The effect of an increase in the incidence of water-borne diseases in the family resulting from poor canal irrigation or from the pollution of rivers and ponds due to pesticide runoffs are felt mostly by women as they take care of the sick.

## Microlevel Studies: Field Work, 1991

Field work was undertaken in three villages in West Bengal in 1991 to examine the status of and gender discrimination against females in landless and land-poor families as well as to ascertain whether the all India picture differs greatly from that of West Bengal. West Bengal was chosen partly because it has been at the forefront of the movement for women's emancipation, some form of democratic government has existed at the village level, and the level of political consciousness among the masses is probably the highest of all Indian states. Therefore it was expected that the types of gender discrimination against women found in other states would not be found in West Bengal. Also, K. C. Roy is a Bengali and is intimately familiar with rural areas.

A random survey was undertaken in three villages in a rainfed paddy-growing district covering 59 landless and land-poor families with 148 male and 140 female members. The results indicate the presence of gender discrimination among these families in the following forms:

1. The share of educated female (minimum of first-grade education in primary school) among total females is significantly lower than that of educated males in total males.

2. Women do suffer more frequently from common water-borne diseases than men.

3. Men get better and prompter treatment than women.

4. Adult male members get to eat better food and in larger quantities than females.

5. Female members take their meals only after male members have eaten and eat only what is left.

6. Female members work longer hours than men.

7. Wage rates of female laborers are less than that of male laborers for the same kind of job.

It would appear that these types of gender discrimination are also found in other Indian states. However, some of these practices are not perceived by women as being discrimination against them.

### Field Work, 1992–1993

Further field work was undertaken in 1992–1993 in a rural town in West Bengal. Since women's education and employment are crucial to their gaining independence and eliminating discrimination against them and since a larger number of educated females would be found in a rural town than in a village, one suburb of Midnapore town was chosen for the survey. All educated females (those who have completed a university degree) were first identified and then randomly selected for the interview. A total of seventy-one respondents were interviewed.

Midnapore town is the district headquarter of Midnapore District, which borders three states—West Bengal, Bihar, and Orissa. Centuries-old customs, practices, and taboos continue to govern social relations and shape females' lives even today in this town.

Since all respondents came from upper caste families, the ideology of seclusion governed the movement of females of these families. Therefore expert assistance from well-qualified and well-mannered females with persuasive power was required. The assistance was provided by Smriti Kana Maiti and Bithika Datta of Midnapore town. Each respondent was approached beforehand to explain the purpose of the interview, to obtain the permission of the respondent and her family, and to set a date and time for the interview. It took two months to complete the work and the interview was carried out in the presence of K. C. Roy. Without the enormous patience, tolerance, skill, and dedication of Smriti and Bithika, the field work would not have ben completed. Hence the authors gratefully acknowledge the invaluable contribution made by Smriti and Bithika to this project. The results of the survey are presented in Table 7.5.

## Results

Although the responses to questions 2, 3(a,b,c,d), 5, and 7(a,b,c,d) were not overwhelmingly affirmative, they nevertheless do indicate that the presence of gender bias in some families adversely affected females' education, health, family life, and performance at work. Females also faced some form of gender discrimination in their search for employment (7a,b). However, more than 73 percent of respondents agreed that although they contribute more than men to their families' welfare in terms of time and proportion of income spent, they receive less appreciation than men.

About 93 percent agreed that lack of technical skill limited the scope for employment of educated females and about 79 percent agreed that if guidance and opportunities were given, they would have completed technology-oriented degrees. When asked if male members in their families were given such guidance and help, the affirmative response was slightly over 56 percent. Also, 83 percent reported that technology is more accessible to males than females. More than 97 percent agreed that information about the availability of technology, adequate facilities for training, credit to obtain and utilize technology, equal opportunity to males and females in obtaining technology, and equal opportunities for employment after obtaining skills would improve their access to technology. Nearly 99 percent agreed that for the survival of societies, adequate and equal opportunities with males for employment of females are necessary. When asked about the difficulties in creating equal opportunities for employment, about 99 percent agreed that lack of government support and action was one of the factors and 100 percent affirmed that excessive political interference in employment generation scheme and absence of legal course of action against injustice were the other two factors.

Thus it would seem that even if they are educated, women cannot escape from gender discrimination in many aspects of their lives both within and outside their family environment. So, apart from education and employment, what else is necessary for women's economic independence?

Several young respondents reported after the interview that even if employment opportunities arise, they cannot utilize those because of the strict enforcement of the "ideology of seclusion" by grandparents or other family elders who are influenced less by the welfare considerations of granddaughters and more by what neighbors would say. Hence they are forced to marry anyone chosen for them against their wishes and procreate children. It would, therefore, seem that education and

**Table 7.5**
**Educated Females in a Rural Town in West Bengal: Socioeconomic Status and Gender Discrimination, 1992–1993**

| Serial Nos. | Items | Nos. Yes | % of Total |
|---|---|---|---|
| | | Responses | |
| 1. | Total no. of respondents | 71 | 100 |
| 2. | In pursuing your studies you faced greater difficulty than male members in your family | 16 | 22.5 |
| 3. | The type of difficulties faced: | | |
| | (a) Guidance and encouragement not received from the family regarding the choice of a career | 16 | 22.5 |
| | (b) Less financial and other support than a male member received from the family | 16 | 22.5 |
| | (c) Although aware of better career paths, these were not available within the proximity of home | 16 | 22.5 |
| | (d) Being female, movements were confined to the surroundings of homes | 16 | 22.5 |
| 4. | Although you work longer hours than men and your income is mostly spent on family's welfare, these receive less appreciation than those of male members | 52 | 73.2 |
| 5. | Tension and unhappiness due to the presence of male bias in family and society have adversely affected health, family life, and performance at work | 30 | 42.3 |
| 6. | No. of respondents employed on a full-time basis | 35 | 49.3 |
| 7. | Difficulties experienced in obtaining employment: | | |
| | (a) Male bias in the selection committee | 4 | 5.6 |
| | (b) Unfair selection method | 19 | 26.8 |
| | (c) Interference of the dominant political party in the selection process | 14 | 19.7 |
| | (d) Financial donation to local party fund and tribes | 11 | 15.5 |
| 8. | Population growth and increased pressure of modern living have made the social environment more difficult for women to obtain suitable employment | 61 | 85.9 |
| 9. | Techonological change and lack of technical skill have limited the scope for employment of educated females | 66 | 92.9 |
| 10. | If guidance and opportunities were given, you would have completed a technology-oriented degree | 56 | 78.9 |

Table 7.5 (continued)

| | | Responses | |
|---|---|---|---|
| Serial Nos. | Items | Nos. Yes | % of Total |
| 11. | Male members in your family were given such guidance and help | 40 | 56.3 |
| 12. | Technology is more accessible to males than females | 59 | 83.0 |
| 13. | How many of the following factors would improve your access to technology? | | |
| | (a) Information about the availability of technology | 69 | 97.2 |
| | (b) Adequate facilities for training | 69 | 97.2 |
| | (c) Credit to obtain and utilize technology | 69 | 97.2 |
| | (d) Equal opportunity to male and female in obtaining technology | 69 | 97.2 |
| | (e) Equal opportunities for employment after obtaining skills | 69 | 97.2 |
| 14. | For the survival of societies, adequate and equal opportunities with males for employment of females is necessary | 70 | 98.6 |
| 15. | What are the difficulties in creating such opportunities? | | |
| | (a) Lack of government support and action | 70 | 98.6 |
| | (b) Excessive political interference in employment generation scheme | 71 | 100.0 |
| | (c) Absence of legal course of action against injustice | 71 | 100.0 |

employment opportunities for females ought to be accompanied by social education of all elders.

This leads us to "dowry," which is one of the most pernicious forms of gender discrimination.

## Dowry

In India in the precolonial days, marriage was an important form of social control over women and dowry was practiced by high- or middle-ranking and upwardly mobile castes. However, in contemporary India it has spread to all castes, communities, regions, and religions, including Islam. Under the "ideology of hypergamy" dowry was a form of "travel pass" for a bride from a slightly lower caste family to travel to a higher caste marital home. Both dowry and hypergamy, which reflect status asymmetry between husband and wife, are tied to the upper caste ideology which entailed seclusion of women, their exclusion from productive work, and their categorization as economic burden (Das 1975; Parliwala 1989).

Evidence (Tambiah 1973) suggests that in ancient times the bride had very little control over the dowry. In contemporary India, also, normatively a substantial part of the dowry was meant neither for the bride nor for her husband; rather it was meant for the husband's kin. Dowry ensured the separation of the outgoing woman from the family as well as from land. However, in modern times, instead of being determined by custom, the amount and kind of gifts to be given are being dictated by the demands of the groom's family as well by the status symbols of the groups within which natal and prenatal families wish to project themselves. While the money value of dowry has been increasing, the quality of goods being demanded has also been changing. Dowry, which begins at engagement, does not end in marriage. In fact, there is an extended dowry (Kishwar 1988) system under which the bride's parents with a view to saving their daughter's marriage are forced to comply with the demands of the groom's family throughout the life of the marriage.

Dowry has commercialized the marriage relationship so much so that it is equated now with women. Young girls grow up sensitive to the fact that their marriage can ruin their natal family, and difficulties in accumulating the dowry amount can delay the marriage. To escape from the social humiliation and to save their families from the dowry expense, many have committed suicide. Even when a sufficient amount of dowry is paid, regardless of the financial capability of the bride's parents, the bride may continue to suffer from harassment, humiliation, and torture at the hands of her in-laws at her marital home on the pretext that her parents have not given them what self-respect demands. The social obligation on the part of the bride to adjust and her acceptance of the social custom that once she enters her in-law's home she will leave it permanently only on her funeral pyre is reinforced by the fact that she becomes her dowry for not only her in-laws but also her parents (Parliwala 1989). Instances abound of women being murdered in their marital homes by their husbands and in-laws.

The form of gender discrimination is the most pernicious since it may lead to the death of the victim and is practiced more often than not by women against women, by mother-in-law and her daughters against her daughter-in-law. This adds another important dimension to the much-talked about male-female gender discrimination. A case in point was emptying a glass of flammable liquids over a young bride's body by her brother-in-law and throwing a lighted matchstick at her in front of her husband in her marital home in a village in Birdhum District in West Bengal, India, and the subsequent burning to death of the bride on December 31, 1993, due to the inability of the bride's parents to satisfy the extended dowry demands of their son-in-law.

### Impact of Economic Change on the Socioeconomic Status of Women

Providing women with employment would help them achieve economic independence and improve their socioeconomic status but ensuring that they remain employed would help them stay independent. Obtaining and remaining in employment requires better education and health and diminution of the force of gender-based discrimination, particularly that of the ideology of seclusion. We now proceed to examine the general pattern of the impact of economic change on all these issues.

### Education and Health-Related Indicators

Table 7.6 illustrates the pattern of improvement that has taken place in education and health-related indicators for females in India since the inception of the First Five Year Plan in 1951.

As the table shows, the enrollments of girls in primary, upper primary, and secondary schools increased steadily from 5.4, 0.5, and 0.02 million in 1950–1951 to 41.0, 12.4, and 6.9 million in 1990–1991. The number of teachers at these three levels of school also increased from 0.5, 0.08, and 0.1 million to 1.6, 1.0 and 1.2 million during the same period.

The steady increase in enrollment also helped improve the literacy for females, which increased from a meagre 8.9 percent in 1950–1951 to 39.3 percent in 1990–1991. However, the drop-out rate in 1987–1988 was 47 percent at the primary level and 62 percent for the elementary level as a whole. Since a high literacy rate, specially high female literacy rate, is associated with a low rate of population growth, infant mortality, maternal mortality, and other important indicators of improvement in quality of life of the population, unless this retention rate is improved considerably, any perceptible impact of education on females' socioeconomic status is not likely to be felt.

While the overall literacy rate reached 52.2 percent according to the 1990–1991 census, there are wide variations in the literacy rates recorded by individual states,

**Table 7.6**
**Female Literacy Rate, Enrollment of Girls, and Teachers in Primary and Secondary Schools**

| | Literacy Rate (%) | | Enrollment and Teachers (million) | | | | | | | |
| | | | Primary | | | Upper Primary | | | Secondary | | |
| | Female | Total | Girls | Total | Teachers | Girls | Total | Teachers | Girls | Total | Teachers |
|---|---|---|---|---|---|---|---|---|---|---|---|
| 1950–51 | 8.9 | 8.3 | 5.4 | 19.2 | 0.5 | 0.5 | 3.1 | 0.08 | 0.02 | 1.5 | 0.1 |
| 1960–61 | 15.3 | 28.3 | 11.4 | 35.0 | 0.7 | 1.6 | 6.7 | 0.3 | 0.7 | 3.4 | 0.3 |
| 1970–71 | 22.0 | 34.5 | 21.3 | 57.0 | 1.0 | 3.9 | 13.3 | 0.6 | 1.9 | 7.6 | 0.6 |
| 1980–81 | 29.8 | 43.6 | 28.5 | 73.8 | 1.3 | 6.8 | 20.7 | 0.8 | 3.5 | 1.2 | 0.9 |
| 1990–91 | 39.3 | 52.2 | 41.0 | 99.1 | 1.6 | 12.4 | 33.3 | 1.0 | 6.9 | n.a. | 1.2 |

*Source:* Government of India 1993a.

with the highest, 89.8 percent, being recorded by Kerala and the lowest, 36.5 and 36.6 percent, being recorded by Bihar and Rajasthan. Similarly wide divergence in female literacy rates also would be found among different states.

Economic development was also accompanied by an impressive growth in educational institutions at all levels. Between 1951 and 1991, the number of primary, upper primary, and secondary schools increased by 166.3, 978.5, and 959.7 percent. During the same period, the number of colleges for general education, professional education, and universities increased by 1214.0, 326.0, and 440.7 percent (*India* 1992). Thus it would seem that considerably less emphasis has been placed on primary education and vocational education, the two most important areas in which greatest emphasis should have been placed. This expansion of educational opportunities obviously benefited women also.

Similarly, improvements were recorded in such health related indicators as life expectancy at birth, infant mortality rate, and so on. Females' life expectancy at birth increased from 31.7 years in 1950–1951 to 55.9 years in 1990–1991 and infant mortality rate declined from 129 per thousand in 1971 to 80 in 1990. Once again it should be noted that within this general framework the record of different states would be different.

### Employment

The incidence of poverty is higher in rural areas than in urban areas. Among the rural poor, women in general are poorer than men. While the incidence of poverty declined consistently from 54.1 percent and 41.2 percent in rural and urban areas in 1972–1973 to 33.4 percent and 20.1 percent in 1987–1988, the incidence of poverty in rural areas was 66 percent higher than in urban areas in 1987–1988 (Government of India 1993a). Hence the alleviation of rural poverty requires creating adequate employment-generating activities. With the scope for nonfirm employment being limited in rural areas, much of the burden of employment creation rested on agriculture. During the first phase of the Green Revolution lasting for about ten years from 1967, the technological change consisting of HYV seeds, chemical fertilizers, and water supply through deep tube wells raised the overall demand for labor in the country. But during the second phase, lasting for about ten years, technological change consisting of the increasing use of labor-saving mechanical devices lowered the overall demand for labor in the country. When the overall demand rose, the major part of it was met by male labor, and where the overall demand fell, female laborers suffered significantly greater losses than male laborers.

A study (Banerjee 1989) on women's participation in economic activities between 1971 and 1981 reveals that there was a small but unambiguous increase in the percentage of main workers in the total female population for both rural and urban areas of India as a whole and of major states. In the case of rural women, on the other hand, in almost all states except Uttar Pradesh and Himachal Pradesh in the north and Kerala in the south, there was a significant positive shift in women's workforce participation rate (WFPR). In urban areas, too, except for

Andhra Pradesh, Bihar, Kerala, and Uttar Pradesh, there was a marked improvement in the proportion of main workers in the female population. The period 1971–1981 also roughly coincides with the first phase of the Green Revolution in agriculture. It should be remembered that according to the census definition of work, main workers are those who had worked for no less than 183 days in the previous year. However, during the same period, there was a more pronounced increase in the number of female marginal workers and this increase was higher than the increase in the number of male marginal workers, for both the rural and urban sector as well as for every state. The increase in the number of marginal workers could be an indication of the increase in the extent of unemployment. Over this period, although the rates of unemployment by all concepts had increased for men and declined slightly for women, the significantly higher proportion of marginal workers in the female population was an indication of the extent of underemployment among them. Also during this period, in rural areas there was a marked increase in female child labor while male child labor declined in absolute numbers. Increase in the girls' workforce participation rates might not have been related to fall in income level of families. It might have rather been related to differing cultural traditions of different groups.

Thus the period under review witnessed a number of important changes in the role of women, specially in the rural sector in the Indian economy. First, women came to account for a larger proportion of the rural labor force. Second, this increase in the sex ratio of workers was most marked in agricultural activities. Third, despite the rise in women's share in agriculture in some states, this share had not increased significantly for the country as a whole (Banerjee 1989).

The 1991 census data (Government of India 1992a) reveal that during the decade of the 1980s, the female workforce participation rate increased in the country as a whole. During 1981–1991, the number of female workers increased by 42.26 percent. In the rural areas, the female workforce participation rate increased by 4.14 percent and the number of female workers in the rural areas increased by 40.25 percent. The general trend appears to be that wherever the work participation of males declined, that of females increased.

The female main workers in the country recorded an impressive growth rate of 44,24 percent excluding Assam and Jammu and Kashmir during 1981–1991. In the rural areas the number of female main workers increased from 39.47 million in 1981 to 55.95 million in 1991, registering a growth rate of 41.78 percent. In the urban areas, the number of female main workers increased from 5.34 million to 8.67 million, recording a growth rate of 62.41 percent during this period. The rate of growth of urban main workers was considerably higher among the females than among the males.

However, along with the growth in the number of main workers, the number of marginal workers also increased in the country. The number of female marginal workers increased from 17.83 million in 1981 to 24.49 million in 1991 in the country, excluding Assam and Jammu and Kashmir recording a growth rate of 37.31 percent, which was considerably higher than the 22 percent growth rate recorded by male marginal workers. In rural areas, compared with a 33.12 percent increase in total number of marginal workers, the female marginal workers recorded only 12.48 percent increase. In urban areas, total marginal workers increased by 45.12 percent, whereas male and female marginal workers increased by 35.70 percent and 50.75 percent, respectively.

An analysis of increments in male and female main workers indicates that while a substantial proportion of the increase in the number of male main workers consisted of cultivators and agricultural laborers, a significant proportion of the increase in the number of female main workers consisted of workers in "other services."

However, despite this increase in number of female workers, unemployment rates for women appear to be higher than those for men. Moreover, a larger difference between the "usual" and "weekly" status unemployment rates, on the one hand, and "daily status" unemployment rates, on the other, in the case of women than of men tends to suggest that underemployment is of much higher proportion among females than among males (Government of India 1992a).

Despite such a general trend in females' employment within the country as a whole, the trend in females' employment in different states and in different regions within each state may differ from each. Therefore, microlevel studies of females' employment situation are useful.

### Further Village Studies

In September 1992, household surveys of three villages in Midnapore, West Bengal, were conducted primarily with a view to obtaining information about environmental and technological changes in the villages and their sustainability. Incidentally some questions were asked about how technological and environmental change had affected the position of women and children. Of the three villages, two, namely Barakuli and Maharajpur, consisted exclusively of scheduled tribes (Santals) and the third village, Gokulganja, consisted of non-Muslim families belonging to the upper caste, scheduled class, and scheduled tribes. In all villages it was reported that women had benefited in terms of employment possibilities as a result of recent technological changes in agriculture. However, while 100 percent of households in the exclusively tribal villages, reported this improvement, only 60 percent did so in Gokulganja (Tisdell et al. 1993, 1994). The most likely reason for the difference is that women of high-caste families have not been able to share equally in employment possibilities with tribal members and scheduled castes because of cultural restrictions. Thus if the policy prescription of Agnihotri (1994) for raising the socioeconomic status of women applies, the socioeconomic status of women in the scheduled castes and scheduled tribes may be increasing at a faster rate than that of women in higher castes.

Although in the surveys mentioned employment prospects for women were generally reported to have improved, environmental deterioration was also placing an increasing burden on women and children. It was now more difficult to collect fruit, wood, wild medicines, and herbs and the "fruits of nature" as well as to find suitable grazing for livestock on common land. There was no indication that the work burden of women had decreased and that their life had materially improved as a result of technological change in the rural villages surveyed. It seems that most women continue to work almost to the limits of physical endurance even though some mechanical improvements in agriculture have slightly reduced the arduousness of agricultural work.

### Educated Urban Middle-Class Working Women: Socioeconomic Profile

With economic change, the profile of urban middle-class families is also changing. Economic necessities and the desire to satisfy various sociopsychological needs are forcing educated women to fulfill their traditional housekeeping role and also to take up various types of white collar jobs. By reducing time allotted for "work inside," leisure, and sleep, they make time for "work outside," work on a very tight time schedule, and in the process, perhaps, overstrain themselves causing adverse physical and mental health effects. A recent study by the Indian Statistical Institute compared one hundred working mothers (all college teachers) with an equal number of nonworking (pure housewife) mothers to find out (a) whether working mothers spend less time on work inside, leisure, and sleep and more time on work outside than nonworking mothers and, if so, is the difference statistically significant; (b) is there a corresponding significant difference between the health of the two groups? The results show that the two groups did differ statistically significantly on the time each allocated to various activities, but these differences had hardly any effect on such health-related indicators as psychological stress level, blood pressure, pulse rate and anemic status, and so on. However, working mothers did suffer more from such stress-related ailments as asthma, colitis, migraine, hypertension, and so on, than their nonworking counterparts, although the difference in general was not statistically significant.

The absence of any significant difference between the two groups of women may imply that while working mothers may feel stressed in the effort to take care of two worlds, a full-time housewife may also feel stressed due to her lack of financial independence, low status in the family, and the monotony of household work.

It is also possible that working mothers can avoid any role conflict by employing paid domestic staff to take care of their household duties and may find that "working outside" provides a vent for accumulated stress instead of aggravating it (Mukhopadhayay 1994). Thus it would appear that economic development is producing an irreversible change in the socioeconomic role of urban educated middle-class housewives in a traditional society.

### Impact of Economic Change on Discrimination Against Females

Although an increasing number of rural girls are getting higher education, the enforcement by family, village, and neighborhood elders of age-old-social customs and traditions embodying gender restrictions seem to continue unabated in villages and in rural towns. Forces of such restrictions are still very strong in rural areas of Bihar, Uttar Pradesh, Madya Pradesh, Andhra Pradesh, Tamil Nadu, Gujarat, and so on, whereas they seem to be weakening in rural areas of educationally advanced and politically conscious states such as West Bengal, Maharashtra, and Kerala. The larger and more economically powerful the cities, the lesser the force of restrictions. Advancement of education among and greater need for employment of females, a newly developed consciousness about the rights of women, and the changing demand for women's labor as a result of capitalist developments in agriculture and industry have been leading women to challenge the forces of "classic patriarchy." The pressures of increasing poverty in the countryside are forcing a renegotiation of structures of authority. As women are moving out of their homestead in search of work and therefore away from the direct control of the family patriarchs, they are entering "male space" and taking off their veils in search of wage labor. The dominant trend in challenge to the patriarchal control is to expose and agitate around the most extreme manifestations of women's subordination in India such as dowry murders, police rape, abortion of female fetuses after amniocentesis, and so on, by condemning these as social evils and mobilizing public support in favor of such condemnation. The less dominant trend is to give publicity to the works of women's groups which relate such extreme forms of discrimination to the structural violence against women within the existing patriarchal family system (Chhachhi 1989).

The challenge to dowry has also been taking place through various forms of struggle ranging from legal actions, seminars to street corner meetings and demonstrations, petitions, and public marches. The emphasis has been on public campaign in order to build the necessary political and social will to ensure action that would be effective in eradicating dowry and the increasing harassment of brides. The fact that the citadel of "patriarchy" is being threatened is borne out by the attempts by religious fundamentalists (both Hindus and Muslims) to reassert their control and reimpose their domination over women. Perhaps as a reaction to the challenge to their power and authority, the Hindu fundamentalists, while being vociferous over the issue of Muslim women's rights, do not condemn the burning of Hindu brides. It should be noted here that the practice of "dowry," although still prevalent in rural areas, is fast disappearing from marriages in urban educated middle class families in West Bengal, Maharashtra, and Kerala.

### Empowering and Utilizing Women in the Economic Development Process

The task of empowering and utilizing women in the economic development process is a complex one requiring action by governments (both national and state), nongovernment organizations (NGOs), and women's grass-roots organizations. Government action is required in three areas: (a) creation of sustainable employment opportunities which can enable women to gain economic independence;

(b) provision of appropriate legal framework under which women's rights of inheritance to paternal land is given both de jure and de facto recognition, and gender-based violence against women is curbed; and (c) massive social education programs to convince the family, village, and neighborhood elders of villages and rural towns of the futility of enforcing gender-based discrimination against women.

### Government Action: Employment

Government intervention with respect to women, which has mainly been confined to creating employment opportunities, has been broadly in two fronts: (i) programs to raise the income level of the poor households mainly through the Integrated Rural Development Programme (IRDC) and (ii) programs to raise the general health level through the institution of various mother and child programs.

Evaluation of two earlier programs, "Food for Work" and Employment Guarantee Scheme (EGS), reveals that whereas under the former scheme women accounted for only 20 percent of the beneficiaries and several states reported no women beneficiaries, under the latter scheme, although the income from EGS accounted for 73 percent of beneficiaries' income, this 73 percent amounted to only Rs443. This would tend to suggest that for most of the female workers, there were little alternative employment opportunities (Duvvury 1989).

A critical evaluation (Rath 1985) of the impact of the IRDP program points to the ineffectiveness of the program both in terms of identification of beneficiaries (with about 15 percent of beneficiaries being misclassified) and of the actual level of increase in income with only 3 percent of the rural poor being able to cross the poverty line). Only in the case of the training of rural youth for self-employment (TRYSEM) with a target of filling up 30 percent of beneficiary positions with women, did women account for 20 percent of the beneficiaries. The problems of procuring raw materials and marketing faced by individual women under TRYSEM could have been resolved more economically if, for example, loans were provided to groups of women.

Under The Norwegian Agency for International Development (NORAD) assisted scheme which operated from 1982–1983 to 1990 funds were made available for various employment-cum-training programs. The programs were implemented through public sector undertakings, corporations, autonomous bodies, and voluntary organizations. Another program, Support to Training-Cum-Employment Programme (STEP), launched in 1986–1987, was intended to take up series of action projects to strengthen and improve women's work in the core sectors of agriculture, animal husbandry, dairying, fisheries, handlooms, handicrafts, khadi and village industries, sericulture, and so on. The focus is on marginalized, poor, and assetless women. Central and state government corporations, universities, social welfare advisory boards, semigovernment agencies and NGOs are eligible for assistance under the program.

Apart from these a number of other programs and projects which have been or are being executed for improving the socioeconomic status of women are hostels for working women, condensed courses of education and vocational training for women, women's development corporations, short-stay homes for women and girls, awareness generation projects for rural poor women, education work for prevention of atrocities against women, and training centers for rehabilitation of women in distress (*India* 1992).

Under the Eighth Five Year Plan (1992–1997), the employment strategy for women forming nearly half of the country's total population and recognized as a target group for employment generation is integrated with the respective sectoral planning.

It is based on promotion of opportunities for self-employment and creation of wage employment. The existing programs such as IRDP, TRYSEM, Jawahar Rozgar Yojana, and so on, would ensure that the target set for women beneficiaries is reached. A major thrust in the strategy is on the formation and strengthening of grass-roots level women's groups which will articulate local women's needs and play an important role in decentralized planning and implementation of programs.

However, the total employment of women under IRDP and TRYSEM reached only 3.9 million (Government of India 1992b). Such programs neither create sustainable employment opportunities nor cover a substantial proportion of females in need of employment. Nevertheless they have helped many women achieve economic independence.

### Appropriate Legal Framework

Enforcing women's rights to paternal land has always been difficult in India. Where women as sisters and daughters in traditionally patrilineal groups do not voluntarily give up their rights in favor of their brothers and instead file claims, male kin have been noted to resort to various methods of circumventing modern laws. After marriage, a sister's absence from her parents' home can become a significant factor in favor of preventing women from claiming land where village exogamy is usually mandatory. Apart from West Bengal and Kerala, in very few of the other states, land reform programs were implemented with reasonable success. Official policies and programs have continued to reflect and reinforce traditional attitudes. Prevailing biases tend to affect both court judgments and the formulation and implementation of government policies including the land reform program.

Instead of empowering women, existing laws to protect women against violence tend to strengthen the power of the state against weaker citizens, most of whom are women. The amendment of the rape laws enacted in 1983 was the culmination of a substantial campaign against the antiquated laws which remained unchanged in the statute book since 1860.

Under the 1986 amendment of the Dowry Prohibition Act of 1961, although the fine was increased to Rs15,000, presents given to the bride or to the bridegroom were not considered as dowry (Agnes 1992). Although the 1986 amendment plugged many loopholes, women continued to be burned in their homes. Under the existing provisions of the Indian penal code, police refuse to register complaints of women seeking protection against domestic violence. The Eighth Plan document states that the existing legal safeguards for women against injustice and atrocities need to be reviewed, loopholes removed, and their implementation monitored. It also acknowledges the need to bring about changes in the laws relating to inheritance of property to fully protect the interests of women and enable them to get an equal share in the paternal property whether inherited or self-acquired.

## Social Education of Elders

The scheme of nonformal education focuses only on children who are unable to attend formal schools for various reasons. For the education of adults, the National Literacy Mission launched in 1988 adopted a specific time-bound approach to achieve total literacy through the involvement of nongovernment organizations. The total literacy campaign was introduced with a special focus on literacy for rural women (*India* 1992). However, since the primary aim of both schemes is to make the target groups reasonably proficient in elementary reading, writing, and arithmetic, the social education of elders is not within the curriculum of any government program of education.

## Nongovernment Organizations (NGO)

A large number of NGOs which operate in India undertake rural development programs with assistance from the national government and, more importantly, from overseas governments and organizations. Many overseas NGOs also undertake such programs and projects on their own. Apart from these, the World Bank, Regional Development Banks, and the U.N. agencies such as UNICEF and WHO have all been involved in such activities. A number of World Bank funded projects which target women's health have been running successfully in south India. However, what is usually found is that where development assistance is directed to women, it often presupposes their role as passive recipients of aid rather than as active agents of change. However, some NGOs such as OXFAM and Christian Aid take a more positive view of women in development. But NGOs have limited resources at their disposal to improve women's capacity on a massive scale. Therefore, while NGOs are an important agent in the process of empowerment of women, the government's commitment to this issue is very essential. As Chambers (1987) observed: "It is by starting with the priorities of the poorer, and enabling them to gain the livelihoods they want and need, that both they and sustainable development can best be served."

## Women's Grass-Roots Organizations

Women's grass-roots organizations have played a valuable role in improving their socioeconomic status and lessening gender based discrimination against them. The amendments to the Dowry Prohibition Act of 1961 and changes being proposed to rape laws would not have been possible without women's grass-roots movements demanding such changes.

The decade of the 1970s witnessed (a) the emergence of a large number of grass-roots, nonparty initiatives involving tribal members, Dalits, the poor, and especially women in these communities, around issues such as land, wages, upper caste oppression, and ecology; (b) a growing recognition in many of these groups of the need to give greater consideration to gender issues; (c) the emergence of separate women's groups; and (d) the focus on poor women's specific concerns in the women's associations linked to the left-wing political parties (Agarwal 1989).

Poor women's grass-roots movements led to the formation of the Comprehensive Rural Operations Service Society (CROSS) in 1976–1977 in Nalgonda District in Andhra Pradesh for higher wages, land, access to government economic programs, and action against male alcoholism and domestic violence. The movement by Dalit women belonging to Vivsaya Cooligan Iyakkam (VCI, Landless Labor Association) against a taboo which prevented them from making use of community wells and ponds on grounds of untouchability led to the storming by these women of the village pond.

The famous Chipko movement, which began in 1972–1973 by the action of the people of Chamoli district in Uttar Pradesh against the auctioning of 300 ash trees to a sports goods manufacturer while the local labor cooperative was refused permission by the state to cut even a few trees to make agricultural implements, has today grown into a wider movement embracing ecology and other issues relating to gender-related inequalities.

A series of village meetings that started in 1982 gave birth to a women's forum called Mahila Mangal Dal (MMD), of which all female members of Gadkharkh households were members. To protect the Panchayat Forest from the unauthorized felling of trees and to revitalize it, one morning eighteen women from MMD marched to the Panchayat Forest with sickles in their hands and surrounded it. A man from the village was caught with a load of freshly cut wood. Acting against all patriarchal norms the women brought the culprit before the village court and the culprit had to pay a fine of Rs25. Since that incident, rotating teams of two women, sickles in hand, guard the forest every day (Dankelman and Davidson 1989). Apart from these, a number of exclusively women's organizations also emerged during the same period. The Self-Employed Women's Association (SEWA), formed in 1972 as a trade union to take up women's economic problems in the urban informal sector of Ahmedabad city, spread beyond the rural sector of Gujarat to other states as well. The Working Women's Forum (WWF), formed in 1978 as an organization of poor women in the informal sector of Madras city, has now spread to the urban and rural sector of several other states (Agarwal 1989). These are just a few of quite a number of women's grass-roots movements which sprang up in the 1970s and early 1980s and have been effective in bringing out the close interrelationship between economic and social oppressions in poor women's lives as experienced both within and outside the family.

## NGOs AND THE EMPOWERMENT OF WOMEN
## IN BANGLADESH—CASES

The socioeconomic status of women in Bangladesh is among the lowest in South Asia. The situation of widowed, divorced, and abandoned women is nothing short of wretched. In relation to women in Bangladesh, Chowdhury (1976: 9) observes:

The greatest single cause of the tragedy of Bangladesh is the place that has been allotted by history, society, and life itself to the women of the nation. Chained by culture, ignorance, fear, poverty, she is, in the words of a paramedic, "not a wife or a woman, but a slave." Hard and continuous labor with always the last portion of food, she cannot afford to fall sick. A slave unable to work is discarded, and this would be her fate as well. Divorced, not accepted by her parents for whom she would only be another mouth to feed, and a disgrace, being separated from her husband, neither can she find employment to support herself. Now she can choose. As a beggar she can go to town and there discard the last shred of any human dignity she may have had, or she can take the more attractive way out of insecticide poisoning.

Zafrullah Chowdhury heads the People's Health Centre (Gonoshasthaya Kendra, GSK), located in the town of Savar about 22 miles from Dhaka, and has established,

**Box 7.1**
**State and Women's Cooperation in Empowering Women in Rajasthan**

The Rajasthan Women's Development Programme (WDP) is the first of the state-sponsored efforts aimed at 'empowering' women through their involvement and participation at all levels of the program.

The women from Datan Village applied through the sarpanch for two hand pumps to be installed in the village—one in the harijan basti and another in the Gujar basti. This was following the information brought by the sathin about the hand pump 'abhijan' in Ajmer district. When the team from the relevant government department arrived to install the hand pumps, they were prevented by the men from the upper caste who did not want the pump to be installed in the lower caste basti. The team however managed to install one in the harijan basti despite the outbreak of violence. The team came twice after that but were prevented every time from putting the hand pump in Gujar basti. The women requested them to come for the fourth time and by standing throughout the day in Gujar basti succeeded in getting the hand pump installed.

The conflict was local between the upper caste and lower caste people in the village which obstructed the government scheme of providing drinking water to the village from reaching the poor. The government for its part was committed enough to send the team five times to the village to install two hand pumps despite the threat of violence.

*Source: Economic and Political Weekly*, Vol. 27, No. 5, 1992.

in connection with this, Centre Narikendra (a Women's Centre) to provide vocational training to widowed, divorced, or young village women. Although the primary mission of the NGO GSK is health care for the poor and underprivileged villagers, Chowdhury realized that many health care problems in fact arise from social problems, for example, the relative status of women in Bangladesh. To tackle such health problems on a long-term basis, social change is needed, and in immediate cases the female victims must be provided with a means to uplift and empower themselves. It was apparent that the long-term treatment of women who presented at his clinic with attempted poisoning and abuse-related health problems would need to proceed in this way. He reasoned, "If women could be provided with some form of economic independence, they would eventually gain their freedom and enter into the various streams of life with new interests and new hopes" (Chowdhury 1976: 9–10).

When women first enter the Women's Centre at Savar, they must first be taught to be literate since it is believed that this is a vital step toward the empowerment of women. After gaining their basic literacy, women are then assigned to vocational training and production groups. Many of these groups engage in occupations not traditionally undertaken by women such as furniture making and welding and fitting. As well, there is printing and publishing, handicrafts, and sewing. Women appear to carry out their tasks with self-confidence. To what extent, however, these skills can be transferred back to the villages by these females and how many females return to their villages is uncertain.

However, Chowdhury (personal communication, January 1993) related an example of social success. In Bangladesh, it is not socially usual for women to drive cars. He decided to train one abandoned woman as a car driver for GSK, a task which she performed very well. Given her improved status, her husband returned to her and valued her more highly. Indeed, it is part of the program of GSK to encourage women to engage in activities that are often frowned on in Bangladeshi society. In the villages, for example, when GSK provides health care, they encourage their female paramedics to ride bicycles, an activity which women should not engage in according to local customs, most of which reinforce the low status of females. In this respect, Ray (1986: 18) comments:

Cycling is essential for work in villages. But in Bangladeshi villages, where superstitions dominate social life, it is an extraordinarily difficult task to establish and legitimise this as far as women (workers) are concerned. Initially, GSK's lady paramedics had to face abuse, censure and humiliation, largely instigated by the *Matbars* (traditional village chiefs) and *Mullahs* (Islamic religious leaders). Occasionally, they were even threatened with violence, and driven out of their homes and villages. Nevertheless, superstition suffered at least a limited defeat in the face of the courage, determination and social consciousness of GSK's workers.

Ray explains that women paramedics in the village are supposed to provide "a glowing symbol of social transformation" and emancipation and rouse confidence among downtrodden village women. Social transformation, self-confidence in women, and their economic independence go hand in hand. This is the basic philosophy underlying GSK as far as the emancipation of Bangladeshi women is concerned. Many examples of GSK's efforts in that regard are to be found in Ray (1986).

It is not that the approach of GSK has been an unqualified success but its action and concern underlies the immensity of the problem of discrimination against women in Bangladesh as well as in a number of other parts of South Asia. Furthermore, GSK has been subjected to political criticism by the more conservative elements of Bangladesh society (as one might expect because of its social reform agenda) and accused of promoting socialism of the worst sort.

Another Bangladeshi NGO whose mission is to assist women is POUSH. This it tries to do through its afforestation program, which is designed for the improvement of the environment, preservation of biodiversity, and the betterment of women. POUSH claims that all women participating in its afforestation program have been taught the Bangladeshi alphabet and they can now sign their names and read simple statements. It claims that the basis of sustainable development is a literate populace (POUSH 1992: 6). With support from the World Food Programme (WFP), POUSH motivates "farmers to allow the use of their fallow land on a production-sharing basis, and selects poor and destitute women from the neighborhood to work as maintenance workers to raise and nurse trees" (Majumder 1992: 14). In return the women are assured of daily wheat rations for three years from POUSH's granaries. Preference is given to poor, landless, destitute, widowed, and divorced women. The main question which hangs over the scheme is what will happen at the end of three years when grain supplies for the maintenance (women) workers are no longer assured from POUSH. The details of the scheme need not concern us here, but the fact that the scheme exists underlies the absence of social safety nets in Bangladesh for the class of women mentioned above. The social status of most women is poor in Bangladesh, but that of completely landless females, widows, and the divorced is from all accounts appalling.

## CONCLUSION

In this chapter we have analyzed the socioeconomic status of women in South Asia under economic change with particular reference to India. Issues such as discrimination against females, impact of economic change on the socioeconomic status of women, and empowering and utilizing women in the economic development process have figured prominently in this analysis. Changes in social customs, traditions, and institutions are very slow to take place in India. Illiteracy is still rampant in rural India. The Indian government and the NGOs have not undertaken any program of social education to convince the elders of the need to do away with social customs and practices embodying gender-based discrimination against women. There are other problems too. Under India's federal system, effective implementation of any law passed by the center depends to a great extent on the willingness of individual states. The social structure in almost the whole of northern India is based on the classic patriarchy. A substantial proportion of members of the federal parliament come from Bihar, Madya Pradesh, and Uttar Pradesh (the Hindu belt). These rural oligarchies generally are not in favor of any action or program to improve the socioeconomic status of women. Therefore it can also be said that the political will on the part of the government is lacking and economic policies were formulated and implemented to serve the interests of the elite class. Even if laws are passed to protect women from discrimination, the entrenched male bias in the administrative and judicial machinery would make its effective implementation difficult indeed. Even if the government possesses political will, such biases could not be done away with quickly. The programs undertaken by the government and the NGOs to improve women's economic status have been mainly of a short-run nature. Unless they are of a long-term nature sustainable improvement in the socioeconomic status of women may not be achieved. The forward-looking strategies document of the 1985 Nairobi conference on women mentioned that effective development requires the full integration of women in the development process as both agents and beneficiaries and that development agencies should take full cognizance of women as a development source (Dankelman and Davidson 1989). However, in implementing development programs affecting women, very few NGOs have taken note of and acted upon this suggestion. There are very few well-organized and powerful women's grass-roots organizations which can be called "all India." It is difficult to mobilize public opinion in favor of or against any issue on a national scale in a vast country with 900 million people. Nevertheless, economic development by raising the society's level of awareness relating to issues affecting women and by creating greater scope for improving the economic well-being of women has set in motion an irreversible process of change. Although the process is slow, it nevertheless has begun.

# 8

# Women and Development in Sub-Saharan Africa with Special Reference to Tanzania

*Felix J. Mlay, Kartik C. Roy, and Clement A. Tisdell*

## INTRODUCTION

In 1991 the total gross national product for Africa south of the Sahara (excluding South Africa) was U.S.$204.7 billion (*World Development Report* 1993), shared by a population of about 500 million. This was slightly higher than the gross national product of Belgium, which has a population of 10 million people. Eighteen of the twenty poorest countries in the world are African. Yet Africa has the potential to generate wealth, and its economy could be turned around with peace, political will, and commitment.

However, the possibility of this change calls for, among other things, liberalization of the gender division of labor and raising the status of women who constitute more than half of the population and who produce the bulk of subsistence and cash crops in addition to reproducing the society. It is often said that if gender roles are abandoned, cash farm incomes could increase considerably and productivity of labor and capital would improve greatly. Liberalizing the division of labor is also likely to lead to higher labor supply as it will improve on-farm employment opportunities for men. Asymmetric gender division of labor may lead to allocative inefficiency such that farms produce at less than their carrying capacity. Research during the U.N. Decade for Women showed the position of women in many parts of the world, especially Africa, to be worsening. Changes in agricultural systems, patterns of development, and institutional changes could be held responsible. This chapter discusses the impact of economic development on the socioeconomic status of women in Sub-Saharan Africa, with particular reference to Tanzania.

## WOMEN'S SOCIOECONOMIC STATUS IN AFRICA: A HISTORICAL PERSPECTIVE

The current socioeconomic status of women in Africa cannot be adequately conceptualized without looking, albeit briefly, into the past.

Historically, the social division of labor in the classic "patriarchal" societies of Africa was associated with different spheres of control over land, labor, and income (Whitehead 1990). As such women had claims to land to farm on their own account and to dispose of their products as well as of income acquired from other independent activities like trading.

Part of women's time was committed as "family labor" to farms assigned for common (household) provisioning and sometimes to work on the personal fields of senior men like fathers and husbands.

Various tensions and processes of negotiations implicit in such arrangements were likely to shift and intensify with new opportunities and risk accompanying commoditization. As a result men specialized in labor migration and cash cropping while women were restricted to traditional food farming (the feminization of subsistence).

The beginning of animal husbandry (the first form of private property) enriched men relative to women (Engels 1972) and necessitated male dominance.[1] For example, almost everywhere in Africa the animal-drawn plow, husbandry, and hunting were in the province of men and this, together with the demands of child care, which initially prevented women from participation in animal husbandry, created the conditions for the growth of inequality.[2]

Slave trade and colonialism accelerated the division of the population into classes and, according to Leacock (1972), Rodney (1972), and Boserup (1970), resulted in deterioration of African women's status, for example, the lesser significance of the stool of the Ashanti queen mother (Christian 1959), the absence of women's freedom to choose a husband due to inflated bride-price (Suret-Canale 1971), and the disequilibrium resulting from the modification of traditional marriage by colonial laws (Dobkin 1968: 36).

Colonialism often resulted in differentiation of social and domestic labor, introduction of large-scale cash-crop production (a domain of men) for exchange, and transformation of productive resources into private property (Hafkin and Bay 1976) in which the colonial personnel excluded women from cash-crop cultivation, taught men modern techniques, and gave men access to machinery that could raise the level of production (Boserup 1970). With the development of cash cropping, and the expansion of commodity economy, women's labor (which continued to cultivate food crops) became inferior and private: It did not produce the cash needed to enter the money economy and its function was now limited to the domestic group.

Colonialism also made land, which was initially communally owned and utilized, a commodity that could be acquired by the colonial power. As women (and the majority of men) were not in the category of formal "ownership," they often fell in the lower strata as stratification based on land ownership developed.

The study of contemporary gender role differentiation in Africa has also been identified by Engels (1972), Nyerere (1967), Gough (1971), and Leacock (1972), who analyzed the position of women in the context of the basic social relations prevailing within society in any given epoch. They found that ownership of resources appeared to be communal and distribution egalitarian in hunting and gathering populations despite the division of labor there.

Generally, men were able to enter the money sector of the economy more easily than women through the recruitment of labor to the plantations which was often restricted to men (Boserup 1970); men also had the advantage in obtaining whatever education was available to the indigenous population (Little 1973). In addition to having to support themselves and their children when compulsory labor took the men away from home, women found themselves in a money economy where the products of their labor were inferior and where they had no longer access to the resources of the society (Hafkin and Bay 1976).

## CONTEMPORARY SOCIOECONOMIC FACTORS AFFECTING THE STATUS OF WOMEN IN AFRICA

Unlike their counterparts in the developed world, most women in Africa must depend on a husband, a father, or whomever due to their limited access to societal resources.

The presence of women in policy and decision-making positions in government and parliament is negligible in Africa no matter how educated they may be. African women have very little say in society and community's day-to-day decisions let alone their personal matters although it is women who basically feed the family, are responsible for its social well being, and manage the household's resources. Women constitute over half of the total population but they are not sharing power equally. Moreover, the educated and professional woman is never considered equal to her male colleagues and peers regardless of her capability.

The notion that educating a girl is a waste of resources as she will "get married after all" has deprived women of an important asset for their development and the development of their societies. On the other hand, girls are valuable because they bring wealth to the family in the form of the bride-price. In some cultures like the Wasukuma of Mwanza, a girl can fetch as much as fifty head of cattle (or more) and this varies with beauty. As a result, many girls are forced by their fathers to leave school "prematurely" to get married (sometimes without their consent) and earn the family an income. The personal experience of one of the authors (Felix Mlay) in Mwanza (Tanzania) in 1979 reveals that villagers went to the extent of bribing primary school head teachers for dismissal of their daughters from school so that they could offer them for marriage,[3] although, by law, it is an offence for a pupil to abscond from school and any parent who encourages that is fined.

The dowry or bride-price which is paid to the girls' family legitimates her as the husband's wife and property. The important rationale behind polygamous marriages in Africa has been to acquire labor force for tilling the land. In Swaziland, for example, "a woman is like a field" in the sense that men aim at possessing both women and fields and protect from encroachment of other men their rights over the products of both children and harvests.

Inequality in education is a vital constraint on women's progress in both rural and urban areas. In African societies women are treated as legal minors in the sense that they will always be owned by someone: a father, a family, or a husband. This is further intensified by traditional customary and sometimes religious values of the society which generally hold that women are weak, incapable of being independent, and that men are the "heads" of the house and the providers of daily bread. In some cultures women are not allowed to eat certain types of foods (e.g., eggs and liver) regarded as taboo, which actually undermines their nutritional status. In some religious cultures, men prevent women (even highly educated ones) from going out or to work on the pretext that they might indulge in sexual malpractice. This limits their labor participation rates and so their opportunity of accumulating wealth.

Needless to say, girls are prepared to take their inferior status when they grow up, as they are brought up as social inferiors to boys. The most unhygienic and cruel humiliation of all times to women has been in some tribes women's "genital mutilation" at puberty, which is meant to psychologically subjugate them to the level of sex objects. Women are considered as born specifically to be used as work hands and to marry and procreate.

At her husband's death, the wife can be passed together with other wives to the husband's eldest son or brother. The wife may be sent to her parents' home "empty handed" because of failure to meet the society's expectations of being able to reproduce sons, a discovery of a relationship with another man, or not being obedient and subservient. These old conservative customs serve only to reinforce the concept that a woman is no more than a piece of property.

It is also true that women's rights regarding inheritance, marriage and divorce, ownership of property, freedom of movement, and the like are practically nonexistent in many countries in Africa. This is because the power of the national constitution to accord women "equal rights" is severely circumscribed by patriarchal values and male dominance. Such women, having no access to the family's wealth or property, become economically and socially impotent. Evidently, women in Africa, and specifically in the rural areas, are said to produce the bulk of the farm produce both for subsistence and export purposes. They produce more than 80 percent of the subsistence food (Foster 1986) and actively participate by spending more time than men in export production. In Nigeria, women work more hours than men in cocoa plantations, in coffee production, and in national market crops like rice, grain, maize, and cassava. In Kenya, women are responsible for over 80 percent of food crops and a substantial proportion of cash crop production (Davidson 1988) but own in their own names only 5 percent of the land (Dankelman and Davidson 1989). The average 15-year-old-girl's workload is two-thirds of that of the workload of both men and women. Men own all land used for both food and cash-crop production.

The advent of colonial capitalism drastically changed former patterns of land use and occupancy in many places, gradually allocating to men once abundant agricultural land in many areas, through government policies that favored the consolidation of scattered tracts in the hands of the male owners and production of cash crops for exports.

Through these processes women's productive-procreative labor, particularly in subsistence production, had been devalued by capitalist production relations and continues to be uncompensated while men's labor assumes a surplus exchange value and the trend toward increased export crop production affects women's nutritional status and that of their children (Meena 1991).

Colonial administration in the 1950s and immediately after independence failed to understand the significance of indigenous land tenure practices based upon principles of obligation and responsibility that guaranteed women access to land and control over certain crops. The Swynnerton Plan in Kenya set a precedent for male domination of income-producing agriculture.

Land reform programs often work to place the most reproductive land in the hands of the able and rich few. As a result, the poorest are squeezed onto marginal land that is steep, infertile, dry, subject to pests, or covered with rainforest (Dankelman and Davidson 1989). Boserup (1970) documents cases in Rhodesia and the Union of South Africa where European "reform" resulted in the transfer of women's land to men.

Nationalization of land, which is the most important factor of production in Africa, does not necessarily lead to equal accesses to land by men and women. In postrevolutionary Ethiopia nationalization of land there gave women neither direct access to land nor a role in agricultural decisions that affected agricultural production. Given the high population growth rate (Davidson 1988) and the youthful structure of the population in Africa, the need for increased agriculture production cannot be overemphasised.

However, technological innovations that will lessen women's procreative and household labor remain low in African nations' development priorities. In many countries although technological change has increased crop yield and brought about significant improvement in economic conditions of large and medium-sized farms, in dry land and rainfed agriculture, land poor women and environment have failed to benefit from this change.

Other socioeconomic factors like Western colonization, the increasing dependence of African countries on the Western monetary economy, developments in technology (agriculture modernization), international trade, increasing religious fundamentalism, and state development policies have contributed to the deterioration of the position of women. Due to the current threat of accelerating degradation of the living environment and to pressure on farming and rural livelihoods as a consequence of commoditization and class differentiation, women find themselves poor and in a dependent situation which leaves them very insecure in times of crisis. Exacerbated by the current economic and social crisis in Africa, a "tug of war" is taking place in the villages where men are claiming and confiscating the product of the labor of their wives to solve their problems. The growing number of poor female-headed households and the crisis of marriage in Africa are evidence of this (Whitehead 1990).

Women in Africa, in carrying out their primary responsibility of providing food for the family, make use of communal resources which serve as a source of various types of food, medical herbs, fodder, timber, water, manure, house-building and handicraft material, resin, gum, and fuelwood. As a result of environmental degradation, these resources have become scarcer and of poorer quality, making the collection of food, water, and fuel more time consuming. Time available for food preparation within the household is thus reduced, leading to the deterioration of the health and the nutritional status of the household.

It is important to note that the African poor woman's primary resource is time, and to accomplish her triple tasks of production, reproduction, and household management, she has to work harder and longer hours, which leaves her with little time for leisure. She then trades off leisure for more work, so as to earn extra income if the family's income declines. Assigned an economic value and added to the family's cash, this may account for a substantial contribution by women and children to the family's income.

Judging from their numerical strength and the place African women hold in the household and in their national economies at large, deliberate efforts must be made, among other things, by changing social structures and women's attitudes, to improve their status, if absolute poverty is to be eliminated in the rural areas. Such efforts must include the provision of more education, training, greater access to the basic factors of production, and appropriate technology for the respective environments they work in. This will no doubt enhance their productivity and hence their income, especially where women's income is either the only means of survival or a major component of household income.

## WOMEN IN TANZANIA

Women in Tanzania are responsible for 70 percent of the food production and supply about 80 percent of their working time for such production (Kisanga 1990). Apart from their reproductive tasks, they cultivate, weed, harvest, process, store, tend the cattle, and take part in tending the cash crops.

### National Policy for Empowering Women

At independence Tanzania inherited a mixture of tribal customs and feudal-like hierarchies among most of the tribal groups which placed men in a significantly advantageous position compared to women (Wiley 1985). Eighty years of colonialism had exacerbated traditional gender inequalities. With independence and the socialism of the 1960s, the issue of human equality became a major government concern, though it tended to focus on questions of equality among socioeconomic classes rather than on gender issues (Mascarenhans and Mbilinyi 1983), thus neglecting women are a big majority of the underprivileged population.

National policy in the past took for granted that women's needs will be met through general programs and policies affecting all citizens. Women's development only received special attention in their traditional roles as bearers and caretakers of children.

## New Laws

Official recognition of the low status of women in Tanzania has gained momentum, and a ministry which caters specifically for women's and children's issues has been formed, although it partly serves to segregate women as a special "group." The Marriage Act of 1971 ensured the equality of women in marriage and specified the right of wives to keep their union monogamous. It also established a minimum age for marriage and made some provision for inheritance by widows.

Primary schooling has been compulsory for girls and boys (thanks to Universal Primary Education) and women have been particularly encouraged to participate in adult literary classes. Programs for establishing boarding facilities for girls at secondary schools and universities have been underway for some years. The Musoma Resolution provided for girls to enter the university immediately after National Service before working for two years, which was compulsory. Girls now comprise 48 percent of primary school students, 20 percent of secondary school entrants, and 15 percent of university students (Wiley 1985).

Women's issues in the Party and the government programs are communicated through the National Women Organization, which is not well-supported financially. Despite its political ends, the main aim of the organization is the promotion of women's income-generating and training projects, which are unfortunately mostly related to their domestic roles.

The National Women Organization gets little support from village women as most of them are either ignorant or uninformed of the benefits of this important organization. As a result, local chapters do not last very long due to leadership, planning, and financial management constraints.

## Nationalization of Land

The nationalization of land after independence in 1961 declared all land (cultivable and residential) as public, allowing any citizen to take up and cultivate a piece of unused land. The intention was to prevent the growth of a class of speculators and absentee landlords. This has however caused problems in Tanzania where most of the cultivation is on shifting basis and where land rights are allocated on the basis of descent.

Nationalization of land, though theoretically implying equal access to land, has not necessarily led to the same access between men and women in Tanzania. In most rural households, women have a minimal role in decisions related to either land distribution or agricultural production, bringing little change in women's relationship to land as their rights to hold it is still through husbands. In coffee-growing areas like the Kilimanjaro region (this may also apply to most permanent cash-crop lands), land is owned and can only be inherited by married sons. However, women's rights to cultivate land are acquired through a husband and even on a husband's death or divorce they cannot inherit it. In these areas land can be scarce and very expensive to the extent that few villagers, let alone poor women whose customary rights to hold land continue to be eroded in the name of development, can afford to purchase land. Worse still, rural women cannot secure government loans to purchase land, farm inputs, and equipment because of their ignorance of the existence of such a facility and their inability of meeting the conditions for repaying these loans. The new Banking Act following privatization requires borrowers to provide security for loans; given that smallholder farmers who produce over 80 percent of the total agriculture production in Tanzania do not have title to their farms or houses, they and other entrepreneurs without secure assets are now excluded from formal credit. Women particularly find themselves disadvantaged because they have no savings and so cannot obtain credit to make purchases. It is only "the well-to-do" women assisted by their husbands who can secure these loans as they can meet collateral conditions. This only serves to intensify inequality in income distribution.

## Impact of Socialist Transformation of the Country on Women

Women's role in relation to land tenure and agricultural production has been little altered under the socialist government in the postcolonial period since 1961 (Croll 1986). As primary smallholder producers in agriculture, peasant women still perform both the bulk of subsistence and often cash-crop labor but have very little control over the allocation of resources and products of their labor. In Mbeya region in early 1981 and late 1982 women protested bitterly against the regulations governing access to and control over land, labor, cash, farm inputs and equipment, the division of farm income, and organization of the labor process with its differential work loads for women and men.

Socialist transformation did not take into account the current social, economic, political, and legal (among others) factors which contributed to class and gender imbalances. The work pattern, and economic and social status of women are influenced by family structures, traditions, and environmental and technological conditions but most importantly by the decision-making process and control of essential resources.

Women's participation in decision making at both the household and community level in Tanzania is minimal. This conclusion is supported by a recent study in the Iringa and Kagera regions (Kavishe 1993) where women account for only about 10 percent of the membership of the village councils in which women deal with issues perceived as women's. Minor decisions on farm activities (like planting, weeding, harvesting, and food preservation), which are mostly handled by women, are shared by both, while decisions related to food and kitchen can be made by wives so long as it does not interfere with the husband's budget. Wives are considered as being unnecessarily extravagant with money, necessitating tight control of it by men, who control all major means of production including land and livestock. In patrilineal tribes of rural Tanzania men pay bride-price, which imposes labor obligation on women so that women's workload becomes another service that they are expected to perform for their husbands and households. Bride-price also legitimizes women as a property of the husband. Wife bashing then becomes a common phenomenon in most tribes. The Wakuria of Musoma are notable for wife beating and some cases have been reported where women have been seriously injured.[4] Village bylaws to arrest the situation have not been very effective because they are executed by men who dominate "village reconciliation (legal) councils."

## Women and Village Policies in Tanzania

At independence in 1961, Tanzania embarked on a program of grouping the scattered rural masses into villages through self-help and settlement schemes which aimed at facilitating the delivery of social-economic services by the government, thereby increasing rural productivity and improving the living standards of the people.

Villagization was the most fundamental and dramatic socialist transformation program in the mid-1970s and is said to have brought more than 90 percent of the mainland rural population into new villages.[5] Like the colonial settlement schemes it aimed at directing the people into new agricultural techniques (Ingle 1972), but unlike them villagization had a communal element (Seavoy 1989).

By the end of the decade, 72 percent of the rural population was within 5 kilometers of a health facility, each village had a primary school, and over half of the villages had improved water supplies (UNESCO 1988) but the quantity and quality of these facilities were undermined by the economic crisis that followed.

These schemes were overcapitalized in relation to their capacity to generate economic returns. They emphasized mechanization but its ineffective use failed to make it economically viable. In addition, all projects were viewed as public sector rather than village projects, which resulted in the schemes developing excessive dependence on the government. As a vehicle for agricultural development, village settlement schemes were a failure and were abandoned in 1966.

Suffice it to say also that the schemes widened interrural and intrarural (men and women) income differentials, the former because a bigger share of the public resources was concentrated in few settlements. Women were excluded from the decision-making process of these schemes, and in the final analysis, they did not benefit much from income accruing from the schemes.

Villagization failed to reduce the distance to water points and to offer better child care and educational facilities because women found themselves considerably worse off in the new "Ujamaa" villages than in their former villages. This is because most of the planners in Tanzania assumed that all people who were moved to these villages were allocated land and housing. Planners and administrators did not take into account the many rights and autonomy women possessed in many parts of the country under the traditional system and in particular that they had land of their own in their own right, independent of their husbands (Caplan 1991). The increased inability of the government to provide these villages with the promised essential amenities affected women more than men. Women who still do most of the work found it difficult to adapt to the new environments and felt dislocated. They still have to walk long distances to windmills, wells, or most likely water taps to fetch water, to the dispensary or health centers when the children get sick, and to the fields which are located far away from the village center.

### Structural Adjustment Programs and Village Women's Status in Tanzania

The major economic indicators began to exhibit unfavourable developments since mid-1970s. The trends became stronger during the first half of the 1980s. For example, during the period 1982–1984, GDP per capita and exports recorded a substantial decline annually, the debt to exports ratio recorded substantial increase annually, and inflation recorded more than 30 percent growth annually. The consequent economic crisis saw the country accepting structural adjustment programs conditioned by policy "reforms" directed by the World Bank and IMF, as it realized that the socialist model was not working adequately. Consequently, from 1984 the Tanzanian shilling has been drastically devalued, subsidies on maize and fertilizers have been removed, producer prices of maize, rice, and export crops have been raised, and internal barriers to agricultural products were removed. Moreover, liberalization of price and foreign exchange controls and removal of restrictions on privatization have gradually been implemented. These conditions could have far-reaching gender implications, more so for rural women, who are already marginalized by the existing political and social orders.

The devaluation by eroding the real wages of both rural and urban population alike led to migration of the rural workforce (mainly men) to the urban areas to seek wage employment. The agricultural workforce has been reduced and women in the rural areas have been left with a bigger workload than before. They also work in the informal sector to subsidize the household income.

### Liberalization of Price and Foreign Exchange Controls and the Removal of Subsidies

The abolition by the government of Tanzania of price and foreign exchange controls and subsidies acted as a disincentive to agricultural production by favoring urban dwellers who bought the agricultural products at low prices. The government taxation system failed to facilitate agricultural producers' control of the realized surplus as well as the reduction of the government's budget by taxing farm products to manage its crisis. Women as usual do not automatically benefit from improvement in agriculture, especially in cash crops, which are mainly controlled by men. Recent studies in Tanzania show that increased producer prices which are supposed to motivate farmers do not seem to have generated improvements in household income (Meena 1991). At farm level, women do not control family resources, including income accruing from the sale of cash crops.

Suffice it to say that the effect of liberalizing prices and foreign exchange controls and the removal of subsidies has been to increase the price of farm implements and inputs. It has also considerably limited the ability of farmers, in particular women, to make use of incentives for crop production because they have to work harder and produce more now to acquire the same item at current prices. Due to increased costs of hiring factor inputs such as tractors women still do back-breaking chores like weeding, digging, and harvesting with tools of very low productivity like the hand hoe, which can be very inefficient and detrimental to their health.

The small amounts of money they get from the sale of vegetables, fruits, and so on, is used to buy food for the family or sometimes is confiscated by men for their personal uses. *ok, there's something to stop*

In addition, increased producer prices for export crops have forced women to spend a big part of their own time on cash crops (the income from which they do not control) and less on food crops. This has no doubt affected their own and their families' nutritional status. In Mwanza region cotton production has been emphasized at the expense of other (horticultural) crops mainly produced by women and for which very low prices are paid.

In most parts of rural Tanzania, most feeder roads are impassable, especially in the rainy seasons, and coupled with increased inability to afford "intermediate means of transport" (IMT),[6] women more than men suffer from rural transport problems. Men and women in Mwanza region used bicycles and ox-carts to ferry cotton from farms, but due to increased prices, these items are no longer affordable. A study of village transport in Makete district of Tanzania in 1986 and 1987 revealed that men contributed only 25 percent of the time women did to transport and were performing approximately 11 percent of the load carriage effort. Walking was the predominant form of transport and these involved the head carriage associated with basic-need provisioning and crop marketing, which are mainly women's work. On the other hand men's role is to "pocket" the money accruing from the sales of the crops. This money is owned and managed by men and may be used to buy food and clothes, to educate children, and sometimes for drinking beer and womanizing in towns or cities. "We work from morning till night" or "Transporting harvest from the farm on the head is difficult because the farms are far away or cultivating by hand with a baby on your back—is a problem" were some of the cries of women in Mbeya region (Mbilinyi 1990).

### Reduction in Public Expenditure

Structural adjustment policies generally requires a reduction in public expenditure which required the government of Tanzania to redirect investment from what the Fund called the "non-productive" (social service) sectors to productive sectors as well as to impose a wage freeze on wage expenditure. Notably, the ability of the government to invest in the service sector was already incapacitated by the economic crisis so much so that further cuts undermined earlier achievements and tortured the people.

### Reduction in Health and Education Expenditures *(using School Fees)*

Structural adjustment approval necessitated the imposition of "user" fees in education and health[7] and so placed an obligation to provide for these amenities on the people as recommended by IMF. The total expenditure for health decreased from the highest 9 percent in 1973–1974 to 5.2 percent in 1984–1985 (according to information from the Ministry of Health) and further to 4.9 percent in 1985–1986 (Meena 1990).

Clearly, the declining budget and incomes of the people not only undermined the achievements already made, but also negatively affected the people in general and particularly women and children. The government was unable to provide sufficient funds to purchase necessary medicines for its hospitals while people's purchasing power was too low to afford the access to the facilities. People criticized the government by pointing out the inadequacy of village medical, water, and transport services (Mbilinyi 1990).

Consequently, these cuts reduced the number of pregnant women (95 percent of all by 1978) visiting Maternal and Child Services (MCH) and deliveries (53 percent) which took place under the supervision of trained medical personnel. More than that, the deterioration in the health services, especially in the MCH, caused alarming increases in maternal death. Maternal deaths due to poor services and increasing malnourishment among pregnant women were approximately 3000–4000 per year.

Women's worsening health condition can be attributed to the heavy burden of both productive and reproductive roles. Traditional attitudes dictate that women bear the number of children men want without regard to the effect on woman's health. The history of the average Tanzanian woman can be described as that of bearing children "too early, too often, and for too long." Apart from their productive tasks rural mothers in Tanzania spend seventeen to twenty years being pregnant and breastfeeding their children (Havenvik 1988). This unfortunately coincides with their prime productive years. *(us)*

Again, the unequal distribution of labor makes women's labor very crucial. Havenvik et al.'s (1988) study showed that agricultural production depends more upon the labor input of women than men (71 and 19 percent, respectively), which is in turn determined by their health and education status.

The allocation of resources to education fell from 18 percent in 1981–1982 to 8 percent of the total budget in 1984–1985 (Meena 1990). This undoubtedly undermined achievements of the early 1970s, notably the Universal Primary Education (UPE) and Mass Literacy Campaigns (MLC) schemes under which half of primary school girls[8] and a very significant proportion of the 85 percent literate adults were women (according to information from the government).

In addition, women had to construct the primary schools in areas where men migrated to urban areas in search of employment opportunities, adding further to their already heavy labor burden. In Isongole (Mbeya), women argued that they helped build the village school and the local party center but did not receive reciprocal help from male villagers or the village government to build a women's cooperative house (Mbilinyi 1990). Although men are expected to pay school fees, cost-sharing in school fees made women work harder.

Allowing market forces to control enrollments at all levels subjects women to undue competition based on financial power rather than intellectual ability. Coupled with the notion that education for girls is a waste,[9] such competition eliminates them from education regardless of their competence.

Coupled with "user charges" the quantity and quality of education at all levels has been reported to be declining. Reduction in government expenditure has thus made the education system turn out illiterates (UNESCO 1988). Moreover enrollments rates have been declining while drop-out rates at primary school level for both girls and boys is alarming. For example, drop-out rates increased from 2.2 percent in 1980–1981 to 9.1 in 1985 and between 1982 and 1986 the enrollment rates decreased by 68 percent (according to sources at the Ministry of Education). The drop-out rate for girls has however been higher than that of boys due to early marriages, pregnancies of mothers, and housework.

It is unrealistic to try to improve the state of production while the health and education of the producers is left unattended (Kavishe 1993: 119).

## CONCLUSION

In Tanzania and most of Sub-Saharan Africa, women play the triple role of producers, reproducers, and major providers of care. Allocation of time between productive (income-generating) and reproductive (domestic) work, her access to essential services and supplies like water, fuel, and education, and her economic as well as her social status in the household dictate her capacity as a mother and determine her ability to affect decisions which will ensure the health and well-being of the family and the nation.

There has been some deliberate and positive efforts (albeit scant)[10] by governments, individuals, and organizations to empower women, but their effort has been frustrated by entrenched social, economic, and political ideologies and customs. The burden of work on women and their inaccessibility to the decision-making processes, for example, are main constraints to productivity.

The rural transformation and sustainable development strategies will fail if over half of the population in this way remains underprivileged. However, for women themselves and for the advocates of gender equality, the task of emancipation of rural women remains an uphill one.

# NOTES

1. Among the Nuer of East Africa cattle had not yet developed into a commodity; although men "owned" the cattle, only girls and the uninitiated boys were permitted to milk them.

2. In Somalia, where livestock have exchange value, women were forced under threat of physical violence from their husbands to perform all the manual and heavy work and were allowed to tend sheep and goats. Somali men considered it beyond their dignity to tend anything but camels, cattle, ponies, the most valuable economic assets of the Somali.

3. Boys were victims too: They had to look after the cattle but many would finish school with inadequate primary education.

4. Personal communication quoted with the permission of Mr. Nsiima Mberwa who has worked in this region as an extension officer for five years.

5. Some rural communities such as the Chagga, the Haya, the Nyakyusa, and the Arusha already lived in permanent villages with permanent cash crops.

6. Between the traditional method of transport and the mode of transporting goods on the head.

7. Prior to this these services were provided free of charge to the people with the exception of private schools and hospitals.

8. Only less than one quarter of school-age children attended school in 1960.

9. It is still believed by some that educating a girl has no economic value.

10. Between 1985 and 1990 out of 248 members of Tanzania parliament only 27 (11 percent—mostly nominated and not elected) were women (UNICEF 1990).

# 9

## Finnish Gender Contracts

### Harriet Silius

### INTRODUCTION

In worldwide comparisons, the position of Finnish women is often at the very top of the scale. United Nations reports on the position of women in different parts of the world sometimes rank women in Finland at first place, sometimes second or third. For many observers Finland is a woman-friendly paradise or, at least, one of the paradises. Finnish women got the right to vote as early as 1906. Women constitute almost 40 percent of the Parliament. The position of women in education has been steadily improving. Among women under the age of forty-five, the level of education is even higher than among men. Finnish women are an integral part of the labor market. Young parents share fairly equally the joys and responsibilities of parenthood. Single mothers do not constitute any social problem, although some of them are not very well off economically.

In common with other Nordic or Scandinavian countries,[1] Finland has an advanced, extensive welfare system, with the state having a full impact on the life of all its citizens. In this welfare context, the Nordic countries share the practice: Women in large numbers work on the labor market. This in turn is supported by intended (e.g., the day-care system) and unintended means (e.g., earnings-related social security). Finnish women have traditionally participated actively in education (including higher education) and in working life. Today they form half of the labor force (47 percent in December 1993).[2] In contrast to the other Scandinavian countries (Denmark, Norway, and Sweden), the vast majority of the Finnish women work full-time, including mothers of children in preschool age. Finnish legislation assures women reproductive rights[3] and offers paid parental leave up to a year. Additionally, since 1991, municipalities are legally obliged to organize day care for all children under the age of three.

Later than the other Nordic countries, Finland introduced legislation on equality between women and men in the 1980s. The aim of this legislation is to prohibit gender inequality in working life. Finnish society is also committed to a policy of equality in general, the consequence of which makes some forms of inequality between women and men considered illegitimate.

Scandinavian feminist researchers of the welfare state have since several years discussed whether the Nordic welfare state could be characterized as women friendly or not (see, e.g., Anttonen 1990, 1992, 1994; Dahlerup 1987, 1992a; Julkunen 1992; Julkunen and Rantalaiho 1989; Siim 1987, 1988). A common result of this vast body of research is a comprehension of the importance of women as active citizens, as policymakers in the extension of the welfare state, and as its largest group of employees. The emergence of the welfare state gave rise to paid work for large groups of women, giving them at the same time economic independence from men. Women have participated in the creation of the Nordic welfare state model. One of the traits of this model is the transition from unpaid caring in the homes, performed by uneducated family, to public, waged caring, performed by educated professionals. The development of the welfare state involved a professionalization of its services in, for example, health, caring, education, and administration, carried out through the demands for education, expertise, and experience made by women. A prerequisite for this view of the character of the welfare state is, however, the existence of state mechanisms, embraced by common consent, moderating between the market demands and caring demands. The Nordic view differs from many Anglo-American assessments of the welfare state, which often are discussing the patriarchal or controlling nature of the welfare state. In my opinion, the differences are due to different welfare state contexts but also to elaborate theorizing on women, gender, and gender systems in the Nordic countries. In sum, a feminist theorizing of the welfare state puts the focus on the relations between women and men and highlights aspects which are not dealt with within mainstream welfare state approaches.

Feminist researchers analyzing the specific Finnish case are more reluctant to accept the paradise description of Finland or to agree on its woman-friendliness. When looking more closely, problems rise. Finnish women work hard, have low wages, use a lot of time fitting everyday life and working life together and so on, on very specific conditions. Among the prominent features of contemporary Finnish society one can identify a strongly segregated labor market, women-only economic conditions, a heavy workload, and a sexist culture.

## THE CONCEPTS OF GENDER AND GENDER CONTRACT

This chapter will present the specific conditions of Finnish women using the concept of gender contract. I will argue that gender makes a decisive difference. In this context *gender* should be understood as a relation between men and women. Gender refers to patterned socially produced, distinctions between female and male, feminine and masculine. Gender is not something that people are, in some inherent sense, although we may consciously think of ourselves in this way (Acker 1992). Rather, for the individual as well as for the collective, it is a daily accomplishment that occurs in the course of participation in work organizations as well as in many other locations. The interesting question is how this relation is constructed in different societies or social contexts at different times.

In the early days of contemporary feminist theorizing, feminist social scientists made a distinction between gender and sex,[4] with gender as socially constructed and sex as biologically given. Today, that distinction is more and more problematic as the social construction of the body is further examined (see, e.g., Lorber 1994). Focusing on the relations between men and women and on the social and cultural construction of these relations, men, and not only women, will finally be gendered. In order to elaborate views on gendered conditions around the world, it is not sufficient to equate women and gender. Media reports regarding Finland as a women's paradise might use gendered (male) norms, standards, or concepts, for example, on citizenship, when comparing women.

The concept of *gender contract* has been introduced into the Nordic context by Joan Acker (1989) in order to explain the subordinated position of women in the labor market in advanced welfare states and their primary responsibility for reproduction and care. The concept of gender contract implies an invisible, unconscious, and tacit contract between women as a group and patriarchal structures such as the state and the labor market. The concept is, however, not only suitable for present-day analyses but also useful in a historical context. Swedish historian Yvonne Hirdman (1994) describes different gender contracts in the Swedish society in a time perspective. She differentiates between (1) the "housewife's contract," which is divided into the first one of the 1920s and 1930s and the second one of the 1940s and 1950s; (2) the "equality contract" from 1960 to 1975, and (3) the "equal status contract"[5] from 1976 to 1990. Liisa Rantalaiho (1994) identifies the first Finnish gender contract as the one of "social motherhood." It emerged in the beginning of this century when Finnish women became political citizens and within their own arenas, out of which the welfare state later developed. The second and modern contract Rantalaiho calls "the contract of the working mother." It outdated the former one in the late 1960s.

Simplifying the gender contract describes social institutions and practices by which the relations between women and men, or between femininity and masculinity, are arranged. It includes the tacit rules, mutual responsibilities, and rights which define the relations between the genders, the generations, and finally production and reproduction (Rantalaiho 1994). Many Nordic feminist scholars agree on Hirdman's (1988, 1990) characterization of the gender contract or the gender system, according to whom its two main logics are distinction and hierarchy. Distinction, division, separation, segregation, or differentness means that women, the female and femininity, should be distinctly discernible from men, the male and masculinity (and not the other way around), no matter whether discourses or practices are in focus (Rantalaiho 1994). The principle of hierarchy implies the primacy of the male norm (Hirdman 1990), meaning that in every instance the male or the masculine should take precedence and be the primary norm. The male figure of Man is the basic norm of, for example, abstract humanity. This same logic applies to the representation of the Citizen or the Worker. They are gendered male. The male and the masculine carry cultural prestige whereas the female and the feminine lack significance, cultural glamor, regardless of the concrete individual women and men in question (Rantalaiho 1993). Thus hierarchy stands for the asymmetry in gender relations. This asymmetry, analyzed within a vast body of research (see, e.g., Acker 1990, 1992; Flax 1987; Harding 1991; Scott 1988) implies that power is distortedly distributed. Often power is systematically ascribed only to one gender, usually the male. Gender, as patterned differences, usually involves the subordination of women, either concretely or symbolically (Acker 1992). To Joan Scott (1986) gender is a pervasive symbol of power.

## THE ORIGINS OF CONTEMPORARY GENDER RELATIONS IN FINLAND: THE RURAL PARTNERSHIP CONTRACT

The specific gender contract of a society has its own structural, historical, and social roots. In order to understand the contemporary gender relations, it is important to trace these origins. According to Liisa Rantalaiho (1994), three features are specific to the Finnish case: Finland's smallness, its state-centeredness, and its recent rapid changes.

For centuries Finland used to be a poor, small, homogenous country living on agriculture. Finland is still small with reference to population. Its five million inhabitants could be compared to, for example, the ten million of London. Finland's area is however bigger than that of the British isles, implying a country with low population density and long distances between people.

Finland was a predominantly rural country until the 1960s. Before the World War II, the majority of Finns worked in agriculture. The structure of agriculture was a Scandinavian type, with small, poor, but independent family farms. Rich gentry was very scarce. Higher state officials and clergy constituted a small upper class. Also the middle class was quite thin. Agrarian poverty in a Northern arctic climate meant that everybody—both men and women—had to work hard for their survival. Socioeconomic differences were small and not at all of the same size as in many other countries on the European continent. The structures of relative poverty and sparsely populated areas produced specific gender relations. Men and women needed the work participation of each other. Marriage was a partnership, including mutual responsibility to work for the survival of the family. Men and women performed mostly different tasks, complementing each other, but women taking over if men for some reason were absent. In agrarian Finland men needed women as labor. Liisa Rantalaiho (1994) has expressively remarked that women were needed more by the cows than by men's sexual demands.[6] In this agrarian society a "good woman" was first a good worker and only second a good mother. Full-time motherhood was nonexistent both as discourse and as praxis.[7] A woman's pride was to be a good housekeeper. Although it happened that women did "men's work," men did more seldom do "women's" (at least not in front of a stranger, i.e., not a family member). While practice varied, discourse did not:

Women and men were separate species "by nature." On the discursive level it was important to be different. Because of long distances also men spent their leisure with the family, not for example, in a street café or some other public space. Poor and cramped housing accommodation forced women and men to share the private space of the home. Gendered work, home, or leisure locations did not occur until the post–Word War II period in Finland.

Smallness produced intense relations between the state and civil society from its modern creation in the middle of the last century onwards.[8] The nation state was built as "our own" shelter against "foreign" oppression.[9] State, nation, and civil societies were synonymous in practice (Alapuro 1988). Through economic, political, and administrative institutions, already established in the Swedish era before 1808, and by the help of the cultural and ideological social movements of the last century, the state was created as a common arena for political progress and reformist change (Silius 1992).

The participants in the building of this nation-state, whether they were state officials, (political) leaders of popular movements, or intellectuals, formed a circle with close networks between the participants. The state organized the professions and education, both primary ways of social mobility, first for men, later for women. It integrated capital and different interest groups, such as the corporations. Feminist movements in Finland early embraced the idea of education. For decades access to education, professions, and state offices were the main issues of women's campaigns. From a principal goal, education later turned into an important strategy for women trying to improve their position. Thus Finnish women entered higher education gradually, for example, already outnumbering men leaving upper secondary education in the 1930s (Anttalainen 1993). Many professions, especially either those with a female tradition as the health-related ones or the ones which did not have time enough to establish male traditions (e.g., architects), absorbed large numbers of women. Today, for example, 40 percent of the physicians are women (Riska and Wegar 1993).

## THE URBAN, INDIVIDUALISTIC WELFARE STATE CONTRACT

If traditional Finland could be labeled poor and agrarian, modern Finland is often described by its late, rapid, and radical changes (see, e.g., Alestalo 1986; Alestalo and Uusitalo 1986). In the beginning of the 1960s, Finland was still an agrarian, rural, and socially homogenous society. Looking at the economically active population in 1960 confirms this impression, with 36 percent working in agriculture, 31 percent in manufacturing, and 33 percent in the services. To gender the figures gives you a different picture. Almost half of the economically active women already in 1960 worked in the services (46 percent), only a third in agriculture, and a fifth in manufacturing (Kovalainen 1993: 27). For men, agriculture and manufacturing were equally important, both comprising over a third (38 and 38 percent), but with only a fourth of all economically active men in the services. Twenty years later, the tripartite distribution of the economically active population had disappeared completely. In less than two decades, agriculture declined steadily and the proportion of the population engaged in the services grew markedly (Kovalainen 1993). The industrial structure of the late 1980s included, in the case of women, 57 percent in the services, 20 percent in manufacturing, and 8 percent in agriculture. For men the corresponding figures were 42 percent in the services, 45 percent in manufacturing, and 13 percent in agriculture (Kovalainen 1993). The changes in the industrial structure implied urbanization for women and for young families. For men the changes meant industrialization and the substitution of services for agriculture. Urbanization changed the traditional relations between men and women. The unity of the farm with the heterosexual couple—the hardworking, de-erotized partners, working together on the farm and in the home for the survival and prosperity of their family—was split into two separate halves. Both halves still had to be economically active in order to support the family, but they worked in different locations. Women left the home or farmyard for paid work. Mothers continued to work, because Finnish society is still organized in a way which presupposes and rewards dual-earner families. The main reasons for this is high taxation and high living costs, especially housing. The Continental European male breadwinner model never gained any foothold in practice. Many researchers have argued that the (wage) working mother—the mother citizen in the words of Helga Maria Hernes (1987) or the woman worker citizen in Barbara Hobson's (1990)—could be regarded as the main representation of the present-day gender contract of Finland as well as of other Scandinavian countries (Leira 1992; Julkunen 1994a; Rantalaiho 1994). Anneli Anttonen (1994) again compares the discursive status of the Finnish woman wage worker with that of the "hero of labor" in socialist USSR.

## GENDERED WORK PRACTICES

Statistics on women's labor force participation are often poorer than the corresponding ones concerning men. Sometimes women do not report themselves as "economically active"; sometimes the statistics makers do not recognize them. Christine Hakim (1993) calls the rising Western female labor market participation a myth. This applies particularly to all so-called assisting family members (Kovalainen 1993), for example, in agriculture. According to official statistics in Finland, women's labor force participation rose from 57 percent in 1950 to 72 percent in 1985. If agricultural labor—waged or not—is accounted for, Tuovi Allén (1993: 157) argues that about 65 percent of all women of working age have been economically active in Finland since the 1860s. She thus concludes that there has been no remarkable increase in women's participation rates, but instead a transformation of female labor from agriculture to the industrial and service sectors.

In the mid-1980s, 74 percent of Finnish women in working age (20–65) were employed. The figures of the other Nordic countries were almost exactly the same, with the exception of Sweden (Haavio-Mannila and Kauppinen 1992: 235). In Sweden the rates were over 80 percent in this period. If the age group 15–74 is considered, 73 percent of Finnish men and 64 percent of the women participated in the labor force in 1990 (*Finnish Labour Review* 4/1993). Due to the present deep recession, the corresponding figures of 1994[10] were 68 percent for men and 61 percent for women. In the late 1980s, unemployment rates were about 5 percent. Severe unemployment hit the Finnish society in 1992, when the unemployment rate for the first time rose over 10 percent. In 1993 it was about 17 percent and in 1994, 19.5 percent,[11] today the highest in the Nordic countries. The high unemployment of the last two years is gendered. The rates for men are higher than for women (22.1 percent versus 16.7 percent). The rates for women began to rise in the second half of 1992, later than for men. The differences are due to the fact that unemployment first hit the private, manufacturing sector and only afterward the public, service sector.

In the Nordic countries women work part-time more often than men, with the exception of Finland. In 1986 one-third of the women in Denmark, Iceland, Norway, and Sweden had a part-time job, whereas in Finland the proportion was only 12 percent[12] (Haavio-Mannila and Kauppinen 1992). Of mothers with children in preschool age the proportion of part-time workers was still higher in the other Nordic countries, but not in Finland. In 1991, 10 percent of these mothers had a part-time job in Finland, whereas 54 percent of the Swedish ones worked part-time (Julkunen 1994b).

Despite their higher level of education and despite their active participation in working life, women's position in the labor market is far from equal to men's (Anttalainen 1993; Haavio-Mannila and Kauppinen 1992). Women do women's work, men do men's. Gender segregation in the labor market is a fact in all Nordic countries, as well as in other industrialized countries. In Finland eight women out of ten work in industries where the majority of all employees are women, and similarly, eight men out of ten work in male-dominated trades. Only 6–7 percent of all employees have experience of jobs where both genders are about equally represented (Anttalainen 1993). In the 1980s, about half of all employed women in Finland, Norway, and Sweden worked in totally female-dominated occupations (Haavio-Mannila and Kauppinen 1992). Among the Nordic countries, the horizontal segregation by gender in Denmark was less sharp: The corresponding figure for Denmark was less than a third. The segregation of the Finnish labor market has remained stable for decades (Anttalainen 1986). Education supports and consolidates the segregation. The educational choices are gendered: Girls choose services and care, boys go for technical vocations. This division has also remained stable for already four decades and is clearest at the lowest levels of the educational scale (Anttalainen 1993).

Women (four out of ten) in Finland work more often in the public sector than men (two out of ten). Most of these women are employed by local government, most men being in state government service. About two-thirds of the local government employees are women. The explanation is that municipalities in Finland are largely responsible for health care, social work, and education. Gendered labor markets seem to correlate in a very specific way with labor market participation, unemployment, and part-time work (Allèn 1993). Hence the higher the labor force participation, the lower the female unemployment rate, and the higher the rate of part-time work of female employment, the higher the rate of segregation.

Women in Finland are usually less paid than men for their work. On an average Finnish women earn 20 percent less than their male colleagues. Finns are, according to Marja-Liisa Anttalainen (1993), only too familiar with the phrase "for a woman, she has a good salary." The while collar labor market is distinctly divided like the labor market into two separate spheres. This is not due to any difference in level of unionization: some 80 percent of both women and men belong to trade unions. Education has not had any impact on the wage gap; rather it has widened it (Anttalainen 1993). Neither does working experience improve women's wages; rather the gap widens with increasing experience (Keinänen 1990). A characteristic of Finnish salary markets is that seven women out of ten remain below a wage limit which is exceeded by seven out of ten men. Finally, Finnish women's wages, when they are at their best, just reach the level when men's wages only begin to rise in earnest (Anttalainen 1993). Because of the wage gap, married women are more dependent on the income of their husbands, than are men on their wives (66 percent of the women earn less than their husbands, compared to 6 percent of the husbands) (Ilmakunnas 1990; see also Hobson 1990 for a comparison of Sweden and the United States).

## THE WORKING MOTHER

One of the main contributions of Nordic feminist theorizing is the elaboration of the concept of caring (for the earliest discussions, see Sørensen 1982; Ve 1983; Wærness 1984). The originally Norwegian theorizing on caring[13] has enlarged the concept of work, the theorizing of the welfare state and of the gender system. Caring work means to take care of children, the elderly, family, and so on, and to run everyday household tasks (e.g., cooking, washing, cleaning, shopping, transporting). This work includes love, attention, and respect as well as planning, organizing, and performing. It requires emotional, bodily, and intellectual efforts. The concept includes, according to Raija Julkunen and Liisa Rantalaiho (1989), both the basic needs of the body (nutrition, cleanliness, and housing) as well as the human need of social integration. Through caring, the continuity of life itself and everyday needs are guaranteed. Caring work requires simultaneity and a flexible perspective of time (Davies 1989).

In Finnish agrarian society women took their children with them when they worked in the fields or in the cowshed. Or, relatives or neighbors took care of the children while the mothers were working, as was the case for working class women. Finnish mothers entered the paid labor before there existed any organized day-care systems (Julkunen 1994a). When structural changes caused urbanization in the 1960s, leaving the older generation in the countryside while the younger migrated to the cities, day care became a social problem to be solved by public measures. Women, also the mothers of small children, were needed (because of low wages) by private industry and services as well as by the growing public sector. Women themselves wanted work in order to improve the standard of living of their family. However, the day-care act was not introduced until 1973.

Postwar feminism in Finland could be defined as maternalism (Nätkin 1994), aiming at the improvement of the situation of women in the family, without striving to change existing family patterns. Before the most crucial improvement, the introduction of the day-care system, other maternity benefits were implemented after persistent work by women politicians and activists. Since 1938, the unique measure of giving a special package to all women who have given birth is in force. The package includes clothes, linen, and different kinds of equipment needed by a baby. The worth of the package is at least twice the amount of money which is given to those few who do not want the package. To buy the things on the market would cost four times this sum. Comprehensive maternity care started in 1944. To many foreign observers, this system is one of the most developed in the world and encompasses today over 90 percent of pregnant women. Universal child allowance was introduced in 1948. It is paid for all children under 17, regardless of the economic state of the family, and it is not taxed. The child allowance is paid to the mother. Until the recession, families with children got important tax reductions. In addition, single parents are entitled to a special tax benefit. School lunch was also introduced in the 1940s. It means that all children have a hot meal in school.[14] School lunches are of decisive importance for employed women, because they do not have to arrange for the reception of their children at home in the middle of the day. Of similar importance for working mothers are school transports and after-school care, which gradually have been expanded during the last two decades.

Paid maternity leave was introduced in 1963. In the beginning, maternity allowance was paid for 12 weeks (a month before and two after birth). Since the 1970s, the period has gradually been prolonged and today covers a year.[15] Mothers without a previous work history get a basic allowance, for others the allowance is income related. During the leave, the mother remains in the labor force and is guaranteed return to her previous work. Until the child is three years old, one parent has the right to be absent from work on nonpaid care leave without losing his or her job. Since 1990, a home-care allowance is paid to parents with a child under three not using the public day-care system, enabling mothers to stay at home after the one-year-long maternity leave.[16]

The period of the maternity leave has since its introduction also been the practice for the length of stay out of active employment. When the period was 3 months, women stayed at home with the baby for 3 months, when 6 they stayed for 6 months, when 9 for 9 months, and so on. Day care has been offered subsequently for children over the age of the maternity period length. Especially professional women, for example, women lawyers, have returned to work immediately after the leave (Silius 1992). A couple of years ago, the female minister of social affairs was the first cabinet minister to take maternity leave (Eeva Kuuskoski[17]). In 1994, the female minister of justice did the same (Hannele Pokka). Although since 1978 it is possible to share the leave between the parents, and in spite of the progressivity of the allowance according to the income of the parent on leave, giving most men a higher compensation than their wives, very few fathers make use of parental leave. Only 2–3 percent of the Finnish fathers have taken this opportunity (Bergman 1989; Julkunen 1994b). The figures of the other Nordic countries are much higher: Foe example, in Sweden 27 percent of the fathers participated in the Swedish 15-month leave (Haavio-Mannila and Kauppinen 1992). In Norway, campaigns have been run to increase the number of fathers on leave, and "media lions" taking parental leave have influenced the behavior of other Scandinavian men. In Sweden a compulsory "daddy month" was introduced in 1994, strongly supported by the male minister of social affairs (Bengt Westerberg).

Day care for children became statutory for all Finnish municipalities in 1973. In spite of a rapid expansion, the demand exceeded the supply in the 1980s. The excess demand was especially severe in the case of small children. Queues were persistent in larger cities where most women worked outside the home. For these reasons the home-care system was introduced as a complement in 1985, in practice from 1990. The public day-care system is organized and financed by the municipalities with state subsidies. The fees for day care are income related and cover, on average, 14 percent of the total expenditures of the services (Ilmakunnas 1993: 131). Within the system there are day-care centers and publicly controlled family day care. On a national level, centers provide around half of the places, but their share in the cities is much larger. Of the children who take part in day care outside the home, over 90 percent attend the public system (Julkunen 1994b). Standards are set nationally and the quality of public day care, especially the centers, is quite high. Professional women prefer day-care centers for their children (Björnberg 1993; Nyberg 1989; Silius 1992). Some of the reasons to this all-Nordic phenomenon are the high educational standard of the personnel, the high-quality facilities, and the elaborate educational programs for the children. Finnish women are proud of their public day-care system for which they, as part of the feminist wave of the late 1960s, fought for decades before its implementation (Julkunen 1994a).

Contrary to many other Western countries, single mothers do not constitute a social or moral problem in Finland. Of all families with children under 18 years of age, 12 percent were lone mother families, while 1.7 percent were sole father families in 1990.[18] The proportions are slightly higher in the other Nordic countries with 16 percent lone mothers in Denmark and Sweden, 17 percent in Norway, and 19 percent in Iceland. The share of lone fathers count from 1 to 3 percent, being lowest in Iceland and highest in Sweden. Although marriage and cohabitation are equally accepted culturally, legally and as far as social policy is concerned, most Finnish couples marry when the first child is born. However, a third of all marriages end in divorce. Divorced people remarry, forming new modes of families.

After the World War II, many Finnish women lived alone with children. They were either war widows or their husbands were away for work (perhaps in Sweden). At the time, the image of the brave mother citizen was created, for example, in the discourse of population policy (Nätkin 1994). Motherhood per se was sublime and honest. The glorification included in particular lone mothers, struggling through the heavy burdens of postwar reconstruction of the late 1940s and 1950s. Women did not need men to be good mothers—if they worked. Women's since long established right to work—in fact an obligation (Rantalaiho 1994)—applied also to lone mothers. Thus there has never been any discussion of lone mothers staying out of work. Liisa Rantalaiho (1994) states that the Finnish lone mother actually has been a cultural heroine, especially after the war.

In spite of public help with day care for children and extensive services for the elderly, women still do more domestic and caring work than men. Women take the responsibility when children are ill and cannot be taken to day care or when the needs of an elderly is not met by public services. Women arrange occasional systems, often with the help of family or friends. Also among professional women (e.g. the Finnish women lawyers), it is up to the woman to be the head organizer and the one who takes full responsibility for the overall arrangements. Compared to the amount of research on women's formal position, there is relatively little research on the nature of the relations between partners within families. This applies also to the relations in domestic work. In professional families with children, mothers spend about 20 hours a week on domestic work whereas fathers spend a third of this time (Silius 1992). Full-time working mothers in general, on average, spend some 25–30 hours a week on unpaid domestic work, according to Finnish (Niemi and Pääkkönen 1989) and Swedish (Nyberg 1989) surveys. According to Lois Bryson (1994), who has used national data collected in 1987 in Australia and Finland, Australian married working women with children did slightly more unpaid household work than corresponding Finnish women. On the other hand, Australian married working men with children participated slightly less than corresponding Finnish men. Consequently Bryson finds a greater degree of gender parity within families in Finland. An unfair division of domestic labor is obvious, however, also in the Finnish case. Finnish fathers still do just half the amount of unpaid work compared to Finnish partnered mothers. Finnish women's time use was not remarkably different from Australian women's, despite differences in labor force participation and provision of day care. Finnish women's reduced domestic load in comparison to Australia is due far less to changes in men's behavior than to the effects of labor force participation (Bryson 1994), although young fathers share child care more equally with mothers (Brandth and Kvande 1991).

## THE NORDIC WELFARE STATE CONTRACT

The subordinated position of women in Finland as well as in the other Nordic countries has, according to Joan Acker (1989), been hidden by the belief that they are the most democratic countries in the world. This idea has been combined with statistics showing figures of increasing equality on different social fields. The fact that the welfare state relied on undervalued female labor and female responsibility for reproduction remained hidden. According to Acker, the gender compromise, a silent part of the compromise between capital and labor, has resulted in a tacit agreement. Women are entitled to paid work and a certain degree of independence from individual men as long as they not only continue to take responsibility for the care of people, both in the service of the welfare state and in the family, but also accept without complaints a subordinated position in paid work, in politics, and in their private relations to men. Finnish feminist researchers (Julkunen and Rantalaiho 1989) have argued that women of the postwar baby-boom generation were the first female cohort to make a gender agreement with the Finnish state. Experiencing feelings of both guilt and thankfulness for the freedom guaranteed by paid work, these women thought that double work was the price they had to pay for their rights.

The Finnish postwar gender contract was made between women—particularly mothers—and the state. This state was represented by women politicians, women government officials—the so-called state feminists—and women organization activists. Together they developed a welfare state, which for women meant a social service state (Anttonen 1994) or a caring state (Leira 1992). It guaranteed women an "exit out of family." It was enabled by the principles of universality, professionality, and equality,[19] embraced, little by little, by common consent in all Nordic societies by both genders. For men the construction of the welfare state implied a social insurance state which guaranteed an "exit out of work." Earnings-based social security, income transfers, and collective wage arrangements were important elements of the male contract. While women made the tacit agreement with each other, men made theirs publicly through male corporative bodies with male employers and the government (the male state). Women benefited from collective bargaining too. The "solidarity" wage policy, in practice until the late 1980s, guaranteed, for example, the same minimum wage for both women and men. Finnish income transfers—by some commentators said to be among the most effective ones—implied an important means of maintaining social homogeneity. Thus Finland is today, even in the days of the deep recession, a country with extreme low differences between the rich ones and the poor ones. For families, especially lone-mother families, this phenomenon is of vital importance. In sum, the state—male and female—met also women's demands, for example, by introducing day care for children and care of elderly.

The Nordic welfare state model thus includes two different discourses, one of production and another of reproduction. The first one deals with work, economic development, working conditions, wages, solidarity and class. The second one deals with women, care, family, equality, and gender. By keeping these two discourses separate, the dominant rationality, based according to Acker (1989) on efficiency, productivity, and profit, could persist as long as a sufficient amount of resources was allocated to caring. In this way, the legitimacy of the welfare state was maintained. The compromise between labor and capital has been visible, conscious, and organized while the gender compromise has been and continues to be hidden and naturalized.

## THE FINNISH GENDERED CONTRACT

I have argued above that women in Finland made their gender contract with each other. Their main responsibility for caring, heavy workload in the home in spite of full-time work, has left men's role almost unchanged. Women are responsible for equality in the family or between the couple. It is up to women to educate men to be good fathers (Kuronen 1994) and to share parenthood, domestic, and other responsibilities. For Finnish women, the education of husbands is a task with a long history. The traditional contract included a power of prohibition (Gordon 1992) which nowadays is replaced by a power of encouragement and guidance. If the private contract is unequal, then the woman has not been successful. Women's duty to work for equality should be fulfilled in such a way that it is not noticed by men (Haavind 1985). Men's self-esteem or identity should not be shaken. One example of this strategy is that Finnish women should behave in public as if they are not feminists, only in favor of equality. Finnish society however, accepts a sexist culture which is insensitive to, for example, sexist language, commercials, and jokes. Until recently sexual harassment, violence against women, pornography, or prostitution were nonissues. The earlier deerotized woman or female body is today sexualized and erotized. Affirmative action programs are nonexistent and it happens that the equality act is enforced in ways which benefit men in female-dominated workplaces instead of promoting measures aimed at improving the situation of the underprivileged gender.

An important aspect of the present contract between women and men is the transition from the mutual partnership relation where both partners worked for the prosperity of the farm toward a new male-only project. Women join the life projects of their partners. The studies, profession, or career of the man today seem to be the common cause which both partners give the highest priority. Women, partnered or not, at the same time have definitely gained status of individuals. When examining relations between private men and women, this looks as a paradox, but it becomes understandable when keeping in mind the public relations.

The Finnish contemporary contract is still a predominantly heterosexual one. Homosexuality was not decriminalized until the 1970s and the gay movement was long forced to an underground existence.

The emotional well-being of the couple or of the family belongs to women's caring responsibilities. Women also maintain the bonds between generations. In the traditional contract, these bonds were part of everyday life. With often long distances between relatives and because of a more individual- than family-oriented ideology, the bonds are looser in Finland than in many other societies, but they are still important. While this relation was once based on shared work and housing, it is today an emotional, friendship relation. Women keep up contacts with family, including the family of their male partner. Judith Stacey (1990) describes this as the feminization of family. Hence, women maintain continuity and integration and are also the main transmitters of culture and tradition.

Finland as well as of the other Nordic countries are today wealthy societies. From being farmers Finns are now members of the middle class. The Finnish society is homogenous with regard not only to class but also to ethnicity, race, and religion. In sharp contrast to other Nordic countries (e.g., Sweden), very few immigrants or refugees are accepted in Finland. Instead of using immigrant workers, the Finnish society has used women for expanding sectors.

I have assumed above that gender contracts are socially constructed and differ according to time, location, and the concrete conditions of women and men. Leaving the content of a gender contract to be filled empirically in different social contexts implies that the concept has a potential to offer meaningful analyses beyond the Finnish or Nordic context.

## A NEW CONTRACT IN THE NEAR FUTURE?

Today the Nordic welfare state model is exposed to severe attacks (see, e.g., Anttonen 1994; Åström and Hirdman 1992). Its legitimacy is threatened by different male discourses. The cuts in resources will have impact on the possibilities for public caring responsibility in the future. Will this situation of the early 1990s, with recession and almost 20 percent unemployed in Finland, be the end of the present contract? Contradictory tendencies seem to offer several possibilities. In the public debate neoliberal ideologies circulate, calling into question women's right to work and the extension of the welfare state. Some demand more earnings-related social insurance and less universal services. Of common undertakings, health care, social services, and education are however highly valued in Finnish nationwide surveys. Assuming that the worst times are behind us and that the private sector recovers, the public sector will struggle with problems for many years. Because it is financed to a great extent by state borrowing and taxation, future taxation policy will be crucial. The question is whether it will be possible in the future to maintain the internationally high level of taxation, which Finns with few protests have been willing to pay. Can the legitimacy of the state remain if men want less taxes, increased private profit, and income combined with earnings-related social security while women want to keep the universal, tax-financed welfare state, providing basic security and possibilities also for women to realize individual projects? Will the peaceful gender relations turn into conflicts, which, for example, Yvonne Hirdman (1994) foresees? These problems lie behind the greater hesitation among Nordic women than men on joining the European Union. Danish women voted no in the first Danish referendum on the Maastricht treaty (Dahlerup 1992b). Before the Finnish referendum, the no side was eager to focus on women-related questions, for example, women's lower mobility on the labor market, while the arguments of the yes side concentrated on male economic interests. Because of the turnout, a majority in favor of a Finnish yes vote, one might ask whether the Finnish women will be the first ones to have to dismantle the Nordic welfare state, the very basis for their position, or whether they will continue to develop it, like the Danish women who joined the European Community several years ago?

## NOTES

1. The Nordic or Scandinavian countries are Denmark, Finland, Iceland, Norway, and Sweden. I am using the terms Nordic and Scandinavian as synonyms.

2. *Source*: Statistics Finland, *Labour Force Survey,* February 1994.

3. Women were entitled to abortion on medical grounds in 1950 and on social grounds in 1970. Abortion is allowed until the twelfth week of pregnancy. The contraceptive pill was approved in 1961 and contraceptives are freely sold.

4. Gayle Rubin introduced the discussion in 1975.

5. The English translation of Hirdman's originally Swedish terms *jämlikhetskontrakt* and *jämställdhetskontrakt* is problematic. For the first mentioned, the term "equality" seems adequate, but for the second one "equality status" does not reveal the different, intrinsic meaning of the Swedish words. The first concept refers to sameness while the second one refers to equal worth, despite differences. One possibility is to call the last contract "the parity contract."

6. The priority of economic needs over sexual, erotic ones or over the striving for personal services produced a different gender contract than the one described by Carole Pateman (1988), who originally introduced the concept of contract for analysis of gender relations. This is one reason why the term "gender contract" is more suitable to the Finnish (or Scandinavian) context than the term "sexual contract," used by Pateman.

7. Increasing wealth later created possibilities for a tiny part of middle-class women to engage in full-time motherhood. The ideology of the housewife or homemaker was, however, widely spread, especially in the 1950s and 1960s (Julkunen 1994b).

8. This applies also to the other Nordic countries, see, for example, Haavio-Mannila and Kauppinen (1992).

9. During a century before Finnish independence in 1917, "foreign" oppression meant czarist Russian efforts to interfere in the affairs of autonomous Finland.

10. *Source:* Statistics Finland, *Labour Force Survey*, February 1994.

11. *Source*: Statistics Finland, *Labour Force Survey*, February 1994.

12. Part-time job is in Finland defined as less than twenty hours a week, but in the other Nordic countries as less than thirty-five hours a week.

13. For an English language version of the early Norwegian discussion, see Holter 1984.

14. Since the 1970s, school meals are also served in secondary schools and vocational schools. The system covers children up to eighteen years, some even later. From the beginning, school meals were only served in primary schools, up to the age of about twelve.

15. The parental-leave period is today 263 days. Sundays and holidays are excluded from these days. During the leave, the parent who stays at home gets 66 percent of her or his previous salary or, if without a work history, minimum about 300 US$ a month (1 US$ = 5 FIM). Before the recession the compensation rate used to be 80 percent of previous earnings.

16. The homecare allowance is a lump sum, which is not income related. Since its introduction, the homecare allowance has became very popular. Nowadays the majority of mothers with babies choose the homecare allowance instead of public daycare (Ilmakunnas 1993). One reason is unemployment, another low female wages, which make the home-care allowance a reasonable choice. The homecare allowance has reduced the labor force participation of mothers with small children from 71 percent in 1989 to 55 percent in 1991, that is, already before the recession (Julkunen 1994b).

17. Ms. Kuuskoski did not use the whole period. Because of this, there was a debate in the newspapers whether she was a good mother or not.

18. Source: *Yearbook of Nordic Statistics.*

19. Feminist movements in the 1960s were pronounced equality movements in the Nordic countries, particularly in Finland and Sweden. Equality denoted, to a very important extent, equality between social classes and regions (poor rural versus rich urban) and almost as a corollary, gender equality.

# 10

---

# Women in the European Union:
# Equality Achieved?

*Hans C. Blomqvist*

## INTRODUCTION

The European Union (EU)[1] was formed by the members of the European Communities (EC) through the Maastricht Treaty in 1993. From the beginning of that year, the member countries also formed a "single market," with free mobility of people, goods, services, and capital. From an economic point of view the twelve member countries can, to a considerable extent, be regarded as one economy. Despite this the member countries are quite different, for example, as far as their level of economic development and socioeconomic characteristics are concerned. Members of the Union are presently Belgium, Denmark, France, Germany, Greece, Ireland, Italy, Luxembourg, the Netherlands, Portugal, Spain, and the United Kingdom.[2] Additionally, Austria, Finland, and Sweden became members in the beginning of 1995. (This chapter will concentrate on the "old," pre-1995 EU, however.)

During the last few decades the status of women in Europe has improved. The differences in pay have diminished and women have gradually started to achieve senior positions in both the private and the public sector. The expansion of the service sector, which traditionally has provided the largest number of jobs to women, apparently has been conducive to that (*Social Europe* 3/91: 6).

Especially when compared to the situation in most developing countries the position of women in society is strong in continental Europe. In a legal sense there is full equality between the genders. In practice, however, there seems to be a "hidden agenda" that militates against establishing a fully equal position for the women of Europe. Institutional and cultural restrictions tend to limit the possibilities for women to participate fully in the economy and society. Particularly, women's reproductive role has been difficult to combine with activities in the formal productive sector. The economic role of women is still widely understood as one closely related to the family and household sector (cf., e.g., Kessler-Harris 1985). The lower participation rates of women in the paid labor force then automatically leads to an underestimation of their contribution to the national economy (since, e.g., household work is not included in the gross national product). The situation is similar in the political realm. Only one of seventeen EU commissioners was a woman when this chapter was written, in the Council there are few women, none of the judges in the EU Court of Justice is a woman, and so on (*Helsingin Sanomat,* March 5, 1994).

The EU is not a homogeneous region socially, culturally, or economically. The different member countries can be divided roughly into three groups, as far as the position of women is concerned, according to Nieminen (1991: 29): (1) Male-dominated, welfare-oriented states: Germany, France, Belgium, the Netherlands, northern Italy, and Luxembourg; (2) market-driven, patrimonial states: the United Kingdom; and (3) states with values strongly influenced by the church and the rural society: Greece, Spain, southern Italy, and Ireland.[3]

The purpose of this chapter is to provide a survey of gender equality in the EU, predominantly from an economic point of view. The chapter concentrates on identifying the issues rather than explaining why inequality occurs, although some discussion on the latter issue is included. Even if the situations in the different member countries differ, it is also important to scrutinize the EU as a whole, partly because the Union has an agenda of equality of its own and partly because it may be assumed that the sheer existence of the Union tends to promote convergence between the different countries in the long run. It should be stressed that "equality" in the context of the EU means specifically equality at work (Nieminen 1991: 169). Family politics is not considered to be of concern to the Union.

## THE EU AND EQUALITY

Even a superficial look at the relevant equality problems in continental Europe suggests that possible problems are not primarily due to deficient legislation. On the contrary, the EC has done much to enhance equality through formal channels. The problems rather seem to be related to the "hidden agenda" concerning socially accepted behavior of men and women. Especially the dual commitment to both traditional family obligations and the demands of the labor market is a major problem when gender equality is concerned. Participation in the paid labor force is seldom chosen at the expense of household duties. Instead work outside home is in excess of household chores, in which men everywhere seem to participate to an insignificant extent (cf., e.g., Nieva 1985; Vianello et al. 1990: 86). Hence, there is a limit to what can be done with the aid of legislation. Without equality within the family it is not possible to achieve equality in public life either (cf. Vianello et al. 1990: 75). Nevertheless, an explicit legal framework may contribute to providing instruments for achieving improvements for women in their activities in economy and society.

Even if the general principle of "same pay for same work" is included in the basic foundation of the Union, the Rome treaty (1957, article 119), it was not until the 1970s that the EC started to work more actively on the issue. The International Women's Year proclaimed by the U.N.in 1975 was also conducive to promoting equality at work in Europe (Utrikesdepartementet 1993: 9–10).

After 1975 the EC has issued five directives concerning equality. Moreover, two other directives have a bearing on women in the labor market and more of the same is on its way through the legislation process (cf. *Social Europe* 1991: 13). Additionally, there are several recommendations and other statements by the Council of the European Communities relevant for this issue. Under the European Commission there is a special department for equality issues, the Equal Opportunities Unit. In addition to this there are several committees and networks for dealing with equality issues. The most important of the committees is the Advisory Committee on Equal Opportunities for Women and Men. Finally, the European Parliament has a committee on women's rights (Utrikesdepartementet 1993: 15; Ministry of Social Affairs 1991: 7).

The EU commission has passed three action programs for gender equality, the latest of which concerns the period 1991–1995 (the program is presented in detail in *Social Europe* 1991). The emphasis of this program is on development of legislation on equality issues to improve the position of women in the labor market and increase the influence of women in the decision-making bodies of the Union. Also entrepreneurship of women is emphasized (Utrikesdepartementet 1993: 10; Moring 1994). A European Women's Lobby (EWL) was set up in 1990 (*Social Europe* 1991: 6, 107).

The five specific equality directives are:

the directive on equal pay for men and women (1975) (75/117/EEC);

the directive on equal treatment, concerning equal treatment of women and men as regards access to employment, vocational training, and promotion and working conditions (1976) (76/207/EEC);

the directive on the principle of equal treatment for men and women in matters of social security (1978) (79/7/EEC);

the directive on the implementation of the principle of equal treatment in occupational social security schemes (1986) (86/378/EEC);

the directive on the application of the principle of equal treatment between men and women engaged in an activity, including agriculture, in a self-employed capacity, and on the protection of self-employed women during pregnancy and motherhood (86/613/EEC).

In this context it must be emphasized that not only a social issue like equality is hard to promote by means of legislation, but it may also be the case that legislation not intended to have a bearing on equality still has such side effects. Legislation on social matters often conceives the family, not the individual, as the relevant unit. Tax laws are a case in point, for example, whether a married couple is taxed separately or not, and whether there are deductions for the spouse earning less (cf. Nieminen 1991: 15, 161). In some cases unemployment benefits for married women are smaller than for men. Still more important are legislation regulating other social issues, such as availability of public child-care facilities, regulations concerning maternal (or parental) leave, and so on. All these factors are decided predominantly at the national level (even if the formation of the single market and the EU are likely to exert pressure toward convergence).

The experience from implementation of the EC equality regulations are rather diverse in the different member countries. In the United Kingdom, Ireland, and the Netherlands the impact has been considerable, as the attitudes toward these rules seem to have been more serious there than in other countries. In other countries, such as Germany, the attitude has been more patronizing, in both official and unofficial contexts (Nieminen 1991: 182). The difficulties with interpreting changes that can be observed in the light of EC rules is, however, that a straightforward causal relation cannot be assumed. For instance, the same ideas pertaining to the policy of the EC would probably have made themselves visible anyway.

## WOMEN IN THE LABOR MARKET

Participation in the organized labor market is often regarded as the most important means for women to improve their socioeconomic status (Moghadam 1990: 13, 19). In the EU women comprise about 40 percent of the paid workforce and the figure has been on the increase over time (Nieminen 1991: 11). The age profile of the participation rate of women typically shows two peaks. The first one occurs between twenty and twenty-four years of age and the second one after 35 (Bruyn-Hundt 1992). (The rate drops during the years when many women concentrate on taking care of young children.)

Even if the judgment of the importance of paid work for the status of women is arguably most relevant in the context of developing countries, the issue is also at the forefront when the equality issue is discussed in developed countries, such as the EU. Nevertheless, for women with access to the formal labor market there are two main problems as regards equality. On the one hand, women earn consistently less than men and, on the other hand, women are concentrated in certain industries and occupations where they are a majority of the employees. Furthermore, women tend to work part-time with little social security much more frequently than men. A study from the mid-1980s indicates that women occupied 90 percent of the part-time jobs in Europe (Landau 1985).

In Europe women are much more independent than in many developing countries in the sense that there is no obstacle for them to own productive assets or take on a job. The extent to which they can make use of this legal equality is closely related to the existence of a service infrastructure, typically provided by the public sector, for taking care of children. It should also be emphasized in this context that the idea of a woman as an independent economic subject, engaged in activities outside the household realm, is quite new in Europe. A wife needed her husband's permission to have a job, in France until 1965 and in (Western) Germany until 1977 (Julkunen 1993).

A major factor behind the subjugation of women in the workplace obviously has to do with their perceived role as homemakers. This assumed role seems to be perceived very similarly all over the world and is a reflection of women's position within the family. Nonmarket production is not counted as part of the gross national product, although nobody denies that it is productive work, too. Thus, the economic contribution of women tends to be undervalued, if only for this reason. At the same time the perceived role of women as homemakers weakens their position in the organized labor market.

Hence, participation in the formal labor market is a necessary but not sufficient condition for equality (cf. Moghadam 1990: 30). Cyclical and also more long run economic considerations have been decisive for the attitudes to women's work in Europe. One important reason for the successful work aiming at gender equality is the aging work force and increasing dependency burden characteristic of Europe; women have been considered a useful reserve pool of labor. On the other hand, this attitude undergoes cyclical variations. In the case of Europe recent sluggish economic growth and high rates of unemployment brings with them a new pressure on women to withdraw from the formal labor market. Hence, the idea of women as a reserve in the labor market has been very strong, more or less consciously.

Women are allegedly disadvantaged through three different mechanisms in the labor market. First, "pure" discrimination (less pay for the same work) may cause earnings of women to be lower than those of men. Second, women tend to concentrate in specific (low-pay) occupations, or industries, where the relative share of women tends to be very high (nurses, primary school teachers, shop assistants, seamstresses, etc.). The ultimate reason for this can probably be found in social attitudes on what is acceptable or "suitable" for women and can be found in the attitudes of women as well as men.[4] Third, the prospect for promotion in any occupation is not as good as it is for men (the "glass ceiling"). (A succinct summary of economic theories of discrimination, comprising all three problems mentioned above, is given in, for example, Lundahl and Wadensjö (1984, Ch. 2).) In continental Europe, the first problem is taken care of, by and large, while the other ones are much more difficult to attack. One way of understanding segregation is in terms of division of labor and "comparative advantage" (women do what they do because they are relatively better at those activities than men are). A full explanation would need some theory for how these comparative advantages have emerged, however (cf. Lundahl and Persson-Tanimura 1983: 7–8). As mentioned already, much of the perceived difference seems to be founded on assumptions and attitudes that are well nigh impossible to falsify. Empirical research has indicated, for instance, that women are regarded as less desirable in a (male-dominated) workplace because "they are too much absent," "they displace men," "they are temperamental," and so on (see Phadnis and Malani 1978). (The similarity to common attitudes toward immigrants in Europe is hardly a coincidence!)

So far the participation rate of women in the labor force has been on the increase in all member countries during the last decades. The level of this participation differs widely between the different countries though. In Spain the participation rate of women increased from 20 to 42 percent between 1980 and 1990. In France, corresponding figures were 34 and 56 percent, and in the United Kingdom, 36 and 64 percent. In the case of Denmark, the participation rate increased from 45 to 78 percent. As a comparison, the figures for Sweden—a country with traditionally high participation rates for women—may be of interest: 65 and 83 percent in 1980 and 1990 (Utrikesdepartementet 1993: 29). Mothers of young children naturally had a much lower activity rate. For instance, in the Netherlands 32 percent of women with children under ten worked outside home; for Germany, Britain, and France the corresponding figure was 38 percent, 46 percent, and 56 percent, respectively. (It may be mentioned, for comparison, that 87 percent of women in Sweden and 78 percent of women in Finland with children under school-age (seven) worked outside the home (Julkunen 1993).)[5]

Against a historical backdrop the rate of unemployment in the EU has been very high during the last few years. The reasons for this are both cyclical and structural. In the case of unemployment among women the difficult situation in the textile and garment industries is a major reason. In early 1993 the overall rate of unemployment was 10.2 percent. Among men the figure was 8.9 percent and among women 12.1 percent. Among young women (under twenty-five) unemployment is much higher, 20.4. percent. The differences between different countries are large, however. In Spain, the rate of unemployment for women was as high as 27.4 percent (41.3 percent for youths) while in Germany only 5.8 percent of all women and 4.4 percent of young women were unemployed.

Women comprise more than half of all unemployed individuals in the EU (Utrikesdepartementet 1993: 29). It is also significant to note that 55 percent of the long-term unemployed are women. The differences between different member countries are great, however (see Statistical Office of the European Communities 1992: 110–111). Hidden unemployment, although rather difficult to measure, is likely to be much more prevalent among women. One factor that evidently contributes to higher unemployment rates for women is the tendency for women to be less geographically mobile than men. Frequently the wife and children stay put when the husband moves on for work. Even when the family moves as a whole, it is usually the work opportunities for the husband that count (Nieminen 1991: 224; Ministry of Social Affairs 1991: 22). Women rather tend to avoid jobs that require relocation (Markham 1987).

The women in Europe work part-time to a great extent. While this no doubt corresponds in many cases to the preferences for flexible work hours of women with young children, it may also be taken as a symptom of the "hidden" factors pertaining to a less than equal situation of women in working life and in society at large. In practice, part-time work is a major reason for "structural" discrimination against women, since part-time workers are almost always women. This de facto discrimination takes place especially when rules on redundancy and social rights are inferior to those prevalent in "normal" full-time employment, as in some seasonal jobs and part-time jobs involving a small number of hours per week. The rules differ widely between different countries (cf., e.g., Nieminen 1991: 149–152,

Sundström 1992). Similarly, part-time work is a major cause of the "feminization of poverty," especially combined with the fact that single mothers have become more and more common (cf. Allén 1992). There are also results that indicate that the return on human capital is lower in part-time than in full-time work (Ermisch and Wright 1992).

In the late 1980s slightly less than a third of all working women in the EC worked part-time. The average is not very informative, however, since the variation between countries is large, perhaps more because legislation and other regulations can make part-time work more or less attractive than because of different attitudes. Part-time work is much more common in the northern part of the EU. In the Netherlands 58 percent of women worked part-time in 1989, in the United Kingdom 44 percent, in Denmark 41 percent, and in (Western) Germany 30 percent. The figures are much lower in southern Europe: 7 percent in Greece, 8 percent in Portugal, 10 percent in Italy, and 11 percent in Spain. The share of part-time workers has been on the increase in all member countries, except Denmark and Greece (Utrikesdepartementet 1993: 31).

As mentioned already, the majority of working women tend to be found in certain well-defined sectors of the economy. The situation in the EU is no exception. Women are strongly overrepresented in the service sector. As a matter of fact, about three-fourths of the working women are in that sector and the percentage has been increasing since the mid-1960s (Equal Opportunities for Women and Men 1991: 25). (The increase in the participation rates of women throughout the EC is reflected in a strong increase of the service sector's share of GDP.) Particularly the health care, distribution, banking and insurance, and (primary) education sectors are strongly dominated by women. The women can be found predominantly in the low-skilled echelons even here, however. Many of the jobs women typically hold are in the public sector (teachers, nurses, social workers, etc.). As noted by, for example, Allén (1992), the typical jobs for women tend to be extensions of the traditional woman's role at home (see also Vianello et al. 1990: 122–123; Jonung 1983: 56). (As a matter of fact, home working is presently on the increase as a form of paid employment, especially in the form of "teleworking." This is also a typically "female" line of work, often with unclear social benefits.)

Segregation in the labor market tends to circumvent formalized rules for equal treatment, making comparisons between the treatment of men and women difficult. Hence, segregation is a major reason for observed discrepancies between "theory" (legislation) and practice. In some instances, however, segregated labor markets may even have offered some advantages to woman workers. Especially public-sector employees, who are often women, benefit from the fact that this sector is less cyclically sensitive than the industrial sector.

Wage differences between men and women in the EU are still large in spite of the agreements and directives mentioned earlier. In most countries the difference has been more or less unchanged or decreased during the last decades, but there are several exceptions from that rule. In manufacturing, the difference is largest in Luxembourg, where the female worker earns only 65 percent of the wages of the

**Table 10.1**
**Women's Pay in Percent of Men's Pay,**
**Hourly Earnings in Manufacturing, 1990**

| | |
|---|---|
| Denmark | 85 |
| Italy | 83 |
| France | 81 |
| Belgium | 76 |
| Greece | 76 |
| The Netherlands | 75 |
| Germany | 73 |
| Spain | 72 |
| Portugal | 72 |
| United Kingdom | 68 |
| Ireland | 68 |
| Luxemberg | 65 |

*Source:* Jokelin (1994).

male worker. In the United Kingdom and Portugal a woman on average earns 68 and 72 percent of what a man earns. The smallest differences are found in Denmark (85 percent) and France (81 percent). See Table 10.1 for full information.

The problems of relatively low pay and of segregation have been attacked—with rather limited success—by developing methods for the valuation of work, aiming at the principle of "same pay for work of the same value" and, with so-called affirmative action, "discrimination" in favor of women in order to break up established gender patterns. This has not gone without questioning, however. It used to be taken as self-evident that women should try to conquer positions traditionally held by men. This old "truth" has recently been challenged in the sense that men's work and a male type of behavior should not automatically be taken as a model for what women should strive for. Instead, crossing occupational border lines by members of both sexes should be natural (cf. Forbes 1993: xxiv).

There seems to be some gender bias in the way the value of work is determined, although the criteria for this are very seldom mentioned explicitly. Straightforward comparisons between the "value" of different work are of course extremely difficult to make. It seems, however, as if the physical strain involved in a job is a major determinant of pay. Mental strain seems less "important" as are characteristics typically conceived of as "female," such as dexterity. In other words, such skills are regarded as "natural," not as occupational skills (Nieminen 1991: 39).

What then is the price paid for the lack of de facto equality in the labor market? For one thing, and as is well known, society does not utilize its economic potential fully as 50 percent of the potential labor force is met with different restrictions as to what they are allowed to do in the labor market (even if it could be maintained that some of the segregation in fact reflects the "comparative advantage" of women and men). A less obvious result is that women evidently do things differently as compared to men. There are, for instance, quite a few studies on the management styles of women. It turns out that the allegedly reconciling and "human-oriented" style of women is visible in their capacity as leaders as well (cf. Ohlin 1976).

All in all, the problems women encounter in the labor market significantly contribute to give women stronger relative incentives to stay at home, as compared to men. While the diversion of part of the potential workforce to household work may reflect the valuation of that work by society, it does not explain why women are supposed to have a "comparative advantage" in household chores. The only possible explanation for the lack of male "housewives" appears to be a social preference for women in that type of work.

## EQUALITY AS A SOCIAL ISSUE

As mentioned before, a condition for women to be able to participate fully in social and economic life is the existence of a certain social infrastructure providing facilities for child care. Recently the falling nativity figures in the Union's member countries have caused concern and discussion, related as they are to women's participation in the workforce. The importance of establishing institutions facilitating participation in working life without sacrificing the well-being of the family has repeatedly been emphasized. The "social dimension" of the Union is rather narrowly defined, however, and is related closely to labor market issues (see, e.g., Ministry of Social Affairs 1991: 50).

In the so-called social protocol (which is part of the Maastricht Treaty) guidelines for cooperation in the social domain are envisaged. The idea is not to replace national policies, but rather to complement them and establish certain minimum levels of social conditions. On the other hand, the protocol does not give the Union competence to harmonize the member countries' social policy (Utrikesdepartementet 1993: 24–26).

Regulations primarily passed for the sake of health and safety may sometimes function as an obstacle to participation of women in the labor market. While special protection of, for example, pregnant women is perfectly commendable, a de facto consequence may be discrimination, especially if a rule concerns all women. Working night shift has traditionally been prohibited for women in many countries. Work in mines and underground is also frequently prohibited for women. According to the EC's second program for equality, only regulations absolutely necessary for protecting the health of women should be allowed to remain in national legislation. One reason for the pervasiveness of this type of rule is, in fact, the support they have had from the trade unions (which allegedly have aimed at gradually widening their coverage to all workers) (Utrikesdepartementet 1993: 31–32; Nieminen 1991: 164, 168; see also Kessler-Harris 1985). Finally, it should be noted that some social legislation intended to improve the position of women, such as the right to maternal leave, may in fact make it worse, as employers sometimes tend to avoid hiring young women who are likely to use that right. Even when this is not the case, long maternal and child-care leaves tend to decrease the earning power of women, as their occupational skills grow obsolete (cf. Allén 1992).

Public day care seems to extend to quite a large percentage of the children in the member countries. For children between three and six years of age about 60 percent of all children are in public child care (whether full-time or not is not clear, however). Belgium, Denmark, France, and Italy all display figures between 80 and 100 percent, while Portugal and the United Kingdom both are below the 40 percent level. For very young children, under three years of age, the situation is rather different. In Denmark the figure is about 50 percent (in 1988) and in Belgium and France about 20 percent. For all the other member countries the enrollment rate is close to zero (Statistical Office of the European Communities 1992).

In many parts of the world, poverty appears to strike women to a greater extent than men (Allén 1992; Paterson 1987). Lately this seems to have been the case in the EC as well. Women-headed households are a case in point here. This phenomenon is partly due to the decreasing importance of the nuclear family as a social institution. As single mothers become more common, for example, many women need to work but may not be able to do so due to the lack of child-care facilities. Often they have to resort to part-time work which is poorly paid and inferior also as regards social security (cf. Nieminen 1991: 220). Even without the part-time problem women's pay is so much lower that more full-time participation in the labor market would not change the general picture of inequality. It has been estimated, however, that the number of poor families in the United States would decrease by about 50 percent if women were paid equally for equal work (Allén 1992). In the case of Europe, this effect would probably be smaller, although there is no doubt about its direction.

## THE CASE FOR INVESTING IN WOMEN

At a general level, women are seen as contributing to the welfare of a country in two ways. First, they add to production, besides in the formal, paid sector, also as the principal providers of unpaid household work effort. Second, women are in a key position as far as family well-being in general is concerned.

In both cases education is a crucial determinant for how great the contribution of women can be (see Moghadam 1993: 17). On the other hand, education seems to be only a necessary, not a sufficient, condition in this context. Women seem to prefer traditional "female" lines of study which may have a bearing on their later status on the labor market. It is not quite clear what is the reason for such preferences. If the choice of education is the outcome of rational decision making, it would appear unwarranted to raise objections. However, the preferences may reflect a situation where women are more discriminated against in some sectors than in others (cf. Lundahl and Persson-Tanimura 1983: 10–11).

The action programs of the Union, mentioned earlier, have to a great extent been geared to improving the level of education. Here again it is the perceived need

**Table 10.2**
**Women's Share of University Students per Field of Study, 1984, percent**

|             | B  | DK | D  | GR | E  | F  | IRL | I  | L  | NL | P  | UK |
|-------------|----|----|----|----|----|----|-----|----|----|----|----|----|
| Arts/human  | 58 | 64 | 60 | 74 | 69 | 67 | 57  | 78 | 61 | 54 | 71 | 61 |
| Medicine    | 68 | 77 | 64 | 52 | 58 | 47 | 45  | 39 | 44 | 37 | 65 | 51 |
| Law         | 43 | 45 | 37 | 56 | 44 | 52 | 41  | 46 | 38 | 40 | 42 | 40 |
| Business    | 48 | 20 | 38 | 41 | 40 | 60 | 38  | 28 | 0  | 20 | 0  | 31 |
| Engineering | 12 | 9  | 6  | 16 | 9  | 16 | 8   | 6  | 3  | 8  | 17 | 4  |

*Source:* Statistical Office of the European Communities, 1992: 61.

for more well-trained labor that is the driving force behind the quest for investing in women's education (cf. Moring 1994). Women appear to be disadvantaged as far as on-the-job training is concerned, however (cf. Allén 1992). This may be due partly to the larger share of women in part-time work but also to a perception on the part of the employers that women are a less stable part of the labor force and, hence, not worthwhile to invest in. Long breaks in working life due to, for example, maternal leaves contribute to this perception.

In Europe the educational level of women is frequently as high, or higher, than that of men. In many fields of study women have been a majority for quite a while already. Table 10.2 illustrates this issue. (See also, e.g., the figures on enrollment in secondary education by females and males, respectively, *World Development Report* 1991.) Engineering is a very male-dominated field everywhere, while the largest variation across countries can be found among business students where women's share varies from zero to nearly 50 percent. In the other fields, the women's share is usually larger, and in the arts, frequently perceived as a typically "female" field of study, the women dominate heavily in all member countries. It must be noted, however, that the figures may be somewhat misleading, in the sense that women often follow shorter courses than men (Statistical Office of the European Commmunities 1992: 61). In the third action program for equality the position of girls at school is specifically stressed. The aim is to encourage girls to take male-dominated courses, such as engineering and sciences (Moring 1994). Considering that 43 percent of industrial firms in Europe, according to a recent survey, regard a shortage of skilled labor as a major obstacle to recruitment (*Social Europe* 1991: 9), it becomes still more obvious that the development of occupational skills is a key to further progress of women in the EU (as it is elsewhere).

Despite their high average level of education, women are predominantly employed in low-wage jobs. As stressed in one of the EC's official equality programs, introduction of new technology brings with it opportunities for training women workers. If the women get a fair share of knowledge on new technology, potential future equality will be enhanced.

## POLITICAL LEVERAGE OF WOMEN IN EUROPE

The role of women in politics has been researched from several points of view. In general, women have been shown to be less interested in politics than men, although the differences seem to have diminished during the last few decades. The largest differences appear in southern Europe where the gap between genders is the largest in many other respects as well (Mossuz-Lavau 1991: 2–3, 6). The difference between men and women tends—with a few exceptions—to diminish as the level of education increases. Similarly, participation in the workforce seems to increase the interest of women in politics (Mossuz-Lavau 1991: 13–15). Family duties do not seem to be a major obstacle to participation in politics any longer (Vianello et al. 1990: 209).

It has been suggested (cf., e.g., Allén 1988; Ramstedt-Silén 1988) that female politicians tend to emphasize somewhat different issues than their male counter-parts. According to some observers, a kind of transfer of "parental" duties has taken place in the case of women decision makers. Instead of taking care of basic services at home, such as education, health care, and so on, women often seem to concentrate on the same type of issues within a "public family" (Ohlin 1976). (This is of course a parallel to the tendency of women to choose occupations close to the "family sphere.")

Against the backdrop just described, it is interesting and significant that women's influence in the realm of politics is rather limited. Women's participation in politics is, in fact, clearly less active than the participation of men, at least when activity is judged from the share of women in parliament and other elected public assemblies. (Their real influence is probably still less, considering that most decisions actually are made within a very small group of key actors.)

In the EU not even the "top" country, Denmark, has more women than 33 percent as members of Parliament. The corresponding share in Germany is 20 percent, in the Netherlands 29 percent, and in Spain 16 percent. At the low end we find Greece, 5 percent; France, 6 percent; and Italy, 8 percent (Jokelin 1994). (This must mean, of course, that women frequently vote for men.) As a matter of fact, women's advancement to key positions in public decision making has often been less successful than their performance in the labor market (cf. Ramstedt-Silén 1988).

Looking at the European parliament, the share of women, after the election in 1989, is roughly 20 percent (Utrikesdepartementet 1993: 37). Still, the parliament has a larger share of women than the member countries' national parliaments have, on average. It should be stressed, however, that the power of the parliament is rather limited, even if it was strengthened somewhat by the Maastricht Treaty. In the Commission, where the real power generally is thought to be, there have been very few women over the years, and no woman has ever been a member of the European Court of Justice (see, e.g., Ministry of Social Affairs 1991: 9). Among the staff of the Union (most of whom work for the Commission) the proportions are close to fifty-fifty, but the women typically occupy the lower echelons even if equal opportunity is official policy of the Union (Utrikesdepartementet 1993: 37; *Social Europe* 1991: 59). The lower degree of participation in politics by women has proved difficult to explain. However, there are some results which indicate that a kind of inferiority complex may be at work here; women seem to have internalized the general image conveyed by the media that women are passive in matters political (Vianello et al. 1990: 210). In any case, it may still be premature to draw strong conclusions. The male "power monopoly" and informal networks in politics may be too strong for many women to overcome, even if they are interested in a career as politician and even if they do not suffer from any inferiority complex.

## CONCLUSIONS

The impressions from a study of the situation of women in the EU are mixed. On the one hand, equality issues have been taken seriously in the Union as well as in its member countries. A common conclusion by researchers is that the equality policy of the EC has been quite successful, even exceeded expectations (Nieminen 1991: 181). At the individual level the rights of women are well protected in a formal sense. On the other hand, the European countries, as indeed most (all?) other countries, have not been able to eliminate the structural characteristics pertaining to inequality, such as the tendency to segregated labor markets. For most women the work done for enhancing equality has not had a very visible effect, which demonstrates the difficulty in correcting the gender bias by means of formalized decision making. Another problem is that the action programs and other measures have not been followed up very actively.

Part of the remaining problem is certainly the fact that such "structural" discrimination may be difficult to detect—as any specific individual "victims" are hard to point out—and even more difficult to eliminate through legislation. It should also be stressed that there is a dynamic dimension in the discussions on equality: The level of demand for equality tends to increase over time and conditions considered satisfactory some years ago may not be satisfactory today. All in all, there may not be very much more that can be done within the present directives and other EU rules. Whether very much more can be done at all by means of legislation is a matter that can be discussed.

## NOTES

1. The term European Community will be used for discussions on earlier events, as the Union proper was established only in November, 1993.

2. The following abbreviations are used below: B, DK, D, GR, E, F, IRL, I, L, NL, P, UK for Belgium, Denmark, Germany, Greece, Spain, France, Ireland, Italy, Luxembourg, the Netherlands, Portugal, and the United Kingdom, respectively.

3. Portugal is not included in Nieminen's list, but the country clearly belongs to the third group.

4. An empirical study of attitudes toward the position of men and women in society, public life, professional careers and obligations to the family is presented in Vianello et al. 1990. As it turns out, the attitudes of men and women are quite similar, contrary perhaps to popular belief.

5. The figures on participation rates are often misleading due to how optional maternal leaves are counted in the data (Julkunen 1993).

# 11

## The Status of American Women: Modernity, Material Progress, But Suffering from an "Individualistic" Culture

*Cal Clark and Janet Clark*

### INTRODUCTION

There are several reasons to believe that the status of women in the United States should be comparatively high. The country has an advanced industrial economy and a system of compulsory mass education that has little gender differentiation. Women are increasingly active in both labor markets and politics; and for the last several decades an activist women's movement has championed women's rights. Thus, many (if not most) women should enjoy material well being and a status that is far less secondary compared to men than exists in poor agricultural societies and developing industrial nations. Furthermore, they should face much less pressure from the dominant culture for socialization into subordinated gender roles.

To some and perhaps a considerable extent, this optimistic picture is justified. Many women enjoy a material standard of living and equalitarian gender status that would be inconceivable to most women around the globe, particularly in the Third World. Yet, problems remain; and, in fact, modernity creates new role conflicts and stress for many women. Patriarchal values have certainly not vanished in America; entrance into the job market liberates women from the bondage of a primary household but burdens them far more than men as housework and child rearing become the "second shift," and the decaying American family has unfortunately produced the "feminization of poverty." In addition, America's highly individualistic political culture exacerbates these stresses of modernity by limiting the "social welfare net" available in most other advanced industrial societies.

## THE AMERICAN POLITICAL ECONOMY AND PROBLEMS
## FOR WOMEN'S STATUS

The United States has had an extremely 'dynamic economy for much of the last 150 years and clearly dominated the international economy during the post–World War II era. Some of the factors that have contributed to this success include a continental expanse with abundant natural resources, by far the first system of mass education that gave America a tremendous advantage in human capital for several generations, a highly individualistic culture that stimulated entrepreneurship and social mobility, leadership in the development of mass production techniques, and government policies favorable to business.

By the 1970s, however, this model of political economy was showing signs of unraveling. In terms of external economic forces, the normal workings of the international product cycle was pricing America out of many basic industries, which exacerbated growing inconsistencies among the elements that had interacted so well in the past. America was being forced into greater concentration on high-tech industries for which the "mass production" approach was inappropriate; America's hyperindividualism undermined universal education and was used to justify growing inequality; the United States abjured the social welfare systems developed in other advanced industrial societies; and the relations between business and government increasingly moved toward legalistic stalemate. Consequently, by the early 1990s the United States appeared to be suffering from an unfortunate combination of decreasing economic dynamism and increasing social stress (Reich 1991; Thurow 1992).

The implications of this political economy for the status of women have been mixed. Initially, the combination of the individualistic political culture and availability of mass education very probably enhanced women's status by minimizing, at least compared to other countries, the constraints of patriarchal norms. During the late nineteenth and early twentieth centuries, the rapid expansion of first industrial and then white collar/clerical employment provided important avenues for social mobility, and the broad-scale movement of married women into the labor force that began in the 1970s produced a substantial decrease in employment discrimination against women. These effects have not been entirely positive, though, and on balance women may now be suffering from the nature of the U.S. political economy. For example, gender segregation in the workplace remains that is generally disadvantageous to women. More broadly and probably more seriously, the lack of social protection and the burgeoning breakdown of social ties have made women more vulnerable to the vagaries of market phenomena.

The somewhat problematic status of women in America is suggested by the data in Table 11.1 comparing health outcomes for American women to those in other OECD nations.

Since these social conditions are correlated with wealth even among these advanced industrial societies (note the $r$'s in the explanatory note in the table), the U.S. score or rate for each of these five items was compared with that predicted for

**Table 11.1**

**Status of U.S. Woman Compared to OECD Nations, 1989**

| | US Rate | Rate for US Predicted from GNP per capita* | Residual Rank Among OECD Nations |
|---|---|---|---|
| Infant Mortality per 1,000 births | 10 | 7 | 22 of 22 |
| % Low-Weight Babies | 7% | 5% | 21 of 21 |
| Female Life Expectancy (Yrs) | 79 | 80 | 18 of 22 |

* Computed from regressions using the log of GNP per capita in 1989 to explain infant mortality ($r = -.43$), percent low-weight babies ($r = -.18$), and women's life expectancy ($r = .55$) for the 22 OECD countries included in the 1991 World Bank tables.

*Source: World Development Report, 1991:* 205, 259, 267.

a country with its level of affluence by a bivariate regression using GNP per capita. These results provide strong empirical confirmation for the supposition that American women fare fairly poorly compared to other OECD societies. America rates last on infant mortality and percentage of low-weight babies and almost as badly on female life expectancy. While the absolute difference between the actual and predicted rates are fairly small, the consistently lagging position of the United States on these key indicators of women's status certainly indicates that women in America face greater problems than those in comparable societies (Collins et al. 1994).

The reasons for this emerge from a comparison of men and women in the United States. Unlike most Third World nations, American women clearly have the educational foundation to challenge patriarchal norms intellectually and to assert their independence economically, as illustrated by the data in Table 11.2. Ninety percent of both women and men have at least some school beyond the primary level, and while men are almost a third more likely to have a college degree (24.5 percent versus 19 percent), the overall distribution of educational achievement is relatively similar between the two sexes.

Relative gender equality in education, however, has certainly not been translated into equality in the economic marketplace, even today. This is especially important because moving to employment outside the home is almost universally considered to be a key step in achieving women's emancipation (Goldin 1990). Before World War II, married women were fairly unlikely to enter the paid labor force, which kept the overall labor participation rates for women fairly low in the 20–25 percent range (see Table 11.3). After World War II, in contrast, married women began to work in much larger numbers—their participation in the paid labor force jumped

**Table 11.2**
**Education by Gender, 1991**

| Education | Men | Women |
| --- | --- | --- |
| 0–8 Years | 10.4% | 9.6% |
| Some High School | 10.5% | 11.5% |
| High School Degree | 36.3% | 41.3% |
| Some College | 18.3% | 18.7% |
| College Degree or More | 24.5% | 18.9% |

*Source:* Adapted from Cynthia Costello and Anne J. Stone.
*The American Woman, 1994–95. Where We Stand.*
New York: W. W. Norton, 1994: 267.

from 12 percent in 1930 to 22 percent in 1950 to 50 percent in 1980. Consequently, women's overall labor force participation rate rose by six percentage points each decade from 30 percent in 1950 to 58 percent in 1992, when women accounted for 45.5 percent of the entire workforce. Thus, it took women until the 1980s to approach gender equality in simply having employment.

It is also important to note that the sharp increases in married women getting paid jobs formed an ongoing and consistent trend throughout the entire postwar period. This indicates that interpretations which explain married women's entrance into the paid labor force was more than a response to the growing economic pressures of the 1970s and 1980s or a result of "civil rights" laws prohibiting job discrimination against married women (Degler 1980; Friedan 1963; Rubin 1976). Rather, women appeared ready to move beyond the confines of home and hearth, probably because of their rising level of education, and the American economy was able to accommodate them in both buoyant and stagnant times. The emancipating potential of outside work is suggested by an angry working-class husband who felt that his wife "doesn't know how to give ... respect because she's working and making money, she thinks that she can argue back whenever she feels like it" (Rubin 1976: 176–177; cited in Goldin 1990: 11).

Simply entering the workforce, though, is no guarantee that one will be treated equally or equitably. As dolefully demonstrated by the final column in Table 11.3, women have never received equal pay. In 1890, women's weekly earnings were only 46 percent of men's, and in the early nineteenth century, they were probably less than half of even that low figure. This ratio rose gradually to about 56 percent in 1930, but then stagnated at about 60 percent from the 1950s through the late 1970s before rising again to 75 percent in 1992. The reasons for the decreasing gender gap in wages stem largely from the conditions in the American labor market. The introduction of machinery in industrialization during the nineteenth century greatly reduced the contribution of "muscle power" to productivity; the tremendous growth in clerical positions between the 1890s and World War II continued

**Table 11.3**
**Women's Labor Force, Participation, and Pay**

|        | Women's Labor Force Partipation Rate, %* | | | Ratio of Women's Earnings to Men's Earnings |
|--------|------|--------|---------|------|
|        | All  | Single | Married |      |
| 1890   | 18.9 | 40.5   | 4.6     | 46.3 |
| 1930   | 24.8 | 50.5   | 11.7    | 55.6 |
| 1950   | 29.5 | 50.6   | 21.6    | —    |
| 1960   | 35.1 | 47.5   | 30.6    | 59.2** |
| 1970   | 41.6 | 51.0   | 39.5    | 60.3 |
| 1980   | 51.1 | 61.5   | 50.1    | 64.4 |
| 1992   | 57.8 | —      | —       | 75.4 |

\* Fifteen and older for 1890–1960; sixteen and older for 1970–1992.
\*\* For 1961.

*Sources:* Adapted from Cynthia Costello and Anne J. Stone. *The American Woman, 1994–95. Where We Stand.* New York: W. W. Norton, 1994: 283, 309; Claudia Goldin. *Understanding the Gender Gap: An Economic History of American Women.* New York: Oxford University Press, 1990: 17, 60, 64.

this trend and put a greater premium on education; and advanced education became increasingly more important over the postwar era. Given America's long history of mass education, these trends obviously made women more valuable vis-à-vis men.

Yet, the growth of clerical and then managerial employment was far from totally beneficial. In fact, wage discrimination against women was generally more pronounced in these occupations than in manufacturing and agriculture as white collar occupations came to be marked by women's segregation into dead-end jobs, company policies requiring that women be fired upon marriage (which obviously limited most women's job experience), and the creation of long career and pay ladders (Corcoran and Duncan 1979; Fuchs 1988; Goldin 1990; O'Neill 1985). While some of this discrimination might be attributed to purely economic factors (e.g., firms' expectations that women will generally not pursue lifetime careers), the prevalence of such practices until recent legal attacks clearly shows substantial gender discrimination per se that can only be explained by the continuance of patriarchal norms.

Most recently, women's gains during the 1980s probably reflect some combination of new laws against gender discrimination, the increase of jobs requiring advanced education, and the gradual erosion of patriarchal norms in American society. Table 11.4 provides some additional insights about these changes by

**Table 11.4**
**Employment Equality by Occupation**

| | Occupational Distribution, 1992 | | Ratio of Women's to Men's Weekly Earnings | |
|---|---|---|---|---|
| | *Men* | *Women* | *1984* | *1992* |
| All Occupations | 100.0 | 100.0 | 67.8 | 75.4 |
| Managerial | 25.7 | 27.4 | 68.7 | 72.3 |
| Executive | 13.5 | 11.4 | 63.9 | 66.2 |
| Professional spec. | 12.2 | 16.0 | 72.6 | 76.4 |
| Technical, Sales & Adm Support | 20.8 | 43.8 | 64.6 | 70.3 |
| Technicians | 3.4 | 3.9 | 69.9 | 73.8 |
| Sales | 11.4 | 12.4 | 54.1 | 59.8 |
| Clerical | 6.0 | 27.5 | 68.8 | 75.5 |
| Service Occupations | 10.2 | 17.9 | 67.9 | 75.2 |
| Precision Production & Crafts | 18.8 | 2.1 | 65.0 | 66.8 |
| Operartors & Laborers | 20.0 | 7.9 | 66.9 | 71.0 |
| Agriculture | 4.6 | 1.0 | 85.0 | 82.9 |

*Source:* Adapted from Cynthia Costello and Anne J. Stone. *The American Woman, 1994–95. Where We Stand.* New York: W. W. Norton, 1994: 296, 310–311.

breaking women's and men's employment patterns and wage differences down by occupational strata. These data suggest several positive trends. The segregation of women into less desirable occupations appears to be muting. Women, in fact, are almost equally represented with men in the top strata of managerial jobs. There is considerable gender segregation lower down the occupational hierarchy with women tending to hold clerical and service jobs, while men predominate in skilled and semiskilled industrial occupations. Yet, the salary differential implied by this is only moderate—precision production jobs pay slightly more than clerical ones and semiskilled laborers earn slightly more than employees in service industries. Furthermore, all the occupational categories exhibit the pattern of decreasing wage differentials between 1984 and 1992, and the previous tendency for salary discrimination to increase at higher level of the occupational hierarchy has mostly (but not completely) disappeared. These results are far from totally sanguine, however. Significant wage differentials remain, and previous progress (i.e., decreasing wage inequality in the early twentieth century) has stalled. Furthermore, women appear to be increasingly divided into a minority with "high-status careers" and the large majority who are "more marginally connected to the labor force" (Jacobs 1989).

Far more importantly, women's economic gains have been far overshadowed by postwar social and political trends that have combined to produce the "feminization of poverty" (Fuchs 1988). In particular, exploding divorce and illegitimacy rates in the 1970s (the former peaked in the 1980s while the latter did not) created a growing group of poor women with families to support as welfare spending for the poor dropped in the 1980s under the conservative Reagan administration (Meyer 1984) and as many husbands and fathers refused to support their children.

Table 11.5 summarizes the impact of these socioeconomic trends. The growing importance of female-headed households over the 1970s and 1980s is readily apparent. In 1970, slightly over a tenth (11 percent) of American households were "headed" by a single woman, and a similar percentage of children lived with only their mother. In just two decades, the percentage of female-headed households rose by over a half to 17 percent and the proportion of children living with a single mother doubled to 23 percent—almost a quarter of the next generation! This pronounced change in American family structure, moreover, is particularly worrisome because of the grave financial burdens that face female-headed families, especially those with children. For example, in 1991 almost half (47 percent) of female-headed families with children lived in poverty, as opposed to only 8 percent of married couples who had children. In terms of median family income, female-headed families have consistently over the last several decades received only slightly more than half the income of male-headed households or of married couples in which the wife does not work, and this ratio was much worse in comparison with two-income families (40 percent in 1970 and 35 percent in 1991). Likewise, female-headed families were only slightly more than half as likely as married-couple households (44 percent to 78 percent) to own their homes (although their disadvantage compared to male-headed households is much less here than in the poverty and median income statistics), suggesting a marked disadvantage in security and equity accrual. Finally, the data on median income over time show that only married couples with a working wife were able to realize a gain in real (i.e., inflation-adjusted) income between 1970 and 1991, indicating the growing social stress induced by U.S. declining economic performance.

## ECONOMIC STRESS AND THE GROWTH OF THE "GENDER GAP" IN POLITICAL ATTITUDES

The last section demonstrated that, while the status of American women might be quite enviable to many developing societies, it is not particularly good by the standards of advanced industrial nations. Furthermore, social and economic trends over the last several decades have made women particularly vulnerable to the problems of poverty and social breakdown. These problems were exacerbated by American public policy. The United States, reflecting its individualist political culture, has traditionally had a much smaller welfare state and net than most other advanced industrial society (Wilensky 1975). During the 1980s, moreover, women

Table 11.5
Changing Family Types and Resources

|  | 1970* | 1980* | 1991 |
|---|---|---|---|
| **Distribution of Household Type, %** | | | |
| Married Couples | 86.7 | 81.7 | 78.1 |
| Wife in paid labor force | — | 41.0 | 46.0 |
| Wife not in paid labor force | — | 40.7 | 32.1 |
| Male-Headed | 2.4 | 3.2 | 4.5 |
| Female-Headed | 10.9 | 15.1 | 17.4 |
| **Children's Living Arrangements, %** | | | |
| Living with two parents | 85.2 | 76.7 | 70.7 |
| Living with mother only | 10.8 | 18.0 | 23.3 |
| Living with father only | 1.1 | 1.7 | 3.3 |
| Other | 2.9 | 3.7 | 2.6 |
| **Poverty Rates, %** | | | |
| Married Couples | | | |
| Children under 18 | | | 8.3 |
| No children under 18 | | | 3.9 |
| Male-Headed | | | |
| Children under 18 | | | 19.6 |
| No children under 18 | | | 6.4 |
| Female-Headed | | | |
| Children under 18 | | | 47.1 |
| No children under 18 | | | 10.6 |
| **Median Family Income** | | | |
| **(in 1991 constant dollars)** | | | |
| Married Couples | | | |
| Wife in paid labor force | $40,617 | $44,211 | $48,169 |
| Wife not in paid labor force | $30,792 | $30,724 | $30,075 |
| Male-Headed | $27,562 | $30,065 | $28,351 |
| Female-Headed | $16,161 | $16,568 | $16,692 |
| **Homeownership Rate, %** | | | |
| Married Couples | | | 78.1 |
| Male-Headed | | | 55.0 |
| Female-Headed | | | 43.9 |

* 1971 and 1981 for median family income.

*Source:* Adapted from Cynthia Costello and Anne J. Stone. *The American Woman, 1994–95.
Where We Stand.* New York: W. W. Norton, 1994: 329, 342.

are generally considered to be among the principal groups who became "losers" from the conservative policies of the Reagan administration (Phillips 1990).

Given women's changing and often deteriorating position in American society, it would not be surprising if they developed a distinctive perspective on political issues. In fact, the 1980s were marked by the emergence of the "gender gap" in political orientations. Until the 1970s, women and men had remarkably similar attitudes on most political issues with a few exceptions, such as women's greater concern for morality issues and opposition to policies that threatened to involve the United States in violent conflict. Over the last two decades, in contrast, significant differences in political attitudes between the sexes emerged or expanded in such areas as women's social and political roles, "social compassion," support for minority rights, protection of the environment, and basic economic issues to greatly augment the previous limited attitudinal gap concerning peace and morality. Consequently, by the mid-1980s gender gaps of 5–10 percent had opened up between men and women in terms of their presidential voting, party identification, and approval of presidential performance (Baxter and Lansing 1980; Bendyna and Lake 1994; Clark and Clark 1993; Kenski 1988; Klein 1984; Mueller 1988; Poole and Zeigler 1985; Stoper 1989).

The image of women as more liberal than men concerning general partisan attachments and support for an expansive role for government is confirmed by the data in Table 11.6 on American public opinion in 1992. In terms of ideological and partisan self-image, women were 8 percent less likely than men to identify themselves as Republicans and as conservatives (approximately 37–45 percent each). Women were particularly supportive compared to men (generally in the range of 10–15 percent) of expanding the role and powers of government, presumably because they believed that redistributive policies were necessary to help them and other marginal groups in society. The data on preferences for increased spending demonstrate that women were generally more favorable than men by 5–15 percent toward increased spending in a wide variety of liberal areas, as well as for fighting crime (suggesting their greater concern with personal protection).

This gender gap has been traced to several distinct elements or sources in American culture and politics. First, women's rising "gender consciousness" and "feminism" have made them more assertive in taking positions independently from their husbands and families (Carroll 1988; Conover 1988; Klein 1984; Rinehart 1992). Second, women's greater (as compared to men's) "compassion" for the less fortunate in society (Clark and Clark 1993; Shapiro and Mahajan 1986) engenders support for a larger and more nurturing set of government programs. Finally, a significant number of women now have a "self-interest" in liberal social policies that was generated by the feminization of poverty (Fuchs 1988; Goldin 1990).

The fact that women's political values came to differ significantly from men's in the United States during the 1980s logically leads to the question of how well they are represented in government, that is, their political status. This can be a critical factor because a variety of research findings suggest that greater representation for women normally makes a government more sensitive to supporting families

**Table 11.6**
**Gender Gap on Social Compassion, 1992**

|  | Male | Female | Gender Gap |
| --- | --- | --- | --- |
| **Ideology. %** |  |  |  |
| Conservative | 45 | 37 | −8 |
| Republican | 44 | 36 | −8 |
| **Role of Government, %** |  |  |  |
| Government should expand | 55 | 70 | 15 |
| Government should become more powerful | 29 | 44 | 15 |
| Strong government over free market | 64 | 76 | 12 |
| Government involved in what people should do for themselves | 45 | 31 | −14 |
| Increase services vs. cut spending | 32 | 42 | 10 |
| Government provides health insurance | 49 | 54 | 5 |
| Government guarantees job and standard of living | 26 | 34 | 8 |
| Government provides child care | 56 | 65 | 9 |
| Willing to pay more taxes | 29 | 31 | 2 |
| **Federal Spending, %** |  |  |  |
| Increase social security spending | 41 | 55 | 14 |
| Increase spending for poor | 48 | 61 | 13 |
| Increase spending for homeless | 68 | 77 | 9 |
| Increase child care spending | 44 | 56 | 12 |
| Increase AIDS spending | 61 | 63 | 2 |
| Increase public school spending | 62 | 69 | 7 |
| Increase college aid | 59 | 61 | 2 |
| Increase spending on unemployed | 35 | 44 | 9 |
| Increase spending for Blacks | 23 | 27 | 4 |
| Increase spending for cities | 21 | 21 | 0 |
| Increase welfare spending | 13 | 21 | 8 |
| Increase food stamp spending | 15 | 21 | 6 |
| Increase spending on crime | 67 | 73 | 6 |
| Increase defense spending | 20 | 19 | −1 |
| Increase environment spending | 59 | 63 | 4 |

*Source:* Computed from the data from the 1992 National Election Study of the Survey Research Center, distributed by the Interuniversity Consortium for Political and Social Research.

**Table 11.7**
**Percentage of Women in Lower House of Parliament, 1982**

| | |
|---|---|
| Sweden | 27.7% |
| Finland | 26.0% |
| Norway | 23.9% |
| Denmark | 22.9% |
| Netherlands | 14.0% |
| Switzerland | 10.5% |
| Austria | 9.8% |
| New Zealand | 8.8% |
| Portugal | 8.8% |
| Italy | 8.2% |
| Belgium | 7.5% |
| Israel | 7.5% |
| West Germany | 7.3% |
| Ireland | 6.8% |
| Spain | 5.4% |
| Iceland | 5.0% |
| Canada | 4.3% |
| France | 4.1% |
| United States | 4.1% |
| Greece | 4.0% |
| Japan | 1.6% |
| Australia | 0.0% |

*Source:* Adapted from Wilma Rule. "Electoral Systems, Contextual Factors, and Women's Opportunity for Election to Parliament in Twenty-three Democracies." *Western Political Quarterly*, 40:3 (September 1987): 483.

and other "women's issues" (Dodson and Carroll 1991; Mezey 1994; Thomas 1994). Thus, if women can gain equitable representation in America's state and federal governments, they might well be able to stimulate a more adequate policy response to the social problems created by the feminization of poverty and the growing marginalization of many women in American society.

The data in Tables 11.7 and 11.8 indicate that women's political representation in America is fairly low, but it has increased appreciably recently. In the comparative figures in Table 11.7, America rates quite poorly, being tied for 18th out of 22 developed democracies for the proportion of women in the lower house of the legislature. The principal reason for this poor performance is probably America's electoral system of single-member districts—women politicians tend to win the most seats in proportional representation systems with large districts (Darcy et al. 1987; Rule 1987)—rather than cultural bias against women per se. In fact, by the 1980s women

**Table 11.8**
**Percentage of Political Offices Held by Women**

|  | 1975 | 1981 | 1987 | 1991 | 1993 |
|---|---|---|---|---|---|
| Presidential Appointees** | 14% | 12% | 12% | 20% | 37% |
| Congress | 4% | 4% | 5% | 6% | 10% |
| Statewide Elected Officials | 10% | 11% | 14% | 18% | 22% |
| State Legislatures | 8% | 12% | 16% | 18% | 20% |
| Mayors | 5% | 8% | 11% | 17% | 18% |

* 1977
** Total presidential appointments subject to Senate confirmation for the entire administration: Carter, 1966–1980; Reagan, 1981–1988; Bush, 1989–1992; Clinton, 1993–.

Source: Cynthia Costello and Anne J. Stone. *The American Woman, 1994–95. Where We Stand.* New York: W. W. Norton, 1994: 350–351.

who entered legislative races in America appeared to face little overt discrimination from voters, party leaders, or campaign contributors (Darcy et al. 1987).

An examination of temporal trends within America in Table 11.8 produces a slightly more optimistic picture since women's representation has clearly made very appreciable gains over the last two decades. At the state and local levels of government, over a fifth of the state legislators, statewide elected officials, and mayors are women—more than double their share of these offices in 1975. At the national level, Presidents Bush and especially Clinton have been much more likely to appoint women to high positions in their administration. While women representation in Congress remains comparatively low at 10 percent, the increase in the number of women Representatives (lower house) and especially Senators (upper house) in the 1992 elections was dramatic enough to earn the title "Year of the Woman" (Cook et al. 1994).

Women's political status in the United States, therefore, has both positive and negative aspects. Positively, there is a significant secular trend toward increasing women's political representation (Cook et al. 1994); direct voter and elite discrimination against women candidates appears minimal (Darcy et al. 1987); women's organizations are beginning to raise and distribute campaign funds in substantial portions (Roberts 1993); and the women's movement has been successful in mobilizing a substantial number of women and in advocating the rejection of patriarchal norms (Sinclair 1983). In contrast, however, women still remain woefully underrepresented at all levels of government, and the very existence of the "gender gap" in political attitudes strongly implies that the polity is not meeting important socioeconomic needs that women have.

## WOMEN'S STATUS IN AMERICA: CONTRADICTIONS AND IRONY

The status of women in America, in sum, resembles a glass whose contents are approximately half gone. Whether the glass is half full or half empty depends more on the perceptual framework of the observer than the mere fact of how high the liquid is in the glass. The combination of positive and negative features, furthermore, suggests some ironic contradictions. First, the gains that women have made from America's high level of "modernization" have been limited and are now perhaps even being challenged by America's "modern" individualistic culture. Second, the success of the women's movement in gaining emancipation (e.g., making divorce easier to obtain) has had some counterproductive side effects because of its indirect contribution to the feminization of poverty. Finally, while women's recent gains in political representation are promising, the conservative dynamics of contemporary American politics may well exacerbate, rather than mitigate, the social problems that a significant minority of American women now face.

# 12

## The Magic of the Market and the Price Women Pay: Examples from Latin America and the Caribbean

*Helen I. Safa and María de los Angeles Crummett*

*periphery*

### INTRODUCTION

Although there were variations by country, the period from 1950 to 1980 in Latin America and the Caribbean was characterized by considerable economic growth. Total product increased fivefold and per capita product doubled. Industry expanded and diversified, with manufacturing output increasing sixfold between 1950 and 1987. The tertiary sector grew at an even faster rate, together with a decline in agricultural employment. Population more than doubled from 1950 to 1980, and there was a marked shift toward urban areas, where the percentage of total population increased from 40.9 percent to 63.3 percent in the same period. Urban growth, which concentrated in large cities, was due largely to internal migration, particularly of women and young adults, and contributed to sharp declines in fertility as well as mortality and infant mortality. As a result, life expectancy increased to over sixty years in most countries, with a growing percentage of aged, especially women. Household size fell, particularly after 1960, and the percentage of households headed by women grew to about 20 percent. Educational levels and employment rates grew for both sexes during this period, but at a faster rate for women than for men (ECLAC 1988a: 7–9; 1988d: 1–3).

The economic crisis which hit Latin America and the Caribbean in the 1980s threatened to overturn the progress of the previous three decades and to halt all attempts at social equity. The crisis was brought on by rising prices of imports, a decline in both the quantity and price of exports, and a steep rise in interest rates on the foreign debt (ECLAC 1988a: 11). The proportion living in poverty grew during the crisis: In 1980 approximately 33 percent of the region's households fell below the poverty line; by 1985 it was 39 percent of households (PREALC 1990). Unemployment increased 48 percent between 1980 and 1985 and real wages declined between 12 and 18 percent in the same period (ECLAC 1988d: 16). In desperation, many countries implemented structural adjustment programs designed by the International Monetary Fund (IMF) and the World Bank to cut government expenditures, improve the balance of trade, and reduce the foreign debt. These policies, however, often resulted in greater hardship for the poor, because they included devaluation of the currency, accelerating the rate of inflation and cost of living; the elimination of government subsidies for basic foods and subsidized credits to farmers; cuts in government expenditures, particularly for social services in areas such as health, education, and employment; and the freezing of real wages (Cornia et al. 1987: 27). The philosophy behind structural adjustment policies is to shift all responsibility for survival from the state to the individual and the family by forcing families to absorb a greater share of the cost of living by reducing government policies aimed at economic well-being.

The economic shocks of the 1980s also prompted a dramatic shift in development thinking. Throughout Latin America and the Caribbean, international lending agencies, governments, the business sector, and a growing number of economists have embraced the "magic of the market." The private sector, along with the participation of foreign capital, not the state, is now viewed as the engine of economic growth and development. With the introduction of neoliberal reforms in the late 1980s and early 1990s, real gross domestic product (GDP) has increased in many Latin American countries, inflation rates and fiscal deficits have declined, foreign investment has risen considerably, and large sectors of national economies have been privatized. Free-trade pacts from the North American Free Trade Agreement (NAFTA) to the Southern Cone Common Market (MERCOSUR), along with the spread of export processing zones, are also key indicators of the accelerated pace of Latin America's integration into the global economy. However, economic restructuring based on the opening of borders and markets has yet to reverse the trend since 1980 of a marked growth in inequality in employment, income distribution, social services, and poverty.

The impact of the economic crisis and neoliberal policies has been particularly severe on women, especially poor women, in Latin America and the Caribbean and threatens to jeopardize the gains previously achieved. Women experience higher rates of unemployment and earn lower wages than men and have been the most affected by cuts in government expenditures on social services and increases in the cost of living (Cornia et al. 1987; ECLAC 1988a; García and Gomáriz 1989; Deere et al. 1990; Aguiar 1990; Benería and Feldman 1992). Women have responded by intensifying their work effort in the household, the labor market, and the community.

The crisis has increased the importance and visibility of women's contribution to the household economy, as additional women enter the labor market to meet the rising cost of living and the decreased wage-earning capacity of men. The new economic orthodoxy advocating free markets and outward-oriented development

*already Shifted to China*

*both*

has heightened the demand for female labor in the *maquiladoras* and nontraditional agricultural exports as Latin American countries shift away from policies emphasizing import substitution based on the domestic economy toward policies stressing trade liberalization and export promotion in the international arena. Women are not only increasing their incorporation into paid wage labor, but also seeking alternative sources of income through the informal sector, migration, artisan production, and domestic outwork (Benería and Roldán 1987; García and Gomáriz 1989; Nash 1993). At the same time, the increased economic importance of women coupled with the rise of female-headed households is challenging the myth of the man as the principal breadwinner in Latin American and Caribbean households.

Although the economic crisis has led to a greater recognition of women's contribution to economic production, most women are relegated to unstable, poorly paid, low-productivity jobs and still face the double burden of holding a job and running a household (Bonilla 1990). The increase in women's paid labor as a result of economic restructuring has generated intense debate over its effects on women's status. Does paid labor merely exploit women as a source of cheap labor, or does it give women greater autonomy and raise their consciousness regarding gender subordination?

This chapter on the impact of recent macroeconomic changes on gender roles in Latin America and the Caribbean provides an important opportunity to investigate this question. Because of the scope of information required in an overview, variations between and within countries have been minimized, and primary attention will be given to poor and low-income women. The chapter will focus on three main areas: (1) increasing labor force participation due to changes in development strategies; (2) the impact of these changes on family structure, especially the growth of female-headed households and the increased contribution of women to the household economy; and (3) the increasing participation by women in social movements demanding the provision of basic services, the recognition of human rights, and other issues which are politicizing women and contributing to the growth of grass-roots feminism.

## INCREASING LABOR FORCE PARTICIPATION

The size of the female labor force increased threefold in Latin America between 1950 and 1980, with overall participation rates rising from almost 18 percent to over 26 percent in the same period (ECLAC 1988a: 15). Participation rates for women grew faster than those for men and included all age groups, although single women between the ages of 20 and 29 continued to be the most active (ECLAC 1988d: 5–7). In 1990, the average labor force participation rate for women is 27 percent in South America and Mexico, 25 percent in Central America, and 47 percent in the Caribbean (Mulhern and Mauzé 1992: 14). Significantly, during the years of the crisis the share of women in the labor force rose from 32 percent in 1980 to 38 percent in 1988 (ECLAC 1992: 59).

According to several studies, greater female involvement is a consequence of several factors, including the erosion of living standards during the 1980s, when women sought to supplement declining family incomes; falling labor force participation rates for men, particularly among the young and old; women's greater access to all levels of education; higher rates of female rural to urban migration; the rise in the proportion of female-headed households; and expanding employment opportunities in the public sector, which has traditionally offered women more equitable access to jobs than the private sector—until public sector employment itself contracted under structural adjustment in the 1980s (Psacharopoulos and Tzannatos 1992; Mulhern and Mauzé 1992; Bonilla 1990).

Higher educational levels are a key factor contributing to increased female labor force participation and employed women generally have higher education levels than nonworking women (Psacharopoulos and Tzannatos 1992: 29). Women's educational levels have risen at an even faster rate than that of men's and this contributed to an increase between 1960 and 1980 of women in white collar work, particularly in the more developed Latin American and Caribbean countries. However, even relatively privileged white collar women face a highly segmented labor market and are found principally in such feminine occupations as clerical work, sales, teaching, and nursing.

Occupational segregation that crowds women into a restricted range of jobs may also account for the earnings gap that exists between women and men. A recent World Bank study on women's employment and pay in fifteen Latin American countries shows that men, on average, earn more than women, even when women have the same education and work experience. The extent of the male earnings advantage differs significantly across countries; in Mexico and Colombia the advantage is around 14 percent, but in Chile, Ecuador, Bolivia, and Jamaica, it is more than 40 percent (Psacharopoulos and Tzannatos 1992). Women are also more likely to be unemployed. For example, in Jamaica female unemployment reached 36.6 percent in 1985, over twice the rate for men (Deere et al. 1990: 52).

Declining fertility levels also contributed to increased female participation rates and can be explained by increased urbanization and educational levels, as well as improved access to contraceptive methods and family planning programs in some Latin American and Caribbean countries. In the period from 1980 to 1985, only three Latin American countries had fertility rates in excess of six children per woman, while eight experienced rates of less than four children per woman (ECLAC 1988d: 2). By the year 2000 projections put the total fertility rate for the region at under 3.0 (*World Development Report 1993* 1993: 291).

Latin America and the Caribbean were characterized by rapid rural to urban migration from 1940 until 1970, when the rate slowed somewhat. Women predominated in this flow due to the limited employment opportunities available to them in the rural area. In addition to stagnation in basic food production, population pressure, and growing landlessness, the economic crisis immediately reverberated on the agricultural sector, exacerbating existing trends. In Mexico, for example, public-sector investment in agriculture fell by 50 percent between 1981 and 1985, while price supports, government credit, and technical assistance were also sharply reduced (Arizpe et al. 1987: 115). Declines in income levels for the landless and small landholders precipitated an increase in the number of *jornaleros agricolas*, or migratory agricultural wage workers, one-third of whom are women (Arizpe et al.: 120).

Women have been incorporated both as field laborers and in processing plants with the growth of agribusiness in Latin American and the Caribbean, particularly in nontraditional export crops such as flowers, winter vegetables, and tropical fruits (Barham et al. 1992). Here, as elsewhere, women command lower wages, work harder, are more likely to hold seasonal or temporary jobs, and are less organized than men. Agricultural laborers face additional health and safety risks. Exposure to dangerous levels of chemical pesticides is especially severe among workers who do stoop labor, such as planting, weeding, and harvesting of export crops. The relatively high percentage of women engaged in such work poses serious health risks both for the women themselves and their unborn children (Mulhern and Mauzé 1992; Barham et al. 1992).

One of the consequences of the civil wars and economic decline in Central America in the 1980s has been the virtual destruction of the small family farm as a result of which agricultural productivity dropped significantly. Rural women have suffered disproportionately. In Central America nearly 20 percent of rural households are headed by women who are fully responsible for agricultural production yet operate without formal land rights and have little access to credit, training programs, production inputs, and extension services (Yudelman 1994: 2). In Latin America as a whole estimates show that nearly 50 percent of family income from the small farm sector comes from activities undertaken by women (Bonilla 1990: 226). Deforestation, the drying of watersheds, and the contamination of water by dangerous chemicals requires women to spend more time collecting clean water and fuel (Yudelman 1994).

International migration has also become an integral component of rural household survival strategies, to which the crisis gave new impetus. Studies of traditional rural sending communities in Mexico show that there is substantially more female participation in U.S.-bound migration, especially single women in their twenties, than there was a decade ago (Cornelius 1992; Crummett 1993). NAFTA and trade liberalization could lead to even greater social dislocation within Mexico and to increased illegal immigration to the United States.

Overall, the volume of the undocumented migrant flow to the United States increased dramatically during the years of the crisis. In the Dominican Republic, for example, a 1991 national-level survey shows that the percentage of families with members who presently or previously resided abroad increased from 15 percent in the early 1980s to over 35 percent from 1985 to 1989. Most migrants are young urban residents under thirty with professional and clerical skills, and about half are women (Ramírez 1992).

The majority of women in Latin America and the Caribbean are concentrated in the service sector, which includes a high proportion of domestic servants as well as white collar workers. In 1980, 65 percent of all economically active women in the region worked in services, compared to 37 percent of men (Bonilla 1990). Domestic service is still the largest occupational group among women in Latin America, although the proportion has fallen markedly, declining from over 37 percent of the economically active female population in some countries in 1960 to a maximum of 22.9 percent in 1980 (ECLAC 1988b: 22). Domestic service has modernized in the most developed countries of the region, with a changeover from resident to nonresident employees and, in some countries, social security coverage, regulation of hours worked and days off, and paid vacations (Chaney and Castro 1989). Vendors have also modernized as "higglers" from Jamaica, Haiti, and the eastern Caribbean who started as farm-to-market vendors now travel between the islands and even as far as Miami buying and selling food, clothing, appliances, and other consumer goods (ECLAC 1988c).

Vending and domestic service are traditional jobs in the informal sector, which is characterized by small-scale, unregulated forms of production and distribution without a formal wage labor contract. Jobs in the informal sector lack protective labor legislation, minimum wages, social security, or other benefits. As employment in the formal sector fell precipitously during the 1980s, the informal sector increased dramatically, as evidenced by the rise in its share in the urban labor force, which climbed from 24 percent to 30 percent during the 1980s (ECLAC 1992: 61). One estimate finds that women make up nearly 60 percent of the labor in the informal sector and that women have higher participation rates in this sector than in the economy as a whole (Otero 1989).

The growth of the informal sector also reflects neoliberal policies, which with international support have identified microenterprises, or the small firms that comprise much of the informal sector, as a component of market-based development strategies in opposition to the state (Safa 1987; Espinal and Grasmuck 1994). Because of their capacity for labor absorption and cost advantages in a highly competitive international market, some microenterprises are receiving support from development agencies such as the Agency for International Development and the World Bank in the form of credit, training, access to raw materials, foreign exchange, and other privileges formerly reserved exclusively for the formal sector. A survey of 200 microenterprises in the Dominican Republic reveals a pattern of gender differences among microentrepreneurs: Women are disproportionately concentrated within clothing and food production, whereas men are more equally distributed among a broader range of business activities which generate higher average monthly incomes, although this is not necessarily reflected in greater household contributions (Espinal and Grasmuck 1994: 15–16).

In an effort to cut labor costs and avoid unions and other labor legislation, manufacturers are also increasingly subcontracting part of their production process to home workers who are not entitled to any fringe benefits. Most of these home workers are married women who must do piecework at home because of child-care responsibilities or because their husbands will not allow them to work outside the home. This allows for greater flexibility in working hours for women, but also for employers who can scale the volume of work up or down with market fluctuations. The piecework rates workers receive generally fall below the minimum wage, as a study of home workers in Mexico City demonstrated (Benería and Roldán 1987). Industrial employment for women in several Latin American and Caribbean countries has increased as a result of the growth of export processing, particularly since the economic crisis of the 1980s. Export promotion has been favored by governments and international agencies as a way of alleviating unemployment and of earning desperately needed foreign exchange to redress the balance-of-payments crisis. However, as an analysis of export-led industrialization in the Dominican Republic has shown, these assembly-type operations have not led to self-sustained growth capable of generating more complex and capital-intensive forms of industrial production, as in East Asia and even Mexico (Deere and Meléndez 1992). Export processing also represents a decided advantage for the United States and other advanced industrial countries, who cut their labor costs by exporting the labor-intensive stages of the manufacturing process to these low-wage countries and by paying only a low value-added duty on these assembled goods when they are reimported back into the United States.

Export manufacturers have shown a preference for women workers, because, like agricultural day workers they are cheaper to employ, are less likely to unionize, and have greater patience for the tedious, monotonous work involved in assembly line production of clothing and electronics, the most popular export processing items. Wage reductions resulting from currency devaluation during the economic crisis along with the opening of economies to global competition in the 1990s have increased the attractiveness of investment in export processing in Mexico and throughout Central America and the Caribbean. In the Dominican Republic, the number of workers grew from 30,802 in 1985 to 140,000 in 1992, exactly when currency devaluations reduced the minimum wage to about U.S. $0.50 an hour, one of the lowest in the Caribbean Basin. Despite a new Dominican Labor Code passed in 1992, rights to collective bargaining are still limited and workers are afraid to organize for fear they will be fired or blacklisted with other plants. Men are still preferred in technical and supervisory positions, though women's educational level is higher, thus re-creating gender hierarchies in a largely female labor force (*Encuesta Nacional de Mano de Obra* 1992). A high percentage of Dominican women workers in export processing zones are married or female heads of households, which departs from the global pattern in which there is a predominance of young, single women employed in export processing (Safa 1990).

Many married women have entered the labor force because of falling household income and the rising cost of living, and some have become the principal breadwinner in the family. Women throughout Latin America and the Caribbean have adopted a variety of strategies to add income and cut expenditures. Households are doubling up, increasing the number of extended families, due both to the shortage and cost of housing and to the need to maintain as many adult wage earners in the family as possible. This appears to be happening in several countries in the region, reversing the trend toward smaller households that occurred prior to the crisis (González de la Rocha 1988; García and Gomáriz 1989). Women in poor households have commonly sought to stretch family income by producing goods at home rather than purchasing them in stores, incorporating additional wage earners to the household, or developing informal social networks for mutual aid among kin and neighbors. They have also cut down on expenses such as clothing, recreation, and even health and education in order to feed their families. Still, consumption of meat, milk, and even basic staples such as rice, beans, and corn has been reduced, resulting in nutritional deficits among the poor. It is estimated that in Mexico the cost of the basic food basket as a percentage of the minimum wage increased from 34.7 percent in 1980 to 49.5 percent in 1987 (González de la Rocha 1993).

Governments have done little to help the poor meet the rising cost of living, although there are food aid programs in some countries. On the contrary, the share of social sector spending fell in the majority of the countries between 1980 and 1985 (ECLAC 1988a: 12). Educational deterioration throughout the region is shown primarily through declining primary school enrollments, a higher incidence of school dropouts, and an increasing loss of teachers. The closure of public health facilities, a lack of medical personnel, medicine, and vital equipment, and growing health care costs have contributed to a sharp increase in infant mortality rates in some Latin American countries (Cornia et al. 1987). These cuts in government services add to the cost of living and increase the pressure on women to join the labor force.

Standing (1989) maintains that this pattern of "global feminization of labor" with increased female labor force participation and declining male participation extends far beyond the Caribbean region to developing countries in Asia and Africa and is due to increased international competition and the growth of export manufacturing, labor deregulation, and structural adjustment measures that have weakened workers' bargaining power in advanced industrial as well as developing countries. The primary beneficiaries of this form of economic restructuring are advanced industrial countries such as the United States, which has promoted this strategy in order to remain competitive within an increasingly global market. Even in these advanced industrial countries, workers, many of whom are women, suffer from a loss of jobs due to relocation of production to other areas of the country and abroad (Safa 1981; Nash 1989).

## FAMILY PATTERNS AND THE HOUSEHOLD ECONOMY

Their increased labor force participation, both in the formal and informal sector, has led women to take more responsibility for the economic support of their families, while the man's role as principal breadwinner is weakening. As a result, women and men are beginning to share decisions regarding the household budget, the children's education, fertility control, and other family matters. This is particularly true of stably married, upwardly mobile couples where both are working and contributing to the household economy (Safa 1995).

The key to understanding the impact of paid labor on women's status is the importance of their contribution to the household economy, particularly among married women. As long as women work but still depend primarily on a male provider, they are defined as supplementary earners. Most women continue to be seen as supplementary earners at the workplace, where they are confined to poorly paid, unstable jobs, and by the state, where their domestic responsibilities as wives and mothers are emphasized over their rights as workers or citizens. However, women themselves are becoming more aware of their critical contribution to the household economy, and this has led many to challenge male dominance, at least within the home, where women have always had more legitimacy than in the public sphere of the workplace and the state. This helps explain why, in our comparative studies of women factory workers in export manufacturing in the Caribbean, women have gained more negotiating power in the household than at the level of the workplace and the state, which is still considered the domain of men. This suggests that there are various levels of gender subordination, in the family, in the workplace, and at the state, and that these different levels, while linked, need to be kept analytically separate (Safa 1995).

In Puerto Rico and the Dominican Republic, where women are major contributors to the household economy, women use their earnings and the family's increased dependence on them to bargain for increased authority and sharing of responsibility within the household. In Puerto Rico, unemployment rates are higher for men than for women, and as in other countries in the region, participation rates for men have been declining, while those for women have steadily increased. In no case in our study of Puerto Rican women industrial workers does the woman's wage represent less than 40 percent of the household income, and it is even higher in the case of married women and female heads of household, who constitute a majority of our respondents. Men no longer feel threatened by their wives working because it is recognized that families can no longer survive on a single wage. For the same reason, most women now continue to be employed even if they are married and have young children, although this places a heavy burden on them. As in the rest of Latin America, the increased employment of married women has not led to any appreciable increase in the male share of domestic work, so that women with families typically face a "double day" (Safa 1990).

However, women gain little from increased employment if they are merely substituting their earnings for those of men. Unfortunately, this is often the case where increased female employment coincides with declining opportunities for men, as has occurred with the shift away from sugar exports in Puerto Rico and the Dominican Republic. Assembly-type export manufacturing has contributed to this change in the gender composition of the labor force in Puerto Rico, the Dominican Republic, Barbados (Coppin 1994), the U.S.-Mexican border (Fernandez Kelly 1983), and other areas by providing more jobs to women than to men.

Where women have to assume the role of breadwinner, this may produce conflict and lead to higher levels of marital instability and female-headed households. Partial figures for 1982 show that the percentage of female heads of household fluctuates between 18 and 23 percent in Latin America and 24 and 46 percent in the Caribbean (ECLAC 1988a: 15). While historical and cultural differences between countries help account for these variations, including a tradition of female economic autonomy dating from slavery in the Caribbean, throughout the region there is a growing importance of socioeconomic factors in the formation of female-headed households, such as male unemployment, migration, urbanization, and the economic crisis.

Female-headed households generally fall into the lowest income categories, even though these women are more likely to be employed than are married or single women. Their low income reflects the disadvantages women face in the labor market, including lower wages, higher unemployment, and less access to remunerative jobs and the fact that female-headed households often have fewer household members employed, due to the absence of a male partner. Female heads of household try to cope with this problem by incorporating other adult kin such as siblings or cousins as additional wage earners in the family or as caretakers for children. Studies have shown that more of the household budget in female heads of household is allocated to food than in male-headed households, reflecting the woman's greater control over expenditures (González de la Rocha 1993).

Poverty is particularly acute among young women with small children, and their numbers are increasing due to the high level of teenage pregnancy in the region (ECLAC 1988a: 26). In Chile, the proportion of births to unmarried teenage mothers doubled from 29 percent in 1960 to 60 percent in 1989 (Buvinic et al. 1992: 270). This increase is not due to adolescent fertility, which has actually declined, but to a lower rate of marriage among young pregnant women. Apparently high unemployment levels among young men have produced a poor "marriage market." Most of these teenage mothers continue to live in their parents' household, and are not even counted as female heads, because they are living as subfamilies in households headed by one or both parents. Adding these new subfamilies increases the incidence of female-headed families in Chile from 20 percent of all household to 26.6 percent of all families (Buvinic et al. 1992: 288). Although the labor force participation rate of young single mothers is higher than for urban women nationally, they are largely poor. In Chile as in the Caribbean, the majority of young single mothers receive little if any support from fathers, many of whom are unemployed, and are forced to rely on their own earnings and some support from the extended family (Safa 1995, Valenzuela et al. 1994).

In short, the redefinition of gender roles within the family in Latin America and the Caribbean depends on a variety of factors, such as the age and marital status of the woman, household composition, and the economic contribution of husband and wife, all of which vary within as well as between countries. While the economic crisis and policies have increased the importance and level of the woman's contribution, they have also led to a deterioration in male employment, which appears to have contributed to an increase in female-headed households, particularly among the young. While this form of economic restructuring may challenge the myth of the male breadwinner, it also shifts the burden of family survival from men to women.

## WOMEN AND SOCIAL MOVEMENTS

The economic crisis and neoliberal policies have also led to a marked increase in participation by women in social movements in Latin America, as workers in trade unions, housewives in squatter settlements, and mothers defending human rights against state repression. While precipitated by economic conditions, many other factors contribute to the increased participation of Latin American women in social movements. Women have long been active at the neighborhood level, both through informal networks and more organized forms of collective action such as squatter settlements and barrio committees. These collective activities took on added importance due to the economic crisis and also received the support of important groups such as the Catholic Church and other nongovernmental agencies. Increased educational and occupational opportunities made women more vocal and contributed to the growth of the feminist movement, which gained visibility during the U.N. Decade for Women from 1975 to 1985. The attention given to poor women by largely middle-class feminists made working class women more receptive to feminism and to issues of gender inequality.

Latin American women have chosen to confront the state directly in voicing their demands, because traditional channels such as political parties and labor unions have neglected women and continue to regard men as the primary spokesmen to the outside world. In addition, labor unions and political parties in countries like Brazil, Argentina, and Chile were extremely weakened due to strong government repression during the years of authoritarian rule. Political parties are seen as a male sphere, in which the poor play essentially a client role, exchanging votes for political favors such as improving roads or setting up a day-care center. This fosters *asistencialismo* (aid dependency) and may lead to the cooptation of women's groups for partisan political ends. In Guadalajara and other Mexican cities, the ruling PRI (Partido Revolucionario Institucional) has established its own women's groups within the *colonias populares,* or low-income neighborhoods, which provide services such as cheap food and educational programs but allow women little role in leadership or decision making (Craske 1993). Women's concerns are addressed basically as a way of winning votes, but the targeting of these women as potential constituents points to the growing political importance of women in electoral politics in Latin America.

Most of the demands that women make on the state arise out of their immediate perceived needs and experience and do not question the existing division of labor. One of the principal demands concerns the provision of public services, such as running water, electricity, and transportation, all of which are sorely lacking in the squatter settlements in which most of these poor women live. Women's reproductive role as housewives and mothers has tended to push them into the foreground as champions of these collective consumption issues and includes protests against the high cost of living and the lack of day care, health services, and even food. One of the most successful and unique collective consumption strategies to combat the economic crisis is the *comedores populares,* or communal kitchens, organized by women in Lima, Santiago, and other Latin American cities. Their number in Lima has grown to over 1,000 (Blondet 1989) and to 700 in Santiago in 1990 (Fisher 1993: 42), despite recent record levels of economic growth in Chile. Their growing number is evidence of women's collective response to continued income inequality aggravated by the crisis and neoliberal reforms in Peru, Chile, and other Latin American countries.

Some feminists have been critical of these women's self-help organizations because they focus almost exclusively on traditional female tasks and continue to identify women with their domestic role. They arise out of what Molyneux (1986) has defined as women's practical gender interests, in contrast to strategic gender interests, which question or transform the sexual division of labor. However, it appears that the collectivization of private tasks such as food preparation and child care is transforming women's roles even though they are not undertaken as conscious challenges to gender subordination. In contrast to some middle-class feminists, these poor women rarely reject their domestic role, but use it as a base to give them strength and legitimacy in their demands on the state (Caldeira 1987: 97). By politicizing the private sphere, women have redefined rather than rejected their domestic role and extended the struggle against the state beyond the workplace into the home and community.

Nowhere is this more apparent than in the demands Latin American women have placed on the state for the recognition of human rights. Perhaps the best known case in contemporary Latin American society are the Mothers of the Plaza de Mayo in Argentina, who played a decisive role in the defeat of the military dictatorship in that country. Composed mostly of middle-aged housewives with no political experience, the Mothers were able to use their traditional roles as mothers and turn them against the state, to protest the disappearance of their children and other loved ones during the military dictatorship. After democratization, their continued demand to prosecute the military and others responsible for the disappearances and their rejection of the legal concessions won by other human rights groups has lost them public support. Despite their reluctance to identify themselves as feminist, women's organizations have supported the Mothers' attempt to make motherhood the basis of an ethical condemnation of society and its values (Fisher 1993: 135). Though the Mothers have lost strength, they have inspired similar human rights movements involving women and their children in Uruguay, Chile, Brazil, Honduras, El Salvador, Guatemala, and other Latin American countries under authoritarian rule (Schirmer 1993; Stephen and Tula 1994).

Many social movements have waned as the locus of power has shifted back to political parties with the transition to democratic rule in countries like Argentina, Brazil, Uruguay, and Chile. Elections rekindle old political divisions between rival political parties and fragment social movements that have arisen not only among women, but among youth, the urban poor, and broader based human rights groups. Nevertheless, certain gains have been made and even institutionalized into legal codes. The new Brazilian constitution adopted in 1988 facilitates divorce, extends maternity leave, and eliminates the prohibition on abortion (without legalizing it).

Argentina has also legalized divorce and modified *patria potestad* to give women more equality in the family and joint custody of children (Jaquette 1989: 199–203). A new Argentine law makes it obligatory for political parties to include a minimum of 30 percent women candidates in election and similar legislation is being considered in Uruguay and other countries (Fisher 1993: 207).

However, perhaps the greatest contribution of women's social movements has been in the growth of popular or grass-roots feminism among poor women in Latin America and the Caribbean. Its emergence can be attributed in part to poor women's dissatisfaction with traditional middle-class feminist organizations and their desire to develop their own agenda, which focuses on practical issues centering on family welfare such as domestic violence, teenage pregnancies, child care, and improvement in women's job opportunities. Their emphasis has not been exclusively on material issues, but has also generated a new collective identity that emphasizes women's solidarity and self-esteem and challenges machismo in political parties, unions, neighborhoods, and at home. The rise of popular feminism highlights the importance of race/ethnicity, class, age, and region in shaping women's multiple identities, as the growing number of organizations of indigenous women, black women, domestic workers, and peasant women underlines. *Encuentros,* or mass meetings, held biannually since 1981 in several Latin American countries and attended by grass-roots and middle-class feminists alike have provided critical forums for debating key issues confronting Latin American feminism (Sternbach et al. 1992).

In the face of persistent poverty and the state's inability or unwillingness to address women's issues, many feminist support groups have transformed themselves into more formal nongovernmental organizations, or NGOs, which seek to act as intermediaries between grass-roots groups and donor agencies. Brazilian NGOs have multiplied dramatically, rising from 60 in the 1970s to over 1,200 in 1994, and are among the most vocal advocates of social justice and democratic values, with a strong emphasis on issues of the environment (Bustani 1994: 1). The NGOs and grass-roots feminist groups challenge a masculine model of the state in which men lead and make decisions and women are passive supporters.

## CONCLUSION

Clearly the changes in gender roles among Latin American and Caribbean women in the postwar period have promoted greater gender consciousness. Women have become increasingly important members of the labor force and contributors to the household economy; they have organized social movements for human rights and social welfare; and they are voicing their demands in labor unions and political parties. Gender consciousness is growing as the contradiction between women's increasingly important economic contribution to the household and their subordination in the family, in the workplace, and in the polity becomes more apparent. The growth of gender consciousness, and particularly popular feminism, has given greater credibility and visibility to women's issues, so that women's organizations are now recognized as a political force, although some may be coopted for partisan political ends.

However, women continue to face formidable obstacles stemming not only from poverty and gender inequality, but from an ideology which continues to identify women as wives and mothers and men as workers and providers. This ideology legitimizes treating women as supplementary income earners who are segregated into poorly paid, low-status jobs, which makes it difficult to support a family on their own. Gender equality will not be achieved until the myth of the male breadwinner (and dependent housewife) is replaced by a more egalitarian model in which women are recognized as equals and can represent their own interests and not have them mediated by men (or other women). But the myth of the male breadwinner is preserved by notions of male dominance embedded in the state and the workplace and to a lesser extent in the household, which continue to profit from women's subordination.

# 13

# Australia: Economic Issues of Women in Paid Employment

*Sukhan Jackson*

## INTRODUCTION

This chapter focuses on Australian women in paid employment as a case study of the Western industrial economy. For the 1990s, the development debate in the world community has centered on human development, which is a broad and comprehensive concept "as concerned with the generation of economic growth as with its distribution, as concerned with basic needs as with the spectrum of human aspirations" (*Human Development Report 1992* 1992: 13). According to the World Bank's Human Development Index (HDI), Australia ranked seventh out of 160 countries, being only behind Canada, Japan, Norway, Switzerland, Sweden, and the United States (*Human Development Report 1992* 1992: 127). Australia was also in the same position on the HDI ranking for industrial countries (*Human Development Report 1992* 1992: 19). The economic issues of working women in Australia are those of income distribution related to the role of the female labor factor in the production of goods and services.

It is apparent that a relationship exists between economic development and women's participation in paid employment. An accelerating economic growth rate in excess of population growth rate would lead to a greater demand for labor, which is normally met by labor reserves not already economically utilized. In newly industrializing economies (NIEs) the reserve labor supply has come from the female population. Women's participation in paid work would continue in the industrialized economies. At this stage, it would be in response to changing labor demand generated by the transformation of the economy from a predominantly primary-based to a tertiary-based one. In those industrialized economies with a low population density such as Australia, the gap in the labor market would be bridged by the immigration of foreign labor, either on a permanent or temporary basis. The scope of this chapter also covers migrant women but space constraints do not permit a separate discussion of them.

## SOME CHARACTERISTICS OF WOMEN LABOR FORCE PARTICIPATION

Women's participation in the labor force, representing women who are either employed or seeking work, is relatively high in Australia. The extent to which people participate in the labor force is measured by the participation rate. It is calculated from the following formula:

$$\text{Participation rate} = \text{number employed or actively seeking work} \times \frac{100}{\text{number in population as a whole}}$$

Therefore, in the case of women,

$$\text{Women's participation rate} = \text{number employed or actively seeking work} \times \frac{100}{\text{total number of women}}$$

According to labor force survey estimates of the Australian Bureau of Statistics, the female participation rate in the civilian labor force for the fifteen to sixty-four age group in April 1994 was 52.3 percent compared with 73.4 percent for males (*Labour Force Australia* 1994: 19).

There has been a net increase in the number of women wage and salary earners as a proportion of total wage and salary earners. The share of women employees has increased from 41.6 percent in November 1985 to 45.8 percent in November 1993. The number of women employees rose from 2,297,800 in November 1985 to a record of 2,793,200 in November 1989, representing a rise of 495,400. Although the recession caused the total to fall to 2,646,100 in November 1993, representing a fall of 147,100 (Australian Bureau of Statistics 1994a: 1–2), there was still a net increase in female employment in Australia.

### More Married Women in Paid Work

The growth in female participation is attributed to the increase in the number of married women joining the labor force in recent decades. Table 13.1 shows the participation rates of married women over a long period, rising slowly up to 1954, and rapidly afterward. For example, in 1921 the participation rate of married women was only 4.2 percent but after World War II there was a threefold increase to 12.6 percent in 1954. The participation rate rose to 32.8 percent in 1971 and to 52.3 percent in 1991 and remained at 52.3 percent in April 1994.

The rise in the participation rates of married women has occurred simultaneously with Australia's employment pattern changing to a predominantly tertiary-based

**Table 13.1**
**Labor Force Participation Rates of Married Women, 1921–1994, %**

| Year | 1921 | 1947 | 1954 | 1961 | 1971 | 1981 | 1991 | 1994 |
|------|------|------|------|------|------|------|------|------|
| %    | 4.2  | 8.0  | 12.6 | 17.3 | 32.8 | 44.3 | 52.3 | 52.3 |

*Source:* Compiled from K. Norris. *The Economics of Australian Labour Markets*, 1993: 39; and Australian Bureau of Statistics. *Labour Force Australia April 1994*. Catalogue No. 6203.0, 1994b: 19.

one. The supply of married female labor into paid work has been influenced mainly by five variables (Norris 1993: 39–41):

1. Wage rates: The real wage rates of female labor have grown both absolutely and relative to those of the males.

2. Fertility rates: an important influence is the trend of decline in the number of children in the family, for example, from a relatively high fertility rate of 3.4 percent during 1956–1960 to a rate of 1.9 percent in 1989.

3. Education level: Women are achieving a higher level of education.

4. Spouse's income: An increase in male wages might have a negative effect on women's participation, but this is weakening in recent years. However, a decrease in the spouse's earnings due to the economic recession would force most women to seek paid work.

5. Social attitudes: There has been a significant change in social attitudes to married women working: "In half a century we have moved from a situation where it was thought unusual for a married woman to work to one where it is thought unusual for a married woman without young children not to work" (Norris 1993: 41).

Equally important to the economic issues of working women (both married and single) is the other side of the labor market equation showing a higher demand for female labor. The outstanding feature in Australia is that this demand is concentrated in a small number of industries.

### Gender Segregation in Paid Work

In the postwar years, the tertiary sector has grown more quickly than at any other time, increasing its share of the country's total employment, and, in particular, the demand for female labor. According to the 1991 census, 78 percent of working women were concentrated in five industry sectors: community services; wholesale and retail trade; finance, property, and business services; recreation and personal services; and manufacturing. Even within the female-dominated industry sectors; 70 percent of women are in lower paying positions such as clerical jobs and sales assistants (Still 1988: 4).

The industrial segregation of female employment is shown in Table 13.2. Most women are employed in service-oriented white collar jobs while most men are in trade-related blue collar jobs. The overrepresentation of female employment in the expanding service sector has been exaggerated by a steady decline of some

**Table 13.2**
**Employment by Industry Sectors in Australia, 1989, 1991 (as percentage of total employed males and total employed females)**

|  | 1991 | 1989 | 1991 | 1989 | 1991 | 1989 |
|---|---|---|---|---|---|---|
|  | Males | | Females | | Persons | |
|  | % | % | % | % | % | % |
| Agriculture | 3.2 | 6.7 | 1.4 | 4.2 | 4.5 | 5.7 |
| Mining | 1.1 | 2.0 | 0.1 | 0.0 | 1.2 | 1.3 |
| Manufacturing | 9.5 | 19.9 | 3.7 | 10.4 | 13.1 | 16.1 |
| Electricity, gas & water | 1.1 | 2.4 | 0.2 | 0.5 | 1.3 | 1.6 |
| Construction | 5.1 | 11.3 | 0.8 | 2.4 | 5.0 | 7.7 |
| Wholesale, retail trade | 10.3 | 19.2 | 8.5 | 23.3 | 18.8 | 20.9 |
| Transport, storage | 3.6 | 7.0 | 1.0 | 2.6 | 4.6 | 5.2 |
| Communication | 1.2 | 2.3 | 0.5 | 1.3 | 1.7 | 1.9 |
| Finance, property, business services | 5.6 | 9.3 | 5.5 | 13.9 | 11.1 | 11.1 |
| Public administration, defence | 3.6 | 4.4 | 2.1 | 3.9 | 5.7 | 4.2 |
| Community services | 6.0 | 10.3 | 11.7 | 27.4 | 17.7 | 17.3 |
| Recreation, personal, other services | 3.1 | 5.1 | 3.9 | 9.8 | 7.0 | 7.0 |

*Note:* Percentages do not add to 100 because employed persons in categories of "not classifiable" and "not stated" (7.5 percent of total employed persons) are excluded.

*Source:* Compiled from Australian Bureau of Statistics. *Census Characteristics of Australia. 1991 Census of Population and Housing*, Cat. No. 2710.0, 1993; and Australian Bureau of Statistics, *Labour Force Australia*, Cat. No. 6203.0, 1989.

industries which were the traditional sources of female industrial work, for example, the clothing, textiles, and footwear industries, whose plight is typical of much light manufacturing in Australia.

Australia has one of the most occupationally segmented workforces of the OECD group of countries (Deery and Plowman 1991: 480). Norris (1993: 152) has listed eight occupations which contribute to the overall employment segregation by gender in Australia. These eight occupations account for 45 percent of total employment. Six of the eight occupations are dominated by women:

1. Stenographers and typists (99 percent);

2. Nurses (93 percent);

3. Bookkeepers and cashiers (81 percent);

4. Housekeepers, cooks, maids , and so forth (78 percent);

5. Clerical workers (64 percent);

6. Proprietors, shopkeepers, shop assistants, and so forth (64 percent);

Male employment is concentrated in two occupation groups:

1. Employers, self-employed, company directors, and so forth (85 percent);
2. Machine toolmakers, metal machinists, mechanics, and so forth (98 percent).

It is not clear to what extent gender segregation by industry and occupation has diminished. However, there has been a decline in the concentration of female employees in industry from 85 percent of all women in paid employment in 1989 (Deery and Plowman 1991) to 78 percent in 1991. Norris (1993: 153) notes that occupational segregation has existed for a very long time in Australia, as female-dominated occupations shifted from domestic service and clothing manufacture in 1911 to clerical work, typing, and sales at the present time.

### Part-Time Employment and Inferior Work Status

In Australia, the number of part-time female employees exceed full-time[1] ones. In the female workforce, 41.9 percent are full-time and 58.1 percent are part-time, compared with part-time male employees who comprise only 7 percent of the male workforce (Norris 1993: 9; Deery and Plowman 1991: 482). There is an interesting change in Australian employment which is also happening in many industrialized economies. In the last two decades, part-time jobs have increased more rapidly than full-time ones, occupying a growing share of employment, from 11.9 percent in 1978 to 23.4 percent in 1992, and three-quarters of part-time employees are women (Norris 1993: 9). The total number of full-time employees (both males and females) dropped by 12.9 percent from a peak of 4,745,600 in November 1989 to 4,134,800 in November 1993. However, the total number of part-time employees grew steadily over a number of years to 1,556,200 in November 1989 and continued to rise to 1,642,600 in November 1993 (Australian Bureau of Statistics 1994b: 2).

The majority of female part-timers are married and between 25 and 45 years of age, as reflected in the gender distribution of income by age groups. The 1991 Census found that women belonging to the 25–34 age group made up the highest number of employees who earned the lowest annual individual income of $8,000 or less. The highest number of males earning the same lowest annual income was found in the 15–19 teenage group. On the other hand, the highest number of both men and women earning an annual individual income of $8000–$12,000 was in the retirement group of 65–74 age group (Australian Bureau of Statistics 1993: 24).

Such income distribution among the age groups of men and women can be explained by an important gender difference in the life cycle of work. It is apparent that women with responsibility for child rearing often substitute full-time for part-time employment. After an interval of caring for their young children, many women return to paid work to occupy only part-time positions, which influence the economic status of these women. Part-time jobs provide very few career opportunities as they are located at the lowest ranks and grades. These low-ranking jobs need very little training and offer scarce opportunities for acquiring transferable skills and promotion. Thus, the time spent in part-time employment would drive many women to the periphery of the labor market.

The return to paid work, both part-time and full-time, after a prolonged absence often implies downward mobility of job and downgrading of skill. The returning women often find themselves in an inferior labor market position because of several reasons. The most important is the pragmatic necessity to combine child rearing with paid work. Another reason is that most supplementary wage earners are prepared to trade off wages for more convenient working hours. For many women, the choices are limited to jobs in which they compete with the more recently qualified youths. The consequences of women temporarily leaving work and then reentering the labor market are twofold. Women are left far behind not only in the promotion up the career ladder but also in the progressive pay increments, in contrast to their male counterparts.

It can be argued that the inferior position of many part-time working women in the periphery of the labor market is a choice-based consequence. However, there are important institution-based factors leading to the inferior employment status of full-time working women.

### Gender Wage Differential in Full-Time Work

Commenting on the low labor status of women Deery and Plowman noted: "Women suffer economically not only because of their workforce participation is skewed in favor of part-time and casual work. In the areas of full-time employment women's wages are substantially lower than those of men" (Deery and Plowman 1991: 485). King reminds us that gender wage differential is an international occurrence. For example, in the early 1970s female average earnings were about 60 percent of the male average in the United States and Canada, and 65–70 percent in France, Finland, Norway, and Israel, but the gap has narrowed in several of these countries (King 1990: 100).

It seems the trend is similar in Australia. Data on award pay rates[2] for adult employees can be used to show that female wages as a percentage of male wages increased from 72 to 93 percent between 1970 and 1980. Since then, the gap is about the same. However, the award pay rate, which varies from industry to industry, is only a *minimum* wage rate enforceable by law. For some people, the award pay is the only component of the individual's pay packet. For many people, especially male employees, it is only one of several components, which can include overtime pay, overaward pay (for skills), merit pay or bonuses (for results), seniority pay (for work experience), and pay rises due to promotion. In the Australian context, the average weekly earning is a more accurate indicator of income distribution. Data on average weekly earnings (for normal time) reveal a greater disparity between men and women, ranging between 80 and 83 percent during 1982–1987 (Dufty and Fells 1989: 302).

## LEGACY OF HISTORICAL DISCRIMINATION
## AGAINST WOMEN

The historical debate on the origin and nature of gender inequalities is inconclusive. One view regards the working women as oppressed victims bearing the brunt of unequal social position and economic status. The alternative argument is that women worked as partners with men in the development of Australia's pioneer economy, especially in the rural sector, and therefore were relatively equal (Alford and Mclean 1986). There is no doubt that by the early twentieth century discrimination against the working women was already institutionalized.

Discrimination against women was incorporated into Australia's wage-fixing process by a series of decisions handed down from the industrial judiciary. In 1907 when Justice Higgins settled the dispute of the famous Harvester case, he also set up a basic wage calculated from the average weekly costs of an unskilled worker supporting a wife and three children. This method of wage-fixing was based on the "needs principle" rather than on labor market conditions. Only the remuneration of skills was determined according to the market, and skilled workers received additional wages or "margins." However, the female wage was not an issue.

The earliest reference to female pay was made in 1912 during the dispute of the rural workers (or fruit pickers) case when there was concern that competition from cheaper female labor might replace the men. At this hearing of the industrial tribunal, Justice Higgins handed down two wage decisions which became the precedents for fixing female pay rates. The first was giving equal pay to women in competitive jobs where male labor could be substituted for cheaper female labor, but this applied only to women considered suitable for men's jobs. The second was that the normal female pay should be a proportion of male pay in jobs for which women were most suitable, and therefore, did not compete with men. On the assumption that women did not have to support their families, they were normally paid about 54 percent of male basic wages and less than 54 percent of male margin rates.

According to competitiveness and skills, three models of female wages had evolved during the 1912–1967 period. First, in competitive jobs where women could force men out of employment if their wages were lower, female wages equaled male basic wages and margins. Second, in jobs which were suited to female labor, women would receive 54–75 percent of male basic wages and also 54–75 percent of male margins since they posed no threat to male employment either in male-dominated or female-dominated industry. Third, for jobs in a male-dominated industry where female competition could threaten male employment, women received less than the male basic wages but equal margins (Short 1986: 316; Dufty and Fells 1989: 302).

After World War II, the female wage was increased to 75 percent of the male basic wage because many women were already paid more than the normal 54 percent of the male basic wage. During 1969–1972, all state governments in Australia eventually passed the equal-pay legislation. However, the equal-pay principle was not applied to all women employees in practice. In 1972, the unions and women's organizations argued that only women in jobs identical to men, or 18 percent of the female workforce, received equal pay (Short 1986: 319; Dufty and Fells 1989: 302). Thus, the rule was changed from "equal pay for equal work" to "equal pay for work of equal value," so that award rates for all jobs would be determined without the gender factor.

It has been argued that wage discrimination against women has continued, and wages of women in full-time employment are lower than those of men. During 1978–1979, the average annual income of men in full-time employment was nearly 40 percent higher than that of women in full-time employment (Deery and Plowman 1992). In a very big number of industries and occupations, men were paid better wages per hour than women of similar education level, work experience, and qualifications. Even within a single occupation, such as the clerical and administration division of the Australian Public Service, it was found that men earned more than women (Deery and Plowman 1991).

Pay equity has been adopted in principle but earnings disparity exists in practice. There are different theories to explain the gender wage differential in a Western industrial economy.

## WHY DO WOMEN GENERALLY EARN LESS THAN MEN?

### Neoclassical Theory of Human Capital

The why and wherefore of gender wage differential is commonly explained by the neoclassical human capital theory. Basically, the theory is concerned with the quality of labor and the long-run supply of it. The time and effort spent by an individual to acquire productive skills and work experience is regarded as a kind of nonmarket work. The opportunity costs do not yield immediate benefits, but the higher level of income gained, in the long run, is the return on investment in human capital.

The human capital theory explains gender wage differentials on the assumption that women have lower expectations than men about their life cycle of workforce participation. Women tend to invest in less human capital and plan to interrupt their work experience for child rearing. Consequently they receive lower lifetime earnings.

In the Australian context, we can no longer use the acquisition of education or skills to explain gender wage differential. The 1991 Census found that for the whole population, a total of 890,881 women and 789,148 men made up all persons holding qualifications in associate diploma, undergraduate diploma, or degree. So there were 100,000 more women than men with some form of further education. By contrast, men dominated the group holding vocational qualifications as there was a total of 1,199,942 males (15 years and above) compared with only 145,546 females. The 1991 Census also showed that there were more female students (288,268) than males (255,521) attending college and university courses either full-time or part-time (Australian Bureau of Statistics 1993: 22 and 23).

Evidently the female population is slightly ahead of the males in human capital investment for the 1990s. The lower earnings of women therefore are more likely to be attributed to the other important factor of human capital, that is, the broken record of employment resulting in less work experience, for which choices were made in favor of family formation.

Critics of the human capital theory are not convinced that the supply side of the labor market fully explains the low employment status of women. There are other relevant factors. An important one is labor market discrimination against women on the demand side.

### Neoclassical Theories of Labor Market Discrimination

Economists have tried to explain the reality of discrimination in the labor market in which a group of people, having the same attributes as the majority, receive lower wages only because of gender or race or some other physical characteristic. In other words, discrimination is seen as the cause of unequal reward for equal productivity. There are three neoclassical models of discrimination based on the profit maximization motive of employers:

1. Distaste model;
2. Statistical discrimination;
3. Monopsonistic discrimination (see King 1990; Norris 1993).

The distaste model can be used to explain the overtly lower pay rates received by the discriminated group such as women. Although capable of the same productivity as the majority, persons belonging to the discriminated group would only be hired by employers with distaste if their wages were lower. Perfect competition in the labor market is assumed, and the employer would maximize profits if the disutility of associating with the discriminated group was compensated by lower labor costs.

Statistical discrimination can occur in the normal practice of screening applicants for jobs, training, or promotion. People are rejected on the basis of their personal characteristics such as gender, race, or other physical attributes, as a result of the employer's past experience or prejudice. Female employees are assumed to have lower productivity because of the perception that absenteeism is high among married women and so is the job turnover rate of young women. Perfect competition in the labor market is assumed, and employers maximize profit by selecting male applicants for training and promotion and generally paying female employees lower wages in expectation of higher costs in recruitment and other aspects of employment.

Under monopsonistic discrimination, employers would have monopsony power in the labor market where the supply of female labor is less elastic than that of male labor. For example, women have lower labor mobility because of family commitments. The cost-minimizing employers would seize the chance to pay lower wages or offer less favorable employment terms. The extent to which monopson-istic exploitation could be reduced would depend on the trade unions. Working for the interests of their members, male-dominated trade unions might allow the exploitation of women but definitely not of men. While female-dominated unions should also protect the interests of their members, many unions in the white collar occupations and service industries are not as powerful as their male counterparts in blue collar occupations and manufacturing industries.

In summary, the distaste model is not relevant to the Australian situation, but the theories of statistical discrimination and monopsonistic discrimination are useful to some extent. Statistical discrimination would account for the unequal opportunities for advancement in the workplace, as reflected in the flatter profile of lifetime earnings for the majority of women. Another result of statistical discrimination is the barrier of a "glass ceiling" against women at the top of their career ladders. It is difficult to estimate the supply inelasticity of female labor in monopsonistic discrimination, but married women normally have less mobility than men. The cost-minimizing employers with monopsony power would have more bargaining powers over women with young children because these employees are willing to trade off higher wages for convenient working hours.

In Australia, wage differentials between men and women are associated with gender segregation in employment. Labor market segmentation theories are help-ful in explaining this phenomenon.

**Radical Economic Theories on Discrimination**

Radical economic theories based on labor market segmentation have been used to explain the concentration of certain groups such as women and ethnic minorities in low-paid jobs (Cain 1976). The characteristics of jobs and the types of people holding these jobs are determined by segmentation of the labor market into different sectors. "The primary sector offers jobs with relatively high wages, good working conditions, chances of advancement and, above all, employment stability. Jobs in the secondary sector, by contrast, tend to be low-paying, with poorer working conditions and little chance of advancement" (Piore 1973: 12).

For the Australian situation, Conroy (1994) has an enlightening discussion on gender segregation by adopting Kelly's (1991) categorization of employers and jobs in a segmented labor market (see Table 13.3). First, there are different classes of employers and they are found in:

1. The core economy firms in businesses such as the large banks, heavy industry, manufacturing, chemicals, pharmaceuticals, automobiles, metals, aircraft, and petroleum. The large companies with monopolistic or oligopolistic powers in the product market can afford to provide good wages and employment conditions.

2. The periphery economy firms in businesses such as restaurants, real estate, textile manufacturing, retailing and services, small computer firms, and law firms. These firms, very large in number and highly competitive, cannot afford as good wages and conditions as the core economy firms. They also operate with a high

**Table 13.3**
**Types of Employers and Jobs in Segmented Labor Market**

| Types of Employers | Primary jobs | Intermediate jobs | Secondary jobs |
|---|---|---|---|
| Core economy firms: monopolistic or oligopolistic | **1** Chemists Engineers Top Managers Bankers Corporate Lawyers Corporate Accountants etc. **MALE-DOMINATED** | **2** Skilled Craft Workers Sales Personnel Insurance Claims Adj. Computer Analysts Middle Managers | **3** Maintenance Workers Clerical Staff Assembly Workers |
| Periphery economy firms: highly competitive, entrepreneurial | **4** Lawyers Doctors Managers Administrators in some hospitals, large chains Social Scientists **MORE WOMEN HERE THAN 1 AND 2** | **5** Bank Tellers Computer Programmers Middle Managers Nurses | **6** Fast-food Workers Operatives Word Processors |
| Public sector: noncompetitive, budgetdriven | **7** Elected Officials High Level Administrators Top Staff Appointed Judges | **8** Mid-range civil servants Teachers Librarians Nurses **HIGH PROPORTIONS OF WOMEN ARE IN 8 AND 9** | **9** Clerical Staff Maintenance Part-time |
| Voluntary sector (including religious institutions) | **10** Clergy CEO of Red Cross Fundraisers | **11** Volunteer Planners Coordinators | **12** Daily and Incidental Workers |

*Source:* Adapted form Kelly (1991) cited in Conroy 1994: 97.

level of labor flexibility by engaging part-time or casual employees who are usually nonunionized. The part-time and casual employees are women.

3. The public sector, which is noncompetitive and budget driven. It is made up of government and nonprofit organizations.

4. The voluntary sector, which is mostly associated with religious institutions (Kelly 1991; cited in Conroy 1994).

Second, labor market segmentation is useful to distinguish between the good and bad jobs in the primary, intermediate and secondary sectors as shown in Table 13.3. Jobs in the primary labor sector of the core economy (cell 1) provide the highest pay and greatest job security and are male-dominated. In the intermediate labor market of the core economy (cell 2), there would be very few women among the skilled craft workers but women would make up one third of computer programmers and salespersons. However, the promotion "pipeline" in this sector would be male-dominated, with implication that most senior positions in the *core economy firms* would be occupied by males. On the other hand, women are concentrated in "pink collar" jobs belonging to the secondary and intermediate sectors (cells 5, 6, 8, and 9) of the periphery economy and public service (Conroy 1994: 97 and 98).

Thus the primary jobs, which are the most desirable, are normally held by men and women occupy the secondary jobs with lower wages and less security. Within the different categories of employer organizations, female labor mobility to senior executive positions would be less restricted in the periphery economy and the public service than the core economy. The differential gender employment status is created, to a large extent, by the rules and procedures of the internal labor market mechanism of the individual firm.

**Internal Labor Markets**

The firm can separate its own workforce into (1) core employees and (2) peripheral employees. The core group of employees is the permanent labor force equipped with skills and knowledge specific to the organization while the peripheral group provides the numerical labor flexibility needed to cope with seasonal requirements. An internal labor market exists when movement up the job hierarchy is available only to the core employees, and the points of job entry are located at the lowest level of the organization. Jobs outside the scope of the internal labor market, offering no security, training, and promotion prospects, belong to a secondary labor market. Most of them are filled by young people and women.

The process of leaving employment for family reasons and then returning, after several years of absence, has excluded the majority of women from the good primary jobs inside the internal labor market. In any case, these jobs often involve long and irregular working hours, overseas travel, and even workplace relocation. The normal assumptions about the family commitments of married women would make many employers doubt their ability to meet such requirements (Deery and Plowman 1991: 488). Thus, gender wage differentials can be attributed to barriers in the internal labor market and the downward job mobility of the majority of women with responsibilities for their children.

Supporting the validity of the segmented market concept, Still (1985) argues that enough evidence in Australia exists to indicate that women usually have poorer job opportunities especially in the management arena. Furthermore, the internal labor market operates in conjunction with the traditional "sex structuring" of organizations which differentiate jobs within the firm into male and female roles (Still 1985: 4). The current debate around the glass ceiling concept relates to the scarcity of women in senior executive positions. In addition, there is a study by Chapman and Mulvey (1986) on the separate contribution of a number of variables to the average wage differences between men and women. Their results suggest that it is the employer's treatment of women and men that largely explains gender difference in earnings.

## GOVERNMENT POLICIES AGAINST WORKPLACE DISCRIMINATION

Employers have a decisive role in the pay structure and employment conditions. They are empowered to define the scope of the firm's internal labor market and eligibility of its participants. The criteria for staff recruitment and promotion up career paths could overtly or covertly discriminate against women (Deery and Plowman 1991: 489).

Three types of workplace discrimination can be distinguished: direct, indirect, and systemic: (1) Direct discrimination results from the specific behavior of an employer who treats some employees less favorably because of gender, race, or other personal characteristics; (2) indirect discrimination exists when the employer sets up a requirement which is irrelevant to the job but would indirectly discriminate against a particular group; and (3) systemic discrimination results from apparently neutral employment practices. They are not intended to be discriminatory and are not easily recognized because they have been accepted as normal in the workplace. Systemic discrimination is not related to individual cases but is reflected in the employment profile of an individual organization, for example, the scarcity of women in senior positions.

The apparent failure of the market mechanism to remove discrimination has made legislation necessary. However, it was only in 1984 when steps were taken to enact the Federal Sex Discrimination Act.

### The Sex Discrimination Act of 1984

The 1984 Sex Discrimination Act was the first attempt to eliminate discrimination on the grounds of sex, marital status, or pregnancy in the areas of employment, education, accommodation, the provision of goods, facilities, and services, the disposal of land, the activities of clubs, and the administration of Commonwealth laws and programs. The legislation also made sexual harassment of employees unlawful in the workplace.

The formal mechanisms set up to redress the grievances of discrimination and sexual harassment include investigation and conciliation by the Sex Discrimination Commission and conciliation and decision by the Human Rights Commission. If necessary, legal proceedings may be lodged in the federal court (Deery and Plowman 1991: 490).

The act deals with individual cases of discrimination and there were some successful prosecutions by individuals against companies. However, the act was designed to address direct and indirect types of discrimination and not all forms of discrimination against women. The problem of systemic discrimination was to be resolved by the federal government's Affirmative Action (Equal Employment Opportunity for Women) Act 1986.

### The Affirmative Action Act of 1986

The affirmative action initiative was imported into Australia from the United States. The act was not intended to find solutions for individual problems but to remove systemic discrimination and to persuade employers to give women a "fair go."

The act was implemented by first targeting educational institutions and employers with 1,000 employees or more. Later in 1989, all organizations with more than 100 employees had to report to the government agency on their implementation of equal opportunity policies and programs. There are three economic arguments to support the removal of systemic discrimination: equity, efficiency, and freedom of choice (see also Still 1988).

1. Equity in the labor market: The guarantee of an individual's right to equal access to job opportunities and rewards, based on merit not gender, would lead to better job competition in the labor market;

2. Efficiency: The optimum use of human resources in the labor market would be realized if the talents and skills of women are rewarded by promotion and equal opportunities. There would be an end to gender segregation in employment.

3. Freedom of choice: In a free-market economy, individuals should have the freedom of choice in their occupations and industries according to ability, inclination, and qualifications. Past practices and prejudices had influenced individual choices on the basis of gender.

It should be noted that affirmative action was not a form of reverse discrimination, whereby the previously disadvantaged female group was to be given preference over male employees. Also, the act did not require employers to fulfill certain quotas by the employment of women (Affirmative Action Agency 1991: 15).

There is a general view in Australia that affirmation action has achieved some limited success. However, the legislation does not carry penalties to ensure compliance by companies. In the case of companies relying on government contracts for a significant income, the government could enforce compliance by giving contracts only to companies implementing affirmative action programs. Companies that were concerned with their public image would also comply but many only made token gestures.

The need for various legislation to remove discrimination against women is a reflection of the community's stubborn resistance to such an attitude change. Government intervention has a positive influence on progress toward addressing the economic issues of women in paid employment. A comparison of the data for 1989 and 1991 in Table 13.2 suggests that there has been a slow breakdown in gender segregation by industry.

## CONCLUSIONS

Female participation in the labor force is relatively high in Australia. A large proportion of women in paid employment are working part-time, and they are the married women with young children. An outstanding feature of the Australian workforce is gender segregation by occupations as well as by industries.

The equal-pay principle was adopted more than 20 years ago to overcome the traditional pay discrimination against women. Pay equity is strictly practiced in the award pay rates, but they are only the minimum rates enforceable by law and do not cover the other components of the wage packet. A better indicator of income distribution is the average weekly earnings, which show a marked pay disparity between men and women, even among full-time employees.

For Australian conditions, the theories of labor market segmentation are useful for explaining some of the gender inequities in employment status. Equally important are the different types workplace discrimination (direct, indirect, and systemic) practiced by employers.

Government intervention was necessary in the form of two legislations to remove all types of discrimination. They were the Anti-Discrimination Act of 1984 and the Affirmative Action (Equal Employment Opportunity) Act of 1986. There is no general agreement on the extent of success. For example, there is still the question of not equally rewarding the female-dominated occupations which are of equal value to the male-dominated occupations. At least, the community is now more aware of gender issues than a decade ago. However, the rising level of consciousness does not speed up action to resolve the economic issues of women in paid employment.

## NOTES

1. The definition of the Australian Bureau of Statistics is that full-time employees are the permanent, temporary, and casual employees who normally work the agreed or awards hours for a full-time employee. If the agreed or award hours do not apply, employees are regarded as full-time if they ordinarily work thirty-five hours or more per week (Australian Bureau of Statistics 1994b: 33).

2. An award pay rate for an occupation group or industry is the minimum wage rate to be enforceable by law. The term "award" is commonly used in Australia to refer to a set of employment conditions covering wages, weekly work hours, holiday loading, and other entitlements of the employee.

# 14

# Conclusions

*Kartik C. Roy, Clement A. Tisdell, and Hans C. Blomqvist*


The overwhelming impression of the present volume is that discrimination and segregation of women is still very much the order of the day, despite the fact that the problem has been recognized for quite some time and despite legislative measures taken in order to counter the problem. As a matter of fact, the general impression is that the status of women rather seems to deteriorate in the early phases of development, after which an improvement can usually be observed.

In developed countries, the socioeconomic status of women is certainly better, and discrimination against females is less prevalent than in developing countries, but the status of women remains somewhat subordinated to that of males. This is not so much a consequence of legislation and formal institutions, however, but emanates largely from the fact that women are still regarded as responsible for household work and the upbringing of children. Moreover, when they enter the paid labor force their contribution is still often seen as complementary, is frequently made on a part-time basis, and is usually heavily concentrated in a small number of industries and occupations where they comprise a majority of the employees.

Some features of social development in the Western world, especially the weakening of the nuclear family as an institution, have aggravated the situation of women in many respects. This is the case particularly in countries where the public welfare net is undeveloped.

In developing countries the discrimination is more pervasive. There is discrimination both within and outside the family, and legal and institutional setups with their built-in bias against women have strengthened instead of lessening the forces of discrimination. In Africa women are often treated as a piece of property, such as land. In South Asia discrimination by women against women, restrictions based on old prejudice, customs, and taboos, and all the major elements of the ideology of seclusion enforced by elders, particularly in rural areas (villages and rural towns) on all categories of women—educated and uneducated, married and single—in nontribal families are the greatest hindrance to improvement in women's socio-economic status. Since the vast majority of the population (74 percent in India, 82 percent in Bangladesh, 78 percent in Sri Lanka, and 67 percent in Pakistan) still live in rural areas, without significant lessening of the force of such restrictions women's status cannot improve.

In most developing countries, some improvements have resulted from economic change, such as better education and health facilities and reduced infant mortality, but commercialization of agriculture, population growth, and increasing pressure on land have strengthened the forces of gender discrimination.

In developed countries also economic change has not been able to do away with discrimination. Built-in male bias in the (often informal) institutional setup is still present. It is also likely that adverse economic circumstances, such as unemployment, may bring into the open previously hidden gender-based discrimination against women. The causal relations are often ambiguous, however. Paradoxically, the severe recessions in the 1980s and 1990s has changed women's relative status for the better in some cases (even if it may have deteriorated absolutely), as the contribution of women to the livelihood of their families has become more important, and indeed is often necessary for the survival of the family.

An especially disadvantaged group is often made up of migrant women, both in formal and informal sectors of production. In Australia, for example, there seems to be considerable discrimination against this group. The editors' private experiences suggest that migrant female workers of ethnic background on factory floors in Australia are usually treated with respect by their male superiors. Discrimination against such female workers by their female superiors, many of whom were their former colleagues, is, indeed, more visible. Being on the factory floor women workers, migrant or not, know the reasons for inefficiencies in the production system and what is to be done to remedy the situation and improve productivity. However, their opinion is never sought and they are not consulted before the introduction of any new workplace practice in which they would be involved. Catchwords such as "workplace reform" and "team work" have seldom developed beyond conferences, meetings, and bundles of paper on which blueprints are drawn. This example tends to support the intuitive feeling that the institutional bias against women in places of employment is still very strong, and discrimination against women continues to hamper progress in efficiency, productivity, and economic growth.[1]

Empowerment of women in developed and developing economies requires somewhat different types of action. In developed economies, the vast majority of women have the freedom to do what they like and most have the freedom of choice they deserve. In a legal sense, there may not be much more to be done in order to enhance the status of women (although some, presumably nongendered legislation tends to produce discrimination as a side effect). Informal institutions and practices are more important, and, unfortunately, much more difficult to deal with.

In many developing countries, on the other hand, women do not even enjoy the freedom to move out of the confines of their homes, to talk to anybody they like, to pursue a career they choose, and to be economically independent. Hence, a prerequisite for empowerment in these countries is reducing the force of gender restrictions based on old customs (sometimes, but not necessarily, based on religion), taboos, and the ideology of seclusion.

Women's grass-roots movements in both developing and developed countries have sprung up in the last few decades to help women in the empowerment process or as part of that process itself. However, the growth of such movements requires women to have the freedom to go out of their homes in order to form such groups in the first place. This freedom is lacking, as obvious from the contributions of this volume, in many developing countries. Thus, for example, in India, many women's grass-roots movements were initiated by tribal members and harijans ("untouchables") who have freedom of movement. But the vast majority of women are nontribal members and nonharijans who sadly lack this freedom.

In China, although old customs, traditions, and taboos exercise considerable influence on women's lives, the ideology of seclusion does not apply. That is true for many other countries as well, while seclusion of sorts is not unusual either. For instance, in Latin America, women traditionally have been kept under close surveillance by husbands, fathers, and brothers. In yet other countries, such as the Philippines and Thailand, there are few restrictions on the movement of women, which in turn has facilitated other forms of abuse.

Thus action needed in empowering women in developed and developing countries on the one hand and in different developing countries on the other hand may seem to be different. However, a closer examination of the types of discrimination and constraints faced by women in both worlds would reveal that the broad nature of action required is similar. In developed countries, discrimination and constraints faced by women are partly (but decreasingly) legalized and partly based on customary practice, whereas in developing countries many of the restrictions on women seem to owe their origin to customs, prejudices, and taboos. Both types of constraints are parts of the overall institutional environment within which socioeconomic relations take shape.

Thus, for example, take the case of South Asia in general and India in particular. The practice of dowry is legally forbidden but has been institutionalized through customary adherence to it by brides' families for many years. But this practice, in a sense, owes its origin to the "classic patriarchy" which, for adherence to it, requires the enforcement on women of the ideology of seclusion. None of these practices, however, has any legal backing.

Hence, the removal of such gender-based restrictions on women would require changing the institutional environment which in turn would necessitate, among other things, changes in society's attitudes to and perceptions of women. Again, take the case of dowry. Even if a bride's parents take legal action against a groom and his parents demanding dowry, it would be difficult to bring down a verdict against the groom and his parents and to force them to pay a penalty, as the practice of dowry is still not being perceived by the bureaucracy, judiciary, and the society at large as being too derogatory to women's socioeconomic status as human beings to be continued. Changes in the attitude to women of legislators, bureaucrats, judges, and of the society at large can come about by, among other things, a massive program of social education of all these who create, implement, uphold, and preserve the institutional environment.

In developed countries, and many developing countries as well, there may not be much left to do from a legal point of view. Actions actually taken may cut both ways too. For example, the Australian universities in implementing the affirmative action program are under obligation to apply the principle of nondiscrimination on the basis of sex, religion, color, and so forth in the matter of employment and to try to raise the share of female staff in their total staff number.

Some universities may be sincerely trying to apply the principle of nondiscrimination and still failing to recruit females on the basis of established criteria. Others may deliberately be trying to increase the share of females in the staff without due regard to the principle of nondiscrimination *and* established criteria. The universities in the first case would probably be criticized and in the second praised for their actions by various lobby groups. Some universities may not be even trying to increase the number of female members on their staff. Of these three cases, the universities in the first case should be praised. However, appropriate monitoring of the actions of universities and other employers is extremely difficult. The principle of nondiscrimination does not, of course, mean discrimination against males and apparent discrimination against a female may turn out to be no discrimination on the basis of the established criteria.

However, some writers argue that *positive* discrimination is justified in order to break what otherwise would be a vicious continuing cycle of social discrimination. Positive discrimination can help to uplift a group socially and provide a demonstrative effect of their social and economic worth. By providing greater hope for the advancement of groups otherwise discriminated against, positive discrimination may provide them with greater motivation to succeed. For example, positive discrimination in favor of women in employment could have these effects. Nevertheless, there is some cause for concern if positive discrimination is a continuing phenomenon. Hopefully, as a result of positive discrimination applying for a limited period of time, the social cycle of discrimination will be broken and positive discrimination will no longer be necessary.

What all these examples say is that passing a law banning discrimination against women in certain respects cannot achieve results unless it is implemented properly. Therefore changes in the institutional environment in the developed countries would also involve among other things social education programs, covering all those who create and uphold the institutional environment.

Informal institutions, comprising, for example, "gender contracts" are formidable obstacles to full equality, however, and are by nature such that it is very hard to eliminate or change them in the short term. The spontaneous development of social institutions seems to evolve toward a gradual phasing out of discriminating practices, though. Instead, other problems are emerging.

The increasing stress of working life and the tendency of dissolution of a central social institution, the nuclear family, has contributed to a new class of underprivileged women, the single mothers. True, this development is undoubtedly likely to be a consequence, to some extent, of the increasing participation of women in economic and social affairs. Still it would be absurd to try to counter these problems by forcing the women back to the kitchens. Comparisons between different developed countries seem to indicate that the existence of a public welfare network, consisting of a functioning daycare system, and so forth may reduce the problems significantly. It is important to realize that this type of institution should not be seen as government handouts but rather as investments in infrastructure necessary to allow the probably most productive members of the society, the parents of young children, to participate fully in the economy and society.

As far as social education is concerned, it is a "pure public good" and hence its provision has to be made by governments. Governments in developing countries are resource-strapped on the one hand and are usually ruled by elites (political, military, rural oligarchs) on the other. They would not be willing to undertake such programs unless they receive financial support and their hands are forced by supranational agencies such as the World Bank and the IMF. These organizations could use their persuasive power to make developing countries take action in this regard, although, admittedly, this would imply a certain change in the agenda of those institutions. Furthermore, by initiating detailed research into gender discrimination in these countries, by publishing the results and by raising such issues in international fora where they can force, to some extent, the hands of those governments. Since efficient and honest implementation of programs aiming at enhancing equality is crucial to their success, much of the task of implementation should probably be contracted out to private agencies, such as NGOs and even commercial enterprises.

Finally, before concluding this chapter, a few more comments should be made on the issue of economic discrimination. As mentioned in several contributions to this volume, there are alternative explanations to pay differences between men and women, some of which may even appear "justified" from a theoretical point of view. The most persuasive of these explanations is probably the one that women, since they may plan to participate less permanently in the paid workforce compared to men, invest less in their human capital and therefore are less productive than their male counterparts. This explanation is clearly becoming less persuasive, as female participation rates are on the rise almost globally, and in any case does little to help us understand the phenomenon of workforce segregation, which is arguably a major reason for differences in earnings between men and women.

Despite the presence in economic literature of theoretical "justification" of economic discrimination against women, it would be difficult to apply the theory to the cases of women who accept the differential rates of pay, do not complain about their inferior status but want to be engaged in socially visible, economically productive employment commensurate with their qualities, knowledge, and skill, and do not want their lives to be ruled by centuries old derogatory customs and prejudices. Even when the male-female wage differential in a practical case can be supported by theory, it is not unlikely that the production conditions may have been maintained in such a way that they prevent women from contributing to the production to their full potential.

Such women live, for example, in the rural areas of many Third World countries in Asia, Africa, and Latin America. Let us take the case of South Asia. In 1994 the population of five South Asian countries, Bangladesh, Nepal, India, Pakistan, and Sri Lanka, stood at roughly 1.19 billion. Of these, 887.4 million, accounting for 74.3 percent of the total lived in rural areas (i.e., villages and rural towns). Assuming the share of females in the total population to be around 49 percent, a rough estimate puts the total female population in rural areas in South Asia at about 435 million, representing about 37 percent of the total population of South Asia. When rural females in other regions of the world are added to this total, the number would reach staggering heights. Discrimination against and restrictions on women which confine them to the surroundings of their homes and prevent them from even trying to contribute to production cannot be economically efficient.

Women's socioeconomic status and GDP growth are interrelated with one impacting on the other. Higher GDP growth rate is necessary for improving the socioeconomic status of women, but the inferior status of women forces the actual GDP growth rate to fall behind the potential growth rate.

What role do women play in the development process for preserving environment and sustaining development and how can this role be strengthened? Sustainable development requires the conservation of the environment, which, among other things, requires preservation of forest and fresh-water resources. However, increased population pressure has contributed to deforestation of vast areas and substantial use of fresh-water resources for domestic and industrial purpose, for example, in countries like Bangladesh and Pakistan. During the ten-year period from 1980 to 1990, Bangladesh and Pakistan have lost over 70 percent of their total natural forest area due to deforestation. If this trend continues, these countries would not have any natural forest left in the foreseeable future. The situation is similar in many other parts of the less developed world, although the extent of environmental degradation in Asia is often more serious due to the fact that this region is so densely populated.

A World Bank study (*Gender and Poverty in India* 1991) on gender and poverty in India suggests that along with education, the ability to earn and control income appears to be one of the most powerful determinants of women's status in the family.

Although the overall resource levels are lower for poor households and those of scheduled caste and tribal groups, women's access to and control over the use of these resources is more egalitarian in such households. However, even among these groups, the inside/outside dichotomy acts as a serious constraint on women's economic productivity and on their ability to secure education and access to health services—because it determines the model of gender relations, the administrative and legal structures, and the social services these women interact with on the "outside." But gender relations are rooted in the private domain of households, and government intervention into such domains is beset with practical and philosophical problems. The most effective means by which public policy can affect intrahousehold processes and reduce women's dependency is to alter the economic environment within the continuously shifting cultural "map" of the inside/outside domains, a change that is ultimately formulated at the household level.

Thus the World Bank study (1991) recognizes the influence of the inside/outside dichotomy on the administrative and legal structures and the social services the poor women interact with emphasizes the need for bringing about changes in the economic environment, and lends strong support to the editors' view that there is the need for changes in the total institutional environment which encompasses administrative, legal social, and economic environment.

Considering population growth, the removal of gender restrictions on women, and improvement in their socioeconomic status are essential for the fulfillment of these twin prerequisites to sustainable growth and development. It is well known that economic development and, in particular, improvement of women's situation are a precondition for bringing down the fertility rate.

Strengthening women's role in the development process would require women's direct involvement and active participation in all stages of this process, from the planning to the implementation stages of programs. Once again, this would require changes in the institutional environment. The process of change, although begun, is a long-term process and can only be completed by concerted action by interested groups and agencies combined with the political commitment of governments.

## NOTE

1. With the official introduction of workforce bargaining in Australia by the Labor Goverment in 1994, a policy which is still in the implementation phase, the position may change, but whether it will do so substantially remains to be seen. It is also worthwhile noting that women have been severely under represented in dominant positions in the labor movement in Australia. However, in 1995, a woman became President of the Australian Council of Trade Unions (ACTU) for the first time. The ACTU is the Australian national umbrella organization for trade unions. Once again, it is too early to say what the impact of this will be but women are demanding greater representation in the organization of trade unions and in the Labor Party, which has been dominated by males and still is.

# References

Acker, J. Proposal for an Umbrella Project for 'Kvinnotemagruppen,' working paper, The Swedish Center for Working Life, Stockholm 1989.

Acker, J. "Hierarchies, Jobs, Bodies: A Theory of Gendered Organizations," *Gender & Society,* 4, 1990.

Acker, J. "Gendering Organizational Theory." In Mills, A. J. and Tancred, P. (eds.). *Gendering Organizational Analysis.* London: Sage, 1992.

Affirmative Action Agency. *Affirmative Action into the 90's: Issues Paper.* Canberra, 1991.

Agarwal, B. "Women, Poverty and Agricultural Growth in India," *Journal of Peasant Studies,* 13, 1986.

Agarwal, B. "Rural Women, Poverty and Natural Resources," *Economic and Political Weekly,* 24, 1989.

Agarwal, B. "Social Security and the Family in Rural India: Coping with Seasonality and Calamity," *Journal of Peasant Studies,* 17, 1990.

Agnes, F. "Protecting Women Against Violence? Review of a Decade of Legislation, 1980–89," *Economic and Political Weekly,* 27, 1992.

Agnihotri, S. B. Missing Females—A Disaggregated Analysis. Mimeo, Orissa Environmental Programme, Government of Orissa, India, 1994.

Aguiar, N. "La mujer y la crisis latinoamericana." In Aguiar, N. (ed.). *Mujer y Crisis: Respuestas ante la recesión.* Caracas: DAWN/MUDAR/Editorial Nueva Sociedad, 1990.

Alapuro, R. *State and Revolution in Finland.* Berkeley: University of California Press, 1988.

Alestalo, M. *Structural Changes, Classes and the State. Finland in a Historical and Comparative Perspective.* Helsinki: Yliopistopaino, 1986.

Alestalo, M. and Uusitalo, H. "Finland." In Flora, P. (ed.). *Growth to Limits. The Western European Welfare States Since World War II.* Berlin: de Gruyter, 1986.

Alford, K. and McLean, M. "Partners or Parasites of Men? Women's Economic Status in Australia, Britain and Canada, 1850–1900," working paper No. 66 (April), Australian National University, Canberra, 1986.

Allén, T. "Naisnäkökulma talouspolitiikkaan—tarvitaanko sitäl a mikä se voisi olla?" In *Naiset ja talous.* Helsinki: Sosiaali-ja terveysministeriö, 1988.

Allén, T. "Economic Development and the Feminisation of Poverty." In Folbre, N.,

Bergmann, B., Agarwal, B., and Floro, M. (eds.). *Women's Work in the World Economy*. Basingstoke and London: Macmillan, 1992.

Allén, T. "The Nordic Model of Gender Equality." In Varsa, H. (ed.). *Shaping Structural Change in Finland. The Role of Women*. Helsinki: Ministry of Social Affairs and Health, 1993.

Andolsen, B. H. "Women's Work and Technological Change in North America." In Fiorenza, E. S. and Carr, A. (eds.). *Women, Work and Poverty*. Edinburgh: T. and T. Clark, 1987.

Anker, R. and Hein, C. (eds.). *Sex Inequalities in Urban Employment in the Third World*. New York: St. Martin's Press, 1986.

*Annual Report of Labor Statistics 1966 & 1986*. Taipei: Directorate-General of Budget, Accounting, and Statistics, Executive Yuan, 1966 and 1986.

Annuar Ali. "Industrial Restructuring: Beyond The Industrial Master Plan." Paper presented at the MIER 1988 National Outlook Conference, November, 1988.

Anttalainen, M.-L. *Sukupuolen mukaan kahtiajakautuneet työmarkkinat Pohjoismaissa*. Helsinki: TANE, 1986.

Anttalainen, M.-L. "Equal Pay?" In Varsa, H. (ed.). *Shaping Structural Change in Finland. The Role of Women*. Helsinki: Ministry of Social Affairs and Health, 1993.

Anttonen, A. "The Feminization of the Scandinavian Welfare State." In Simonen, L. (ed.). *Finnish Debates on Women's Studies*. Tampere, Finland: University of Tampere, Centre for Women's Studies and Gender Relations, 1990.

Anttonen, A. "The Scandinavian Welfare State as a Woman-friendly State." Paper presented at the International Seminar on "Women and the Welfare States in Europe," London, June 1–6, 1992.

Anttonen, A. "Hyvinvointivaltion naisystävälliset kasvot." In Anttonen, A., Henriksson, L., and Nätkin, R. (eds.). *Naisten hyvinvointivaltio*. Tampere, Finland: Vastapaino, 1994.

Ariffin, J. "Rural-Urban Migration and the Status of Factory Women Workers in a Developing Society: A Case Study of Peninsular Malaysia." Paper presented at the conference of the Sociological Association of Australia and New Zealand, Brisbane, 1978.

Ariffin, J. "Impact of Modern Electronics Technology on Women Workers in Malaysia." In Aziz, U. A., Hoong, Y -Y., and Poh, L -C. (eds.). *Technology, Culture and Development*. Kuala Lumpur, Malaysia: University of Malaya Press, 1984a.

Ariffin, J. "Industrial Development and Rural-Urban Migration of Women Workers in Malaysia." Ph.D. Thesis, University of Queensland, Australia, 1984b.

Ariffin, J. *Women and Development in Malaysia*. Petaling Jaya, Malaysia: Pelanduk Publications, 1992.

Ariffin, J. *From Kampung to Urban Factories: Findings from the HAWA Study*. Kuala Lumpur, Malaysia: University of Malaya Press, 1994.

Arizpe, L., Salinas, F., and Velásquez, M. "Effects of the Economic Crisis on the Living Conditions of Peasant Women in Mexico." In *The Invisible Adjustment: Poor Women and the Economic Crisis*. Santiago: UNICEF, 1987.

Arrow, K. J. "Models of Job Discrimination." In Pascal, A. H. (ed.). *Racial Discrimination in Economic Life*. Lexington, MA: Lexington Books, 1972.

Asahi Shimbun. *Japanese Almanac 1994*. Tokyo: Asahi Shimbun, 1993.

Åström, G. and Hirdman, Y. (eds.). *Kontrakt i kris: om kvinnors plats i välfärdsstaten*. Stockholm, Carlssons, 1992.

Australian Bureau of Statistics. *Census Characteristics of Australia: 1991 Census of Population and Housing.* Canberra, 1993.

Australian Bureau of Statistics. *Employed Wage and Salary Earners Australia December Quarter 1993.* Canberra, 1994a.

Australian Bureau of Statistics. *Labour Force Australia.* Canberra, 1989, 1994b.

Banerjee, N. "Trends in Women's Employment, 1971–81: Some Macro-Level Observations," *Economic and Political Weekly,* 24, 1989.

Barham, B., Clark, M., Katz, E., and Schurman, R. "Nontraditional Agricultural Exports in Latin America," *Latin American Research Review,* 27, 1992.

Baxter, S. and Lansing, M. *Women and Politics: The Invisible Majority.* Ann Arbor: University of Michigan Press, 1980.

Becker, G. S. *The Economics of Discrimination.* Chicago: Chicago University Press, 1957.

*Beijing Adult Education,* 5th issue. Beijing: Government of China, 1985.

Bendyna, M. E. and Lake, C. C. "Gender and Voting in the 1992 Presidential Election." In Cook, E. A., Thomas, S., and Wilcox, C. (eds.). *The Year of the Woman: Myths and Realities.* Boulder, CO: Westview, 1994.

Benería, L. and Feldman, S. (eds.). *Unequal Burden: Economic Crises, Persistent Poverty, and Women's Work.* Boulder, CO: Westview, 1992.

Benería, L. and Roldán, M. *The Crossroads of Class and Gender.* Chicago: University of Chicago Press, 1987.

Bergman, S. "Post-War Feminism in Finland." In Bergman, S. (ed.). *Women's Worlds. Finnish Contributions to the Third Interdisciplinary Congress on Women.* Åbo, Finland: Institute of Women's Studies at Åbo Akademi University, 1989.

Bergmann, B. R. and Darity, W., Jr. "Social Relations in the Workplace and Employers Discrimination." In *Proceedings of the Thirty-Third Annual Meeting of the Industrial Research Association.* Madison: University of Wisconsin, 1981.

Bhalla, S. "Technological Change and Women Workers, Evidence from the Expansionary Phase in Haryana Agriculture," *Economic and Political Weekly,* 24, 1989.

Björnberg, U. "Political Parenthood among Women and Men in Sweden." Paper presented at the 17th Nordic Congress of Sociology, Gävle, Sweden, August 13–15, 1993.

Blondet, C. "Women's Organizations and Politics in a Time of Crisis." Paper presented at workshop at the Helen Kellogg Institute for International Studies, University of Notre Dame, Notre Dame, Indiana, 1989.

Bonilla, E. "Working Women in Latin America." In *Economic and Social Progress in Latin America: 1990 Report.* Washington, D.C.: Inter-American Development Bank, 1990.

Boserup, E. *Women's Role in Economic Development.* London: Macmillan, 1970.

Brandth, B. and Kvande, E. "Fra forsorger til omsorger. Om den maskuline utforming av barnomsorg." Paper presented at the 16th Nordic Congress of Sociology, Trondheim, Norway, August 23–25, 1991.

Brett, A. "Why Gender Is a Development Issue." In Wallace, T. and March, C. (eds.). *Changing Perceptions, Writings on Gender and Development.* Oxford: Oxfam, 1991.

Bruyn-Hundt, M. "Economic Independence of Women in the Netherlands." In Folbre, N., Bergmann, B., Agarwal, B., and Floro, M. (eds.). *Women's Work in the World Economy.* Basingstoke and London: Macmillan, 1992.

Bryson, L. "Citizenship, Caring and Commodification." Paper presented at the conference "Crossing Borders," Stockholm, May 27–29, 1994.

Burnstein, H., Crow, B., and Johnson, H. (eds.). *Rural Livelihoods, Crises and Responses.* Oxford: Oxford University Press and the Open University, 1992.

Bustani, C. "The Forest for the Trees: Explaining Change in Brazilian Environmental Policy." Paper presented at the XVIII International Congress of the Latin American Studies Association, March 10–12, Atlanta, Georgia, 1994.

Buvinic, M., Valenzuela, J. P., Molina, T., and González, E. "The Fortunes of Adolescent Mothers and Their Children: The Transmission of Poverty in Santiago, Chile," *Population and Development Review,* 18, 1992.

Cain, G. G. "The Challenge of Segmented Labor Market Theories to Orthodox Theory: A Survey," *Journal of Economic Literature,* 14, 1976.

Caldeira, T. "Mujeres, Cotidianeidad y Política." In Jelin, E. (ed.). *Ciudadania e Identidad: Las Mujeres en los Movimientos Sociales Latinoamericanos.* Geneva: United Nations Research Institute for Social Development (UNRISD), 1987.

Caplan, P. "Development Policies in Tanzania—Some Implications for Women," *Journal of Development Studies,* 17, 1991.

Carroll, S. J. "Women's Autonomy and the Gender Gap: 1980 and 1982." In Mueller, C. M. (ed.). *The Politics of the Gender Gap: The Social Construction of Political Influence.* Beverly Hills, CA: Sage, 1988.

*Census Yearbook of China 1993.* Beijing: China Statistical Publishing House, 1993.

Chambers, R. "Sustainable Rural Livelihoods." Overview of a paper for a conference on Sustainable Development, London: International Institute for Environment and Development, 1987.

Chan, S. "Overachievers and Underachievers: A Cross-national Comparison of Some Policy Performances," *Korean Journal of International Studies,* 19, 1987/1988.

Chan, S. and Clark, C. *Flexibility, Foresight, and Fortuna in Taiwan's Development: Navigating between Scylla and Charybdis.* London: Routledge, 1992.

Chaney, E. and García-Castro, M. *Muchachas No More: Household Workers in Latin America and the Caribbean.* Philadelphia: Temple University Press, 1989.

Chapman, B. J. "Sex Differences in Earnings: Changes over the 1970s in the Australian Public Service." In Chapman, B. J., Isaac, J. E., and Niland, J. R. (eds.). *Australian Labour Economics: Readings,* 3rd ed. Melbourne: Macmillan, 1984.

Chapman, B. J. and Mulvey, C. "An Analysis of the Origins of Sex Differences in Australian Wages," *Journal of Industrial Relations,* 28, 1986.

Chen, M. "Women's Work in Indian Agriculture by Agro Ecologic Zone: Meeting Needs of Landless and Landpoor Women," *Economic and Political Weekly,* 24, 1989.

Chhachhi, A. "The State, Religious Fundamentalism and Women; Trends in South Asia," *Economic and Political Weekly,* 24, 1989.

Chiang, L. H. N. and Ku, Y. L. *Past and Current Status of Women in Taiwan.* Taipei: National Taiwan University, Population Studies Center, Women's Research Program, Monograph No. 4, 1985.

*China Women's News,* May 10, 1991.

*China Women's State Affairs.* Beijing: Information Dept., State Council, June 1994.

Cho, U. and Koo, H. "Capital Accumulation, Women's Work, and Informal Economies in Korea," working paper No. 21, Michigan State University, Women in International Development Program, 1983.

Chodorow, N. *The Reproduction of Mothering.* Berkeley: University of California Press, 1978.

Chou, B.-E., Clark, C., and Clark, J. *Women in Taiwan Politics: Overcoming Barriers to Women's Participation in a Modernizing Society.* Boulder, CO: Lynne Rienner, 1990.

Chowdhury, Z. "The Mother and Child in Bangladesh," *Alternative Approaches to Health Care,* No. 33, Geneva: United Nations Children Fund, 1976.

Christian, A. "The Place of Women in Ghana Society," *African Women,* 3, 1959.

Chung, T. F. and De, K. C. Background paper on Structural Adjustment Policies in Malaysia. Central Bank Conference, November 1988.

Clark, C. and Clark, J. "The Status of Women and the Provision of Basic Human Needs in Developing Societies." In Roy, K. C. and Clark, C. (eds.). *Technological Change and Rural Development in Poor Countries: Neglected Issues.* New Delhi, Oxford University Press, 1994.

Clark, C. and Roy, K. C. *Comparing Development Patterns in South and East Asia: Challenge to Neoclassical Economics.* Boulder, CO: Lynne Rienner, 1995.

Clark, J. and Clark, C. "The Gender Gap 1988: Compassion, Pacifism, and Indirect Feminism." In Duke, L. L. (ed.). *Women in Politics: Outsiders or Insiders?* Englewood Cliffs, NJ: Prentice Hall, 1993.

Collins, K., Scott, D. R., Salganicoff, A., and Chait, E. "Assessing and Improving Women's Health." In Costello, C. and Stone, A. J. (eds.). *The American Woman, 1994–95: Where We Stand.* New York: Norton, 1994.

Conover, P. J. "Feminists and the Gender Gap," *Journal of Politics,* 50, 1988.

Conroy, D. "The Glass Ceiling: Illusory or Real?" In *Affirmative Action Agency Women, Organizations & Economic Policies.* Canberra Bulletin of Public Administration, No. 76, 1994.

Cook, E. A., Thomas, S., and Wilcox, C. (eds.). *The Year of the Woman: Myths and Realities.* Boulder, CO: Westview, 1994.

Coppin, A. Issues of Gender in a Caribbean Labor Market: Barbados. Unpublished manuscript, Dept. of Economics, Oakland University, 1994.

Corcoran, M. and Duncan, G. J. "Work History, Labor Force Attachment, and Earnings Differences between the Races and Sexes," *Journal of Human Resources,* 14, 1979.

Cornelius, W. "Los migrantes de la Crisis: The Changing Profile of Mexican Migration to the United States." In González de la Rocha, M. and Escobar Latapí, A. (eds.). *Social Responses to Mexico's Economic Crisis of the 1980s.* San Diego: University of California, Center for US–Mexican Studies, 1992.

Cornia, G. A., Jolly, R., and Stewart, F. (eds.). *Adjustment with a Human Face.* New York and Oxford: Clarendon Press, 1987.

Craske, N. "Women's Political Participation in Colonias Populares in Guadalajara, Mexico." In Radcliffe, S. and Westwood, S. (eds.). *"Viva": Women and Popular Protest in Latin America.* London: Routledge, 1993.

Croll, E. "Rural Production and Reproduction: Socialist Development Experiences." In Leacock, E. and Safa, H. (eds.). *Women's Work.* South Hadley, MA: Bergin and Garvey, 1986.

Crowther, G., Findlay, H., Raj, P. A., and Wheeler, T. *India,* 3rd ed. Victoria, Australia: Hawthorn, 1990.

Crummett, M. de los Angeles. "Changing Class and Gender Roles After a Decade of Austerity: Rural Households in Calvillo, Aguascalientes, Mexico." Paper presented at the CIESAS/University of Florida seminar on "Structural Adjustment, Women's Work, and Domestic Organization," Guadalajara, Mexico, 1993.

Dahlerup, D. "Confusing Concepts—Confusing Reality: A Theoretical Discussion of the Patriarchal State." In Sassoon, A. S. (ed.). *Women and the State.* London: Hutchinson, 1987.

Dahlerup, D. "Learning to Live with the State. State, Market and Civic Society, Including the Family—the Need for State Intervention in East and West." Paper presented at the first European Conference of Sociology, Vienna, August 26–29, 1992a.

Dahlerup, D. "Vaelferd eller blind vaekst?: Flere kvinder end maend sagde nej til Maastricht." In Carlsen, H. N., Jackson, R., and Meyer, N. (eds.). *Nar et nej er et ja— danske visioner for et andet Europa.* Mörke: Grevas, 1992b.

Dandekar, K. "Has the Proportion of Women in India's Population Been Declining?" *Economic and Political Weekly,* 10, 1975.

Dankelman, I. and Davidson, J. *Women and Environment in the Third World.* London: Earthscan, 1989.

Darcy, R., Welch, S., and Clark, J. *Women, Elections, and Representation.* New York: Longman, 1987.

Das, V. "Marriage Among the Hindus." In Jain, D. (ed.) *Indian Women.* New Delhi: Department of Social Welfare, Government of India, 1975.

Dasgupta, S. and Maity, A. K. *The Rural Energy Crisis, Poverty and Women's Role in Five Indian Villages.* Geneva: ILO, 1986.

Daud, F. "'Minah Karan', The Truth about Malaysian Factory Girls," *Berita,* 1985.

Davidson, J. " 'Without Land We Are Nothing'—The Effect of Land Tenure Policies and Practices upon Rural Women in Kenya," *Rural Africana,* 2, 1987.

Davidson, J. *Agriculture, Women, and Land. The African Experience.* Boulder and London: Westview, 1988.

Davies, K. *Women and Time. Weaving Strands of Everyday Life.* Lund, Sweden: University of Lund, Department of Sociology, 1989.

Deere, C. D., Antrobus, P., Bolles, L., Meléndez, E., Phillips, P., Rivera, M., and Safa, H. *In the Shadows of the Sun: Caribbean Development Alternatives and United States Policy.* Boulder, CO: Westview, 1990.

Deere, C. D. and Melendez, E. "When Export Growth Is not Enough: U. S. Trade Policy and Caribbean Basin Economic Recovery," *Caribbean Affairs,* 5, 1992.

Deery, S. J. and Plowman, D. H. *Australian Industrial Relations,* 3rd ed. Sydney: McGraw-Hill, 1991.

Degler, C. N. *At Odds: Women and the Family in America from the Revolution to the Present.* New York: Oxford University Press, 1980.

Department of Statistics. *Industrial Surveys.* Kuala Lumpur, Malaysia: Government Printers, various years.

Department of Statistics. *Labour Force Survey Report.* Kuala Lumpur, Malaysia: Government Printers, various years.

Dobkin, M. "Colonization and the Legal Status of Women in Francophone Africa," *Cahiers d'Etudes Africaines,* 8, 1968.

Dodson, D. L. and Carroll, S. J. *Reshaping the Agenda: Women in State Legislatures.* New Brunswick, NJ: Center for the American Woman and Politics, 1991.

Doessel, D. and Gounder, R. "International Comparisons of Levels of Living and the Human Development Index: Some Empirical Results," Discussion Paper No. 73, Department of Economics, The University of Queensland, Brisbane, Australia, 1991.

Dufty, N. F. and Fells, R. E. *Dynamics of Industrial Relations in Australia.* Sydney: Prentice Hall, 1989.

Duvvury, N. "Women in Agriculture: A Review of the Indian Literature," *Economic and Political Weekly,* 24, 1989.

ECLAC. *Latin American and Caribbean Women: Between Change and Crisis.* Santiago: United Nations, 1988a.

ECLAC. *Women as a Social Protagonist in the 1980s.* Santiago: United Nations, 1988b.

ECLAC. *Women in the Inter-Island Trade in Agricultural Produce in the Eastern Caribbean.* Santiago: United Nations, 1988c.

ECLAC. *Women, Work and Crisis.* Santiago: United Nations, 1988d.

ECLAC. *Economic Survey of Latin America and the Caribbean 1990,* Vol. 1. Santiago: United Nations, 1992.

*Economic Eye,* 13, 1992.

El Serafy, S. "The Proper Calculation of Income from Depletable National Resources." In Ahmad, S., El Serafy, S., and Lutz, E. (eds.). *Environmental Accounting for Sustainable Development.* Washington, D.C.: World Bank, 1989.

Engels, F. *The Origin of the Family, Private Property and the State.* New York: International Publishers, 1972.

England, P. "The Failure of Human Capital Theory to Explain Occupational Health Segregation," *Journal of Human Resources,* Vol. 17, 1982.

England, P. "Wage Appreciation and Depreciation: A Test of Neoclassical Economic Explanations of Occupational Sex Segregation," *Social Forces,* Vol. 62, 1984.

England, P. and McCreary, L. "Integrating Sociology and Economics to Study Gender and Work." In Stromberg, A., Larwood, L., and Gutek, B. (eds.). *Women and Work: An Annual Review.* Newbury Park, CA: Sage, 1987.

Epstein, T. S. *South India Yesterday, Today and Tomorrow.* London: Macmillan, 1973.

*Equal Opportunities for Women and Men. Third Medium-term Community Action Programme—1991-1995. Women of Europe,* Supplement No. 34. Brussels: European Commission, 1991.

Ermisch, J. F. and Wright, R. E. "Different Returns to Human Capital in Full-time and Part-time Employment." In Folbre, N., Bergmann, B., Agarwal, B., and Floro, M. (eds.). *Women's Work in the World Economy.* Basingstoke and London: Macmillan, 1992.

Espinal, R. and Grasmuck, S. "Gender, Households and Informal Entrepreneurship in the Dominican Republic." Paper presented at the XVIII International Congress of the Latin American Studies Association, March 10–12, Atlanta, Georgia, 1994.

European Commisssion. Social Europe 3/91. *Equal Opportunities for Women and Men.* Brussels: Commission of the European Communities, 1991

Farris, C. S. "The Sociocultural Construction of Femininity in Contemporary Urban Taiwan," working paper No. 131, Michigan State University, Women in International Development Program, 1986.

Fei, J. C. H., Ranis, G., and Kuo, S. W. Y. *Growth with Equity: The Taiwan Case.* New York: Oxford University Press, 1979.

Fernández-Kelly, M. P. *For We Are Sold, I and My People: Women and Industry in Mexico's Frontier.* Albany: State University of New York, 1983.

*Finnish Labour Review,* various issues. Helsinki: Ministry of Labour, 1993.

Fiorenza, E. S. "The Endless Day: Introduction." In Fiorenza, E. S. and Carr, A. (eds.). *Women, Work and Poverty.* Edinburgh: T. and T. Clark, 1987.

*First Malaysia Plan, 1966-1970.* Government of Malaysia, Kuala Lumpur, Malaysia: Government Printers, 1967.

Fisher, J. *Out of the Shadows: Women, Resistance and Politics in South America.* London: Latin America Bureau, 1993.

Flax, J. "Postmodernism and Gender Relations in Feminist Theory," *Signs,* 12, 1987.

Folbre, N. "Introduction: The Feminist Sphinx." In Folbre, N., Bergmann, B., Agarwal,

B., and Floro, M. (eds.). *Women's Work in the World Economy.* Basingstoke and London: Macmillan, 1992.

Foster, T. A. Common Future for Women and Men (and all Living Creatures). A submission to the World Commission on Environment and Development, Ottawa: EDPRA Consulting Inc., 1986.

Friedan, B. *The Feminine Mystique.* New York: Norton, 1963.

Frobel, F., Heirichs, J., and Kreye, O. *The New International Division of Labour.* Cambridge: Cambridge University Press, 1980.

Fuchs, V. R. *Women's Quest for Economic Equality.* Cambridge, MA: Harvard University Press, 1988.

Fukutake, T. *Rural Society in Japan.* Tokyo: University of Tokyo Press, 1980.

Gallin, R. S. "Women, Family, and the Political Economy of Taiwan," *Journal of Peasant Studies,* 12, 1984.

García, A. I. and Gomáriz, E. *Mujeres Centroamericanas: Ante la Crisis, la Guerra y el Proceso de Paz.* San José: FLACSO/CSUCA/Universidad para la Paz, 1989.

Gates, H. "Dependency and the Part-time Proletariat in Taiwan," *Modern China,* 5, 1979.

Gates, H. *Chinese Working-Class Lives: Getting by in Taiwan.* Ithaca: Cornell University Press, 1987.

Goldin, C. *Understanding the Gender Gap: An Economic History of American Women.* New York: Oxford University Press, 1990.

González de la Rocha, M. "Economic Crisis, Domestic Reorganization and Women's Work in Guadalajara, Mexico," *Bulletin of Latin American Research,* 7, 1988.

González de la Rocha, M. Familia Urbana y Pobreza en América Latina. Unpublished manuscript prepared for Economic Commission on Latin America and the Caribbean (ECLAC), 1993.

Gordon, T. "Citizens and Others: Gender, Democracy and Education," *International Studies in Sociology of Education,* 2, 1992.

Gough, K. "The Origins of the Family," *Journal of Marriage and the Family,* 13, 1971.

Government of China. *Statistical Yearbook of China 1993.* Beijing: China Statistical Publishing House, 1993.

Government of India. *Census of India 1991.* New Delhi, 1992a.

Government of India. *Eighth Five Year Plan 1992–97.* New Delhi: Planning Commission, Government of India, 1992b.

Government of India. *Economic Survey 1992–93.* New Delhi: Government of India, 1993a.

Government of India. *India 1992.* New Delhi: Government of India, 1993b.

Government of Malaysia. *Malaysia: The 'Solid State' for Electronics, an Invitation for Investment.* Kuala Lumpur, Malaysia: Federal Industrial Development Authority Malaysia, 1970–71.

Government of Malaysia. *Sixth Malaysia Plan, 1991–1995.* Kuala Lumpur: Government Printers, 1991.

Government of Taiwan. *Social Indicators in Taiwan Area of the Republic of China, 1988.* Taipei, Directorate-General of Budget, Accounting, and Statistics, 1989.

Government of Taiwan. *Social Welfare Indicators, Republic of China, 1989.* Taipei: Council for Planning and Development, 1989.

Greenhalgh, S. "Sexual Stratification: The Other Side of 'Growth with Equity' in East Asia," *Population and Development Review,* 11, 1985.

*Guanming Daily.* "Welcome to Our China." Gran Ville, NSW, Australia: Bitter Holdings, 1988.

Guazzelli, M. J. "Southern Brazil: Breaking with an Imposed Dependence." In *Women and the Environmental Crisis: Report of the Proceedings of the Workshops on Women, Environment and Development*. Nairobi: Environment Liaison Centre, 1985.

Gulati, L. "Profile of a Female Agricultural Labourer," *Economic and Political Weekly*, 13, 1978.

Haavind, H. "Förändringar i förhållandet mellan kvinnor och män." *Kvinnovetenskaplig tidskrift*, 3, 1985.

Haavio-Mannila, E. and Kauppinen, K. "Women and the Welfare State in the Nordic Countries." In Kahne, H. and Giele, J. Z. (eds.). *Women's Work and Women's Lives. The Continuing Struggle Worldwide*. Boulder, CO: Westview, 1992.

Hafkin, J. and Bay, G. *Women in Africa*. Stanford, CA: Stanford University Press, 1976.

Hakim, C. "The Myth of the Rising Female Employment," *Work, Employment & Society*, 7, 1993.

Harding, S. *Whose Science? Whose Knowledge? Thinking from Women's Lives*. Ithaca: Cornell University Press, 1991.

Harris, B. "The Intra-Family Distribution of Hunger in South Asia." Paper prepared for the Project on Hunger and Poverty and presented at the seminar on Food Strategies, July, Helsinki: WIDER, 1986.

Hartman, H. "Capitalism, Patriarchy, and Segregation by Sex." In Blaxall, M. and Reagan, B. (eds.). *Women and the Workplace*. Chicago: University of Chicago Press, 1976.

Havenvik, H. J. (ed.). *Tanzania: A Country Study and Norwegian Aid Review*. Bergen, Norway: University of Bergen, Center of Development Studies, 1988.

*HAWA Draft Report*. Kuala Lumpur, Malaysia: HAWAII, University of Malaya, 1981.

*Helsingin Sanomat*, March 5, 1994.

Hernes, H. M. "The Welfare State Citizenship of Scandinavian Women." In Hernes, H. M. (ed.). *Welfare State and Woman Power. Essays in State Feminism*. Oslo: Scandinavian University Press, 1987.

Hertz, B. "Bringing Women in the Economic Mainstream," *Finance and Development*, 26, 1989.

Hirdman, Y. "Genussystemet—reflexioner kring kvinnors sociala underordning," *Kvinnovetenskaplig tidskrift*, 3, 1988.

Hirdman, Y. "Genussystemet." In *Demokrati och makt i Sverige*. Stockholm: SOU, 1990.

Hirdman, Y. *Women—From Possibility to Problem? Gender Conflict in the Welfare State— The Swedish Model*. Stockholm: The Swedish Center for Working Life, 1994.

Hiroata, H. *Japanese Women Today (Fact Sheet)*. Tokyo: International Society for Educational Information, 1990.

Hirschman, C. and Aghajarian, A. "Women's Labour Force Participation and Socioeconomic Development: The Case of Peninsular Malaysia, 1957–1970," *Journal of Southeast Asian Studies*, 11, 1980.

Ho, S. P. S. *Economic Development in Taiwan, 1860–1970*. New Haven: Yale University Press, 1978.

Ho, S. P. S. "Decentralized Industrialization and Rural Development: Evidence from Taiwan," *Economic Development and Cultural Change*, 28, 1979.

Hobson, B. "No Exit, No Voice: Women's Economic Dependency and the Welfare State," *Acta Sociologica*, 33, 1990.

Hoffman, E. P. "Introduction." In Hoffman, E. P. (ed.). *Essays on the Economics of Discrimination*. Kalamazoo, MI: W. E. Upjohn Institute for Employment Research, 1991.

Holter, H. (ed). *Patriarchy in a Welfare Society*. Oslo: Scandinavian University Press, 1984.

Horiuchi, M. "Measures to Encourage Women's Participation in Society," *Economic Eye,* 13, 1992.

Horowitz, B. and Kishwar, M. "Family Life—The Unequal Debt: Women's Condition and Family Life Among Agricultural Labourers and Small Farmers in a Punjab Village," *Manushi,* 11, 1982.

Huang, P. H. "Modernization of Education in the Republic of China since 1949." In Shaw, Y. M. (ed.).*Chinese Modernization.* San Francisco: Chinese Materials Center, 1984.

*Human Development Report 1992.* UNDP, New York: Oxford University Press, 1992.

*Human Development Report 1993.* UNDP, New York: Oxford University Press, 1993.

Humphrey, J. "The Growth of Female Employment in Brazilian Manufacturing Industry in 1970's," *Journal of Development Studies,* 20, 1984.

Ilmakunnas, S. "Puolisoiden tulot palkansaajaperheissä." In Allén, T. et al. (eds.). *Palkkaa työstä ja sukupuolesta.* Helsinki: Tilastokeskus, 1990.

Ilmakunnas, S. "The Public Day Care System in Transition." In Varsa, H. (ed.). *Shaping Structural Change in Finland. The Role of Women.* Helsinki: Ministry of Social Affairs and Health, 1993.

Ingle, C. *From Village to State in Tanzania. The Politics of Rural Tanzania.* Ithaka: Cornell University Press, 1972.

Inter-American Development Bank. *Encuesta Nacional de Mano de Obra.* Sto. Domingo, 1992.

*Ippan Joho Information Bulletin,* October 12, 1993.

Isotalus, P. "Keinoja palkkaerojen purkamiseen: Työnarviointitutkimukset ja suosiminen." In *Naiset ja talous.* Helsinki: Sosiaali-ja terveysministeriö,1988.

Iwao, S. *The Japanese Woman: Traditional Image and Changing Reality.* Sydney: The Free Press, 1993.

Jacobs, J. A. *Revolving Door: Sex Segregation and Women's Careers.* Stanford: Stanford University Press, 1989.

Japan Institute of Labour. *Japan Labour Bulletin.* Tokyo: Japan Institute of Labour, various issues.

Japan Institute of Labour. *Japanese Working Life Profile.* Tokyo: Japan Institute of Labour, 1991.

Jaquette, J. S. "Women and Modernization Theory: A Decade of Feminist Criticism," *World Politics,* 34, 1982.

Jaquette, J. "Women and the New Democratic Politics." In Jaquette, J. (ed.). *The Women's Movement in Latin America: Feminism and the Transition to Democracy.* Winchester, MA: Unwin and Hyman, 1989.

Jokelin, R. "Euroopan unionin ja Suomen tasa-arvopykälät ovat suunnilleen samanlaisia. Suomi-neito voi eurosisartaan paremmin," *Helsingin Sanomat,* May 7, 1994.

Jomo, K. S. *Growth and Structural Change in the Malaysian Economy.* Basingstoke and London: Macmillan, 1990.

Jonung, C. "Kvinnors och mäns yrken." In Lundahl, M. and Persson-Tanimura, I. (eds.). *Kvinnan i ekonomin.* Malmö: Liber Förlag, 1983.

Julkunen, R. *Hyvinvointivaltio käännekohdassa.* Tampere, Finland: Vastapaino, 1992.

Julkunen, R. "Naisetko kotiin," *Talous ja yhteiskunta,* 21, 1993.

Julkunen, R. "Suomalainen sukupuolimalli." In Anttonen, A., Henriksson, L., and Nätkin, R. (eds.). *Naisten hyvinvointivaltio.* Tampere, Finland: Vastapaino, 1994a.

Julkunen, R. "Työssäkäyvän äidin julkiset ja yksityiset sosiaalipoliitiset suhteet." In Eräsaari, L., Julkunen, R., and Silius, H. (eds.). *Naiset julkisen ja yksityisen rajoilla.* Unpublished, 1994b.

Julkunen, R. and Rantalaiho, L. "Hyvinvointivaltion sukupuolijärjestelmä," working papers, 5, 56. Jyväskylä: University of Jyväskylä, Department of Social Policy, 1989.

Kabeer, N. "Poverty, Purdah and Women's Survival Strategies in Rural Bangladesh." In Burnstein, H. et al. (eds.). *The Food Question: Profits Versus People.* London: Earthscan, 1990.

Kabeer, N. "Gender Dimensions of Rural Poverty: Analysis from Bangladesh," *Journal of Peasant Studies,* 18, 1991

Kandiyoti, D. *Women in Rural Production Systems.* Paris: UNESCO, 1985.

Kardam, N. *Bringing Women In: Women's Issues in International Development Programs.* Boulder, CO: Lynne Rienner, 1991.

Kavishe, P. F. *Nutritional Relevant Actions in Tanzania.* UN/ACC/SCN Country Case Study Supported by UNICEF United Nations Children Fund. A Case Study for the XV Congress of the International Union of Nutritional Sciences, Adelaide, Australia, 1993.

Keinänen, P. "Palkkaerot iän, koulutuksen ja perhevaiheen mukaan." In Allén, T. et al. (eds.). *Palkkaa työstä ja sukupuolesta.* Helsinki: Tilastokeskus, 1990.

Kenski, H. C. "The Gender Factor in a Changing Electorate." In Mueller, C. M. (ed.). *The Politics of the Gender Gap: The Social Construction of Political Influence.* Beverly Hills, CA: Sage, 1988.

Kessler-Harris, A. "The Debate over Equality for Women in the Work Place." In Larwood, L., Stromberg, A. H., and Gutek, B. (eds.). *Women at Work. An Annual Review, Vol.1.* Beverly Hills, CA: Sage, 1985.

King, J. E. *Labour Economics: An Australian Perspective.* Melbourne: Macmillan, 1990.

Kisanga, P. "Women and Nutrition." ACC/SCN Symposium Report. Nutrition Policy Discussion Paper No. 6, United Nations, 1990.

Kishwar, M. "Toiling Without Rights: Ho Women of Singhbhum," *Economic and Political Weekly,* 22, 1987.

Klein, E. *Gender Politics: From Consciousness to Mass Politics.* Cambridge, MA: Harvard University Press, 1984.

*Kodansha Encyclopedia.* Tokyo: Kodansha Limited, 1993.

Kovalainen, A. *At the Margins of the Economy. Women's Self-Employment in Finland 1960–1990.* Turku, Finland: Publications of the Turku School of Economics and Business Administration, 1993.

Kung, L. "Perceptions of Work among Factory Women." In Ahern, E. M. and Gates, H., (eds.). *The Anthropology of Taiwanese Society.* Stanford: Stanford University Press, 1981.

Kung, L. *Factory Women in Taiwan.* Ann Arbor, MI: UMI Research Press, 1983.

Kuronen, M. "Neuvola naisten kohtaamisen paikkana." In Eräsaari, L., Julkunen, R., and Silius, H. (eds.). *Naiset julkisen ja yksityisen rajoilla.* Unpublished, 1994.

Kuznets, S. "Quantitative Aspects of Economic Growth of Nations, Distribution of Income by Size," *Economic Development and Cultural Change,* 1, 1963.

Kuznets, S. "Modern Economic Growth: Findings and Reflections," *American Economic Review,* 63, 1973.

Lam, D. K. K. and Lee, I. "Guerrilla Capitalism and the Limits of Statist Theory." In Clark, C. and Chan, S., (eds.). *The Evolving Pacific Basin in the Global Political Economy: Domestic and International Linkages.* Boulder, CO: Lynne Rienner, 1992.

Landau, E. C. *The Rights of Working Women in the European Community.* Luxemburg: Office for Official Publications of the European Communities, 1985.

Leacock, E. "Introduction." In Engels, F. *The Origin of the Family, Private Property and the State.* New York: International Publishers, 1972.

Leahy, M. E. *Development Strategies and the Status of Women: A Comparative Study of the United States, Mexico, the Soviet Union and Cuba.* Boulder, CO: Lynne Rienner, 1986.

Lee, T. H. *Intersectoral Capital Flows in the Economic Development of Taiwan, 1895–1960.* Ithaca: Cornell University Press, 1971.

Leira, A. *Welfare States and Working Mothers.* Cambridge: Cambridge University Press, 1992.

Lewis, N. B. "The Connection of Uneven Development, Capitalism and Patriarchy: A Case of Prostitution in Asia." In Fiorenza, E. S. and Carr, A. (eds.). *Women, Work and Poverty.* Edinburgh: T. & T. Clark, 1987.

Li, K. T. *The Evolution of Policy Behind Taiwan's Development Success.* New Haven: Yale University Press, 1988.

Lim, D. *Economic Growth and Development in West Malaysia 1947–1970.* Kuala Lumpur, Malaysia: Oxford University Press, 1973.

Lim, L. "Women Workers in Multinational Corporations: The Case of the Electronics Industry in Malaysia and Singapore." Ph.D. Thesis, University of Michigan, 1978.

Little, K. *African Women in Towns: An Aspect of Africa's Social Revolution.* London: Cambridge University Press, 1973.

Lockhead, J. and Rohana-Ariffin. "Retraining for Women Workers in Industry with Special Reference to Those Retrenched." Research paper submitted to HAWA, Prime Minister's Department, Malaysia, 1986.

Lopez, E. P. "Overcoming Barriers: Women and Participation in Public Life." In Wallace, T. and March, C. (eds.). *Changing Perceptions, Writings on Gender and Development.* Oxford: Oxfam, 1991.

Lorber, J. *Paradoxes of Gender.* New Haven: Yale University Press, 1994.

Lundahl, M. and Persson-Tanimura, I. "Inledning." In Lundahl, M. and Persson-Tanimura, I. (eds.). *Kvinnan i ekonomin.* Malmö, Sweden: Liber Förlag, 1983.

Lundahl, M. and Wadensjö, E. *Unequal Treatment. A Study in the Neo-Classical Theory of Discrimination.* Beckenham and New York: Croom Helm and New York University Press, 1984.

Madden, J. F. *The Economics of Sex Discrimination.* Lexington, MA: D.C. Heath, 1973.

Mahani, Z. A. "Alternative Industrial Strategies and Effects of Fiscal Incentives and Trade Policy in Achieving Employment Objectives in Malaysian Industrialization." Unpublished Ph.D thesis, University of Malaya, 1992.

Majumder, M. K. "Food for Afforestation Programme," *POUSH Annual Report 1991.* Dhaka: POUSH, 1992.

Mancke, R. B. "Lower Pay for Women: A Case of Economic Discrimination?" *Industrial Relations,* 10, 1971.

Manimala. "Zameen Kenkar: Jote Onkar," *Manushi,* 14, 1983.

Markham, W. T. "Sex, Relocation, and Occupational Advancement," In Stromberg, A. H., Larwood, L., and Gutek, B. (eds.). *Women at Work. An Annual Review, Vol. 2.* Newbury Park, CA: Sage, 1987.

Mascarenhans, O. and Mbilinyi, M. *Women in Tanzania. An Analytical Bibliography.* Stockholm: Scandinavian Institute of Women Studies, Uppsala, 1983.

Mbilinyi, M. "Structural Adjustment. Agribusiness and Rural Women in Tanzania." In Bernstein, H. et al. (eds.). *The Food Question: Profits Versus People.* London: Earthscan, 1990.

Meena, R. "The Impact of Structural Adjustment on Rural Women in Tanzania." In Gladwin, C. H. (ed.). *Structural Adjustment and African Women Farmers.* Gainesville, FL: University of Florida Press, 1991.

Mencher, J. and Saradamoni, K. "Muddy Feet and Dirty Hands: Rice Production and Female Agricultural Labourers," *Economic and Political Weekly,* 17, 1982.

Meyer, J. A. "Budget Cuts in the Reagan Administration: A Question of Fairness." In Bawden, D. L. (ed.). *The Social Contract Revisited: Aims and Outcomes of President Reagan's Social Welfare Policy.* Washington, D.C.: The Urban Institute, 1984.

Mezey, S. G. "Increasing the Number of Women in Office: Does It Matter?" In Cook, E. A., Thomas, S., and Wilcox, C. (eds.). *The Year of the Woman: Myths & Realities.* Boulder, CO: Westview, 1994.

MIDA. *Annual Report.* Kuala Lumpur: Malaysian Industrial Development Authority, various years.

Mincer, J. and Polachek, S. "Family Investment in Human Capital: Earnings of Women," *Journal of Political Economy,* 82, 1974.

Ministry of Human Resources. *Occupational Wages Survey in the Manufacturing Industries.* Kuala Lumpur, Malaysia: Ministry of Human Resources, various years.

Ministry of Labour. *Japan's Working Women Today.* Tokyo: Ministry of Labour, 1991.

Ministry of Social Affairs. *Naiset ja EY.* Helsinki: Sosiaali-ja terveysministeriö, 1991.

Mithen, S. J. "The Mesolithic Age." In Cunliffe, B. (ed.). *The Oxford Illustrated Prehistory of Europe.* Oxford: Oxford University Press, 1994.

Moghadam, V. M. *Gender, Development, and Policy: Toward Equity and Empowerment.* Helsinki: UNU/WIDER, 1990.

Moghadam, V. M. *Gender and the Development Process in a Changing Global Environment.* Helsinki: UNU/WIDER, 1993.

Molyneux, M. "Mobilization without Emancipation? Women's Interests, State and Revolution." In Fagen, R., Deere, C. D., and Corragio, J. L. (eds.). *Transition and Development: Problems of Third World Socialism.* New York: Monthly Review Press, 1986.

Moon, B. E. *The Political Economy of Basic Human Needs.* Ithaca: Cornell University Press, 1991.

Mori, M. "Evaluating the Effectiveness of the Equal Opportunity Law," *Economic Eye,* 13, 1992.

Moring, K. "EU: naisohjelma painottaa naisten työtä ja koulutusta," *Helsingin Sanomat,* May 7, 1994

Moser, C. O. N. "Gender Planning in the Third World: Meeting Practical and Strategic Gender Needs." In Wallace, T. and March, C. (eds). *Changing Perceptions, Writings on Gender and Development.* Oxford: Oxfam, 1991.

Mossuz-Lavau, J. "Women and Men in Europe Today. Attitudes towards Europe and Politics," *Women of Europe,* Supplement No. 35, 1991.

Mueller, C. M. (ed.). *The Politics of the Gender Gap: The Social Construction of Political Influence.* Beverly Hills, CA: Sage, 1988.

Mukhopadhayay, S. "Between Two Worlds," *Statesman,* January 15, 1994.

Mulhern, M. and Mauzé, S. "Gender and Trade and Investment in Latin America and the Caribbean." GENESYS, Special Studies No. 8. Prepared for United States Agency for International Development. Washington, D.C.: Office of Women in Development and Bureau for Latin America and the Caribbean, 1992.

Nakamura, T. and Grace, B. R. G. *Economic Development of Modern Japan.* Tokyo: Ministry of Foreign Affairs, 1985.

Nash, J. *From Tank Town to High Tech: The Clash of Community and Industrial Cycles.* Albany: State University of New York Press, 1989.

Nash, J. (ed.). *Crafts in the World Market: The Impact of Global Exchange on Middle American Artisans.* Albany: State University of New York Press, 1993.

Nash, J. and Fernandez-Kelly, M. P. (eds.). *Women, Men and the International Division of Labor.* Albany: State University Press of New York, 1983.

Nätkin, R. "Väestöpolitiikka, abortti ja äitiys." In Anttonen, A., Henriksson, L., and Nätkin, R. (eds.). *Naisten hyvinvointivaltio.* Tampere, Finland: Vastapaino, 1994.

Niemi, I. and Pääkkönen, H. *Ajankäytön muutokset 1980-luvulla.* Helsinki: Statistics Finland, 1989.

Nieminen, L. *EY:n tasa-arvopolitiikka.* Helsinki: Lakimiesliiton kustannus, 1991.

Nieva, V. F. "Work and Family Linkages." In Larwood, L., Stromberg, A. H., and Gutek, B. (eds.). *Women at Work. An Annual Review, Vol. 1.* Beverly Hills, CA: Sage, 1985.

Nordic Council of Ministers. *Yearbook of Nordic Statistics, 31.* Copenhagen: Nordic Council of Ministers, 1993.

Norris, K. (ed.). *The Economics of Australian Labour Markets,* 3rd ed. Melbourne: Longman, 1993.

Nyberg, A. *Tekniken—kvinnornas befriare?* Linköping, Sweden: Linköping Studies in Arts and Sciences, 45, 1989.

Nyerere, J. K. *Socialism and Rural Development.* Dar es Salaam: Oxford University Press, 1967.

O'Neill, J. "The Trend in the Male-Female Wage Gap in the United States," *Journal of Labor Economics,* 3, 1985.

Oakley, A. *Sex, Gender and Society,* Aldershot, England: Gower, 1987.

Ohlin, U. "A Case for Women as Co-Managers: The Family as a General Model of Human Social Organization." In Tinker, I. and Branson, M. B. (eds.). *Women and World Development.* Washington, D.C.: Overseas Development Council, 1976.

Otero, M. "Rethinking the Informal Sector," *Grassroots Development,* 13, 1989.

Papanek, H. "Purdah in Pakistan: Seclusion and Modern Occupations for Women." In Papanek, H. and Minault, G. (eds.). *Separate Worlds: Studies of Purdah in South Asia.* Delhi: Chanakya Publications, 1982.

Parliwala, R. "Reaffirming the Anti-Dowry Struggle," *Economic and Political Weekly,* 24, 1989.

Pateman, Carole. *The Sexual Contract.* Cambridge, MA: Polity Press, 1988.

Paterson, J. "The Feminization of Poverty," *Journal of Economic Issues,* 21, 1987.

Phadnis, U. and Malani, I. "Introduction." In Phadnis, U. and Malani, I. (eds.). *Women of the World. Illusion and Reality.* New Delhi: Vikas Publishing House, 1978.

Phillips, K. *The Politics of Rich and Poor: Wealth and the American Electorate in the Reagan Aftermath.* New York: Random House, 1990.

Piore, M. J. "Notes for a Theory of Labor Market Stratification." In Edwards, R. C., Reich, M., and Gordon, D. M. (eds.). *Labor Market Segmentation.* Lexington, MA: D.C. Heath, 1973.

Polachek, S. "Occupation Segregation Among Women: Theory, Evidence and Prognosis." In Lloyd, C. B., Andrews, E. S., and Gilroy, C. L. (eds.). *Women in the Labor Market.* New York: Columbia University Press, 1979.

Polachek, S. "Occupational Self-Selection: A Human Capital Approach to Sex Differences in Occupational Structure," *Review of Economics and Statistics,* Vol. 58, 1981.

Polachek, S. "Occupational Segregation: A Defence of Human Capital Predictions," *Journal of Human Resources,* Vol. 20, 1985.

Poole, K. T. and Zeigler, L. H. *Women, Public Opinion, and Politics: The Changing Political Attitudes of American Women.* New York: Longman, 1985.

POUSH. *POUSH Annual Report 1991.* Mohammadpur, Dhaka, 1992.

PREALC (Programa Regional del Empleo para América Latina y el Caribe). *El rol productivo de la mujer en América Latina.* Santiago, Chile, 1990.

Psacharopoulos, G. and Tzannatos, Z. *Women's Employment and Pay in Latin America: Overview and Methodology.* Washington, D.C.: World Bank, 1992.

Ramirez, N. "Nuevos hallazgos sobre fuerza laboral y migraciones: analisis preliminar de los datos del cuestionario de hogar ampliado de la ENDESA '91M'." In *Población y Desarrollo*, no. 2., Sto. Domingo, Dominican Republic: Profamilia, 1992.

Ramstedt-Silén, V. "Naisten osallistuminen taloudellis-poliittiseen päätöksentekoon—edellytykset ja esteet." In Ministry of Social Affairs. *Naiset ja talous.* Helsinki: Sosiaali-ja terveysministeriö, 1988.

Ranis, G. "Industrial Development." In Galenson, W. (ed.). *Economic Growth and Structural Change in Taiwan: The Postwar Experience of the Republic of China.* Ithaca: Cornell University Press, 1979.

Ranis, G. (ed.). *Taiwan: From Developing to Mature Economy.* Boulder, CO: Westview, 1992.

Rantalaiho, L. "The Gender Contract." In Varsa, H. (ed.). *Shaping Structural Change in Finland. The Role of Women.* Helsinki: Ministry of Social Affairs and Health, 1993.

Rantalaiho, L. "Sukupuolisopimus ja Suomen malli." In Anttonen, A., Henriksson, L., and Nätkin, R. (eds.). *Naisten hyvinvointivaltio.* Tampere, Finland: Vastapaino, 1994.

Rath, N. "Garibi Hotno: Can IRDP Do It?" *Economic and Political Weekly,* 20, 1985.

Ray, J. K. *Organizing Villagers for Self-Reliance.* Hyderabad, India: Orient Longman, 1986.

Reich, R. B. *The Work of Nations: Preparing Ourselves for 21st Century Capitalism.* New York: Knopf, 1991.

Repetto, R., Magrath, A., Wells, M., Beer, C., and Rossini, F. *Wasting Assets: Natural Resources in the National Income Accounts.* Washington, D.C.: World Resources Institute, 1989.

Rinehart, S. T. *Gender Consciousness and Politics.* New York: Routledge, 1992.

Riska, E. and Wegar, K. "Women Physicians: a New Force in Medicine?" In Riska, E. and Wegar, K. (eds.). *Gender, Work and Medicine: Women and the Medical Division of Labour.* London: Sage, 1993.

Roberts, S. L. "Women's PACs: Evolution, Operation, and Outlook." Paper presented at the Annual Meeting of the Southern Political Science Association, Atlanta, 1993.

Rodney, W. *How Europe Underdeveloped Africa.* London: Bogle-L'ouverture Publications, 1972.

Rogers, B. *The Domestication of Women: Discrimination in Development.* New York: St. Martin's Press, 1979.

Roy, K. C. "Landless and Land Poor Women in India under Technological Change: A Case for Technology Transfer." In Roy, K. C. and Clark, C. (eds.). *Technological Change and Rural Development in Poor Countries: Neglected Issues.* New Delhi: Oxford University Press, 1994a.

Roy, K. C. "Neglected Issues in Technological Change and Rural Development, An Overview." In Roy, K. C. and Clark, C., (eds.). *Technological Change and Rural Development in Poor Countries: Neglected Issues.* New Delhi: Oxford University Press, 1994b.

Roy, K. C. and Tisdell, C. A. "Poverty Amongst Females in Rural India: Gender-Based Deprivation and Technological Change," *Economic Studies*, 31, 1993a.

Roy, K. C. and Tisdell, C. A. "Technological Change, Environment and Poor Women, Specially Tribal Women in India," *Savings and Development*, 17, 1993b.

Rubin, G. "The Traffic in Women: Notes on the 'Political Economy' of Sex." In Reiter, R. (ed.). *Toward an Anthropology of Women*. New York: Monthly Review Press, 1975.

Rubin, L. *Worlds of Pain: Life in the Working-Class Family*. New York: Basic Books, 1976.

Rule, W. "Electoral Systems, Contextual Factors, and Women's Opportunity for Election to Parliament in Twenty-three Democracies," *Western Political Quarterly*, 40, 1987.

Ryan, J. R. and Wallace, T. D. *Determinants of Labour Markets: Wages, Participation and Supply in South India*. Hyderabad, India: ICRISAT, 1985.

Safa, H. "Runaway Shops and Female Employment: The Search for Cheap Labor," *Signs*, 7, 1981.

Safa, H. "Urbanization, the Informal Economy and State Policy in Latin America." In Smith, M. P. and Feagin, J. (eds.). *The Capitalist City: Global Restructuring and Community Politics*. London: Basil Blackwell, 1987.

Safa, H. "Women and Industrialization in the Caribbean." In Stichter, S. and Parpart, J. (eds.). *Women, Employment and the Family in the International Division of Labor*. London: Macmillan, 1990.

Safa, H. *The Myth of the Male Breadwinner: Women and Industrialization in the Caribbean*. Boulder, CO: Westview, 1995.

Saffioti, H. I. B. "The Impact of Industrialization on the Structure of Female Employment," working paper No.15, Michigan State University, Women in International Development Program, 1983.

Salih, K. "The Changing Face of the Malaysian Economy." Paper presented at a Seminar on "Business Opportunities and Entrepreneurship," Kuala Lumpur, Malaysia, 1987.

Salih, K. and Mei, L. Y. "Economic Restructuring and the Future of the Semiconductor Industry in Malaysia." In Narayanan, S. et. al. (eds.). *Changing Dimensions of the Electronics Industry in Malaysia: The 1980s and Beyond*. Penang and Kuala Lumpur, Malaysia: Malaysia Economic Association and MIER, 1989.

Saradamoni, K. *Progressive Legislation: A Slide-Back for Women*. Report submitted to the ICSSR on the Project on Changing Land Relation and Women: A Case Study on Palghat, 1980.

Schirmer, J. "The Seeking of Truth and the Gendering of Consciousness: The Comadres of El Salvador and the Conavigua Widows of Guatemala." In Radcliffe, S. and Westwood, S. (eds.). *"Viva": Women and Popular Protest in Latin America*. London: Routledge, 1993.

Schröder, H. "The Economic Impoverishment of Mothers is the Enrichment of Fathers." In Fiorenza, E. S. and Carr, A. (eds.). *Women, Work and Poverty*. Edinburgh: T. and T. Clark, 1987.

Scott, A. M. "Women and Industrialization: Examining the 'Female Marginalization' Thesis," *Journal of Development Studies*, 22, 1986.

Scott, J. "Gender: A Useful Category of Historical Analysis," *American Historical Review*, 91, 1986.

Scott, J. "Deconstructing Equality Versus Difference: Or, the Uses of Poststructuralist Theory for Feminism," *Feminist Studies*, 14, 1988.

Seavoy, R. *Famine in East Africa: Food Production and Food Policies*. New York: Greenwood Press, 1989.

Sen, A. K. and Sengupta, S. "Malnutrition of Rural Children and the Sex Bias," *Economic and Political Weekly*, Annual No., May, 1983.

Shapiro, R. Y. and Mahajan, H. "Gender Differences in Policy Preferences: A Summary of Trends from the 1960s to the 1980s," *Public Opinion Quarterly*, 50, 1986.

Shitamori, M. "Female Experience on the Management Track," *Economic Eye*, 13, 1992.

Shiva, V. "India: The Abundance Myth of the Green Revolution." In *Women and Environmental Crises: Report of the Proceedings of the Workshops on Women, Environment and Development*. Nairobi: Environment Liaison Centre, 1985.

Shiva, V. *Staying Alive, Women, Ecology and Development*. London: Zed Books, 1989.

Short, C. "Equal Pay-What Happened?" *Journal of Industrial Relations*, 28, 1986.

Siim, B. "The Scandinavian Welfare States-Towards Sexual Equality or a New Kind of Male Domination?" *Acta Sociologica*, 30, 1987.

Siim, B. "Towards a Feminist Rethinking of the Welfare State." In Jones, K. and Jónasdóttir, A. (eds.). *The Political Interest of Gender*. London: Sage, 1988.

Silius, H. *Den kringgärdade kvinnligheten. Att vara kvinnlig jurist i Finland.* Åbo, Finland: Åbo Academy Press, 1992.

Sinclair, B. D. *The Women's Movement: Political, Socioeconomic, and Psychological Issues*, 3rd ed. New York: Harper & Row, 1983.

Siwar, Chamhuri. "Revitalisation of Agriculture: The Basis for Industrial Growth and Restructuring." Paper presented at the MIER 1988 National Outlook Conference November, Kuala Lumpur, Malaysia, 1988.

Snow, R. "Some Critical Thoughts on the Social Impact of MNCs in Asia," *Social Europe 3/91. Equal Opportunities for Women and Men*. Brussels: Commission of the European Communities, 1991.

Sørensen, B. A. "Ansvarsrasjonalitet." In Holter, H. (ed.). *Kvinner i felleskap*. Oslo: Universitetsforlaget, 1982.

Stacey, J. *Brave New Families. Stories of Domestic Upheaval in Late Twentieth Century America*. New York: Basic Books, 1990.

Standing, G. "Global Feminization through Flexible Labor," *World Development*, 17, 1989.

Statistical Office of the European Communities. *Women in the European Community*. Brussels, 1992.

Stephen, L. and Tula, M. T. *Hear My Testimony: María Teresa Tula, Human Rights Activist of El Salvador.* Boston: South End Press, 1994.

Sternbach, N. S., Navarro-Arangurn, M., Chuchryk, P., and Alvarez, S. "Feminisms in Latin America: From Bogotá to San Bernardo," *Signs*, 17, 1992.

Still, L. V. "The Marginal Executive: Australian Women Managers." *Women in Management Series*, Paper No. 1, Nepean College of Advanced Education School of Business Working Paper Series, 1985.

Still, L. V. "Affirmative Action: the Case for a Balanced Perspective." *Women in Management Series*, Paper No. 10, Nepean College of Advanced Education School of Business Working Paper Series, 1988.

Stoper, E. "The Gender Gap Concealed and Revealed: 1936–1984," *Journal of Political Science*, 17, 1989.

Sundström, M. "Part-time Work in Sweden and Its Implications for Gender Equality." In Folbre, N., Bergmann, B., Agarwal, B., and Floro, M. (eds.). *Women's Work in the World Economy*. Basingstoke and London: Macmillan, 1992.

Suret-Canale, J. *French Colonialism in Tropical Africa, 1900–1945*. London: Hurst, 1971.

Tambiah, S. J. "Dowry and Bridewealth and the Property Rights of Women in South Asia." In

Goody, J. and Tambiah, S. J. (eds.). *Bridewealth and Dowry.* Cambridge: Cambridge University Press, 1973.

Taylor, C. E. and Faruque, R. *Child and Maternal Services in Rural India: The Narangwar Experiment, Part I.* Baltimore: Johns Hopkins University Press, 1983.

Thelen, K. and Steinmo, S. "Historical Institutionalism in Comparative Politics." In Steinmo, S., Thelen, K., and Longstreth, F. (eds.). *Structuring Politics: Historical Institutionalism in Comparative Analysis.* New York: Cambridge University Press, 1992.

Thomas, S. *How Women Legislate.* New York: Oxford University Press, 1994.

Thurow, L. *Head to Head: The Coming Economic Battle Among Japan, Europe, and America.* New York: Warner, 1992.

Tiano, S. "Gender, Work, and World Capitalism: Third World Women's Role in Development." In Hess, B. B. and Ferree, M. M. (eds.). *Analyzing Gender: A Handbook of Social Science Research.* Beverly Hills, CA: Sage, 1987.

Tinker, I. (ed.). *Persistent Inequalities: Women and World Development.* New York: Oxford University Press, 1990.

Tinker, I. and Bramsen, M. B. (eds.). *Women and World Development.* Washington, D.C.: Overseas Development Council, 1976.

Tisdell, C. A., Roy, K. C., and Gannon, J. "Sustainability of Tribal Villages in West Bengal: The Impact of Technological and Environmental Change at Village Level." Paper presented to IIDS Second International Conference on Development and Future Studies, Perth, 1993.

Tisdell, C. A., Roy, K. C., and Gannon, J. "Environmental and Technological Change and Sustainability: The Bengali Village of Gokulganja—an Indian Microcosm." In Thakur, B. (ed.). *Perspectives in Resource Management in Developing Countries.* New Delhi: Concept Publishing, 1994.

Tsui, E. Y. *Are Married Daughters "Spilled Water"?—A Study of Working Women in Urban Taiwan.* Taipei: National Taiwan University, Population Studies Center, Women's Research Program, Monograph No. 4, 1987.

UNESCO. *Sector Review: The Financing of Education in Tanzania Overview.* Paris: 1988.

UNICEF. *Women and Children in Tanzania.* Dar es Salaam, 1990.

Utrikesdepartementet. *Kvinna i Europa.* Om EG och jämställdheten. Stockholm: Utrikesdepartementet, 1993.

Valanzuela, M. E., Venegas, S., and Andrade, C. (eds.). *De Mujer Sola a Jefa de Hogar.* Santiago, Chile: Servicio Nacional de la Mujer, 1994.

Ve, H. "Likhetsidealer i velferdsstatens skole." In Haavelsruud, M. et al. (eds.). *Utdanning og likhetsidealer.* Oslo: Aschehoug, 1983.

Venkataramani, S. H. "Born to Die," *India Today,* June 15, 1986.

Vianello, M., Siemienska, R., Damian, N., Lupri, E., Coppi, R., D'Arcangelo, E., and Bolasco, S. *Gender Inequality. A Comparative Study of Discrimination and Participation.* London: Sage, 1990.

Wærness, K. "Caring as Women's Work in the Welfare State." In Holter, H. (ed.). *Patriarchy in a Welfare Society.* Oslo: Scandinavian University Press, 1984.

Wallace, T. "The Impact of Global Crises on Women." In Wallace, T. and March, C. (eds.). *Changing Perceptions, Writings on Gender and Development.* Oxford: Oxfam, 1991.

Ward, K. B. "Women in the Global Economy." In Gutek, B., Stromberg, A., and Larwood, L. (eds.). *Women and Work. An Annual Review.* Newbury Park, CA: Sage, 1988.

Wellesley Editorial Committee. *Women and National Development: The Complexities of Change.* Chicago: Chicago University Press, 1977.

Whitehead, A. "Food Crisis and Gender Conflict in the African Countryside." In Bernstein, H., Crow, B., Mackintosh, M., and Martin, C. (eds.). *The Food Question: Profits Versus People.* London: Earthscan, 1990.

Wilensky, H. L. *The Welfare State and Equality: Structural and Ideological Roots of Public Expenditures.* Berkeley: University of California Press, 1975.

Wiley, L. "Tanzania: The Arusha Planning and Village Development Project." In Overholt, C. et al. (eds.). *Gender Roles in Development Projects.* West Hartford, CT: Kumarian Press, 1985.

Wohlstetter, A. and Coleman, S. "Race Differences in Income." In Pascal, A. H. (ed.). *Racial Discrimination in Economic Life.* Lexington, MA: Lexington Books, 1972.

*Work for Women,* 9th issue, 1990.

*World Development Report 1991.* New York: Oxford University Press for the World Bank, 1991.

*World Development Report 1993.* New York: Oxford University Press for the World Bank, 1993.

Yang, M. M. C. *Socio-economic Results of Land Reform in Taiwan.* Honolulu: East-West Center Press, 1970.

Young, M. D. *Sustainable Investment and Resource Use.* Carnforth, England: Parthenon, 1992.

Yudelman, S. "Women Farmers in Central America: Myths, Roles, and Reality," *Grassroots Development,* 17, 1994.

# Index

# About the Editors and Contributors

HANS C. BLOMQVIST is Professor of Economics at the Swedish School of Economics and Business Administration in Vasa, Finland. He has been a Visiting Scholar at the Australian National University, University of Queensland, Australia, Stanford University, and the Institute of Southeast Asian Studies, Singapore. His research interests include development economics, with an emphasis on Southeast Asia, applied macroeconomics, and behavioral economics. He is the author or editor of eight books and has contributed numerous articles to academic journals.

BIH-ER CHOU is Professor and Head of the Department of Sociology and Anthropology at National Tsing Hua University in Taiwan. She has been Visiting Fulbright Professor at the University of New Orleans and the University of Wisconsin. She is the co-author of *Women in Taiwan Politics* and *The Political Representation of Women in a "Reserved Seats" System.* She has served as Director of the Women's Studies Program at National Tsing Hua University and was Co-principal Investigator of a Rockefeller Foundation Grant for the study of "Linkages among Women's Work, Status, and Fertility in the Context of Chinese Family Structure in Taiwan."

CAL CLARK is Professor and Head of Political Science at Auburn University. His primary teaching and research interests include international political economy, East Asian development, comparative public policy, and U.S. competitiveness. He is the author of *Taiwan's Development*, co-author of *Women in Taiwan Politics*, and co-editor of *Studies in Dependency Reversal, State and Development*, and *The Evolving Pacific Basin.* His work has appeared in several leading journals.

JANET CLARK is Professor and Chair of Political Science at West Georgia College. Her primary teaching and research interests include women in politics, American government, and state and local politics. She is the co-author of *Women,*

*Elections, and Representation, Government and Politics in Wyoming* and *Women in Taiwan Politics.* Her work has appeared in numerous leading journals. She has served as president of the Western Social Science Association and of the Women's Caucus for Political Science. She is the current editor of *Women & Politics* and served a term as book review editor of the *Social Science Journal.*

MARÍA DE LOS ANGELES CRUMMETT received her Ph.D. in economics from the New School for Social Research in New York. She has carried out field-work in Mexico and has written numerous articles on Mexican agrarian structure, rural women, and migration. She has worked as a consultant for development agencies including UNIFEM, FAO, UNFPA, ILO, and USAID, and is currently a research associate at the Center for Caribbean and Latin American Studies, University of South Florida, Tampa.

GAO KUN graduated from Beijing University. She is presently a lecturer of sociology at the Department of Sociology, Institute of Sociology in Renmin Univerity of China, Beijing. Her research interests include sociology with an emphasis on the social status of women in China, social work and public administration. She has published a number of articles in relevant journals.

SUKHAN JACKSON lectures on industrial relations in the Department of Economics, University of Queensland, Australia. She publishes in the area of labor relations and is the author of *Chinese Enterprise Management: Reforms in Economic Perspective.*

JAMILAH ARIFFIN is a Professor in the Faculty of Economics and Administration at the University of Malaya in Kuala Lumpur, Malaysia. Her research fields include "Women and Industrial Development" and "The Gender Dimension in Labour Migration." An author and coordinating editor of several books, she was also a member of the Commonwealth Expert Group on "Women and Structural Adjustment" and a member of the ESCAP Expert Group on Women and Development for Asia and the Pacific Region. She prepared the Malaysia Country Report for the Women's World Conference in 1995.

FELIX J. MLAY has worked as a secondary and high school teacher for ten years, most of the time in the rural areas of Tanzania. He is currently employed by the Ministry of Finance in Tanzania since 1990 and he lectures in economics at the Dar es Salaam school of accountancy.

JANE RICHARDSON studied Japanese at the University of Queensland. She has been working in the Queensland office of the Consulate-General of Japan since early 1992. A fluent speaker of Japanese, she is a regular visitor to Japan.

PAUL RIETHMULLER is a Senior Lecturer in the Department of Economics at the University of Queensland. His major research interest is in the food and agricultural industries of Japan and South East Asia. In recent years, he has published papers in *Agribusiness, The Review of Marketing and Agricultural Economics, The Journal of Policy Modelling, The Current Affairs Bulletin,* and *Agricultural Science.*

KARTIK C. ROY is Associate Professor of Economics at the University of Queensland and the Secretary-General of the International Institute for Development Studies. He was educated in India and Australia and obtained two Ph.D. degrees—one of them at the University of Queensland. His major areas of interest include international economics and development economics. He has published several articles in international journals and has eighteen books to his credit, the latest being *Poverty, Female-Headed Households and Sustainable Economic Development* (with Nerina Vecchio) (Greenwood, 1998).

HELEN I. SAFA is currently Professor of Anthropology and Latin American Studies at the University of Florida. She is the author of *The Myth of the Male Breadwinner: Women and Industrialization in the Caribbean,* and *The Urban Poor of Puerto Rico* and co-author of *In the Shadows of the Sun: Caribbean Development Alternatives and US Policy.* She has also edited several books and articles on migration, urbanization, and women and development, particularly on Latin America.

HARRIET SILIUS is a sociologist and is at present researcher at the Finnish Research Council and Director of the Institute of Women's Studies at Åbo Akademi University, Finland. She has written about women and professions, the relations between women and the welfare state, citizenship, and higher education. She is engaged in a national multidisciplinary project on the gender system of the Finnish welfare state and in charge of a project on motherhood.

CLEMENT A. TISDELL is Professor and Head of the Department of Economics at the University of Queensland, Brisbane, Australia. He is a prolific author and has written extensively on development economics, social issues, and environmental economics. Some of his recent books include *Economic Development in the Context of China: Natural Resources, Growth and Development,* (with K. C. Roy and R. K. Sen) *Economic Development and the Environment: A Case Study of India,* (with D. L. McKee) *Developmental Issues in Small Island Economies,* and *Environmental Economics.*

ISBN 0-275-95134-0

HARDCOVER BAR CODE